RUSTIC ITALIAN FOOD

RUSTIC ITALIAN FOOD

Marc Vetri with David Joachim

Beverage Notes by Jeff Benjamin
Photography by Kelly Campbell

TEN SPEED PRESS
BERKELEY

who taught me that the whole is greater than the sum of its parts

and to my three little gnocchis,
Maurice, Catherine, and Mario

{ CONTENTS }

The line it is drawn
The curse it is cast
The slow one now
Will later be fast
As the present now
Will later be past
The order is
Rapidly fadin'.
And the first one now
Will later be last
For the times they are a-changin'.

—Bob Dylan, 1964

Hip: Informed, up-to-date, fashionable, contemporary, relevant. Being modern in dress, attitude and interests. From "hepi," meaning "well-informed" from the West African language of Wolof.

—URBAN DICTIONARY, 2011

FOREWORD BY MARIO BATALI

IT SEEMS THAT NEARLY every month there is a new place in town, mine or yours, with some hipster chef who has spent a couple of weeks or months or years in Italia or France or España or Denmark, working in a legendary place. The chef is back in town with his or her "new" ideas on how to improve the mother country's food and gastronomic culture, all for our delight. As not-hip as I am, I try now to wait a month or two before heading in to check out the "new" freshie and to see if, in fact, there is something new or innovative or provocative or at least delicious to enjoy and subsequently talk about with my ever-growing group of pleasure-interested pals and associates in the field of food, beverage, and hospitality. The result is usually a mishmash of successful and not-so-successful dishes somehow thematically entwined by their faint relationship with the original versions. The problems are usually the same: overambitious creativity for creativity's sake, less than perfect shopping, and hurried technique that can lead to some fine dishes, but overall a cuisine a little less than fully inspired or executed.

My first visit to Vetri in 1999 was an exploration before the "scientist" chefs had yet to invade the United States. I went there hoping to find Italian food inspired by true technique and fine products but practiced by a master. And so it was: perhaps the best meal of true Italian deliciousness with sublime mouthfeel and honest and clear flavor I had ever had outside of the boot, and better than many meals I had eaten inside the boot. I was immediately a huge fan and have been ever since. Marc Vetri is not a practitioner of modern food. He is, however unbeknown to him, a "hipster." His food and style at that time, in 1998, were among the first real things in the gastronomic rebirth of Philadelphia that became a revolution, and these two stylistic components define to this day what hip means to me. His cooking is not trendy, it is not based on ingredients from Asia or South America, and it is decidedly not "creative for creativity's sake." Marc Vetri's take on "hip" is the well-informed part. He has studied and cooked in and around Bergamo in Italia, as well as around the country in the United States, and developed his personal style at the hands of the masters. His food represents and tastes like the truly ethereal and delicious food made in Italia, but maybe just a little bit lighter, just a little bit cleaner, more to the point.

Which brings me to the book in your hands, *Rustic Italian Food*. Like everything Marc does, I truly love it. And like everything Marc does, it really delivers even more on second glance, as I realize just how intensely Vetri observes and catalogs when he is creating the new from the traditional. From the first bread recipe to the pickles and preserves, Marc understands the fundamental building blocks of the real cooking of Italia. It starts at the soil and goes/grows/evolves from there.

This book should in fact be placed in the "reference book" category. The chapter on both rolled and extruded pastas has more useful information than encyclopedias about the noodle. The salumi chapter has enough true and thoughtful information to replace many single topic tomes from the shelves of cookery schools. The vegetable and sides recipes are superbly simple, and yet the dishes are fresh and packed with layers of flavor and complexity.

As the times are a-changin' and the newest is often thought of as the best, *Rustic Italian Food* holds the line with traditional technique, as does Marc Vetri himself. But here, and everywhere in the Vetri world, the technique and the food are lightly and delicately refined, with a sense of true thought, not toward innovation, but toward imaginatively modifying the really good into the great. Being well informed and continuing to improve on delicious is the new "hip." This book is that, too.

INTRODUCTION: A RETURN TO REAL COOKING

I REALLY LIKE TO COOK. I don't say that as a joke—I really, really enjoy cooking. Sniffing out the best ingredients, dreaming up a dish, and then handcrafting something delicious brings me immense satisfaction. That idea might seem odd in the technological age of modern cuisine. Why bother cooking by hand? Why judge doneness with your eyes when you can just put something in an oven, press a button, and take it out when the buzzer goes off? It will be cooked perfectly. You can vacuum-seal a veal medallion in plastic, label it, put the bag in a water bath at a prescribed temperature for a prescribed time, then take it out, cut it open, and serve it. Some people think that this kind of scientific advancement is a godsend. But not me. If I wanted to be a file clerk, I would work at an accounting firm. I don't enjoy filing. I enjoy cooking. I like to touch and smell fresh herbs, to roll them between my fingertips and breathe in their tempting aromas. I like to feel the supple skin on a fresh pear and taste the tannic bite of young artichokes. I want to understand where my food comes from—the earth, the climate, and the place where it was grown. Touching, knowing, and understanding give me more respect for the ingredients I'm working with and help me honor those foods in the kitchen. The fewer things between me and the food, the better. Don't get me wrong—knowing the science of food can certainly make you a better cook. But how you use that knowledge makes all the difference between modern cuisine and rustic preparations. Some chefs use their knowledge to manipulate our medium—food—to its furthest reaches, constructing or deconstructing elaborate dishes with multiple components. Other chefs use food knowledge to expertly pair two ingredients together in a simple preparation like a musician who can move you from your seat with two minimal notes. That musician may have a deep understanding of musical theory but chooses to display his

or her knowledge with an uncomplicated melody. I love knowing how and why things happen in cooking, but I'll take Miles Davis over Wynton Marsalis any day of the week.

This kind of simple, hands-on cooking is the core of Italian cuisine. In the kitchen, my greatest aspiration is to take as few ingredients as possible, cook them perfectly, and make them sing. I try to bring this kind of simplicity to all of my tables—at home and in my restaurants. It's what I teach the cooks who come to work with me, and what I set out to share in this book.

I'm not alone in this straightforward approach. Thomas Keller, the prince of precise French cooking, recently told reporters that a chicken tastes best when simply roasted in the traditional manner: "Clean the chicken, season it inside and out, rub it with butter, truss it and roast it at 425 degrees," says Keller. I couldn't agree more. Even Alain Ducasse, one of the most decorated chefs in the world, recently simplified the menu at his flagship Plaza Athenée restaurant in Paris. "We've never been about bling-bling," he told an international news agency, "but now we are definitely going to get back to essentials. Cuisine has become too complicated—this is about subject, verb, adjective: duck, turnips, sauce."

For many young cooks, the simple basics no longer hold their interest. Some very talented chefs have come to work with me over the years, and I am still amazed at how many of them don't know rudimentary food preparations like butchering animals and making stock. For me, it is an art to make a piece of cured salami with only three ingredients: pork, fat, and salt. Bread, one of the world's most important foods and most beautiful art forms, can be crafted from only flour, water, salt, and yeast. Yet these fundamental procedures are foreign to many cooks. It's not because making bread is hard. It's because few people take the time to show others how simple it is to make.

Think of pickles, jams, and preserves. Cooks have been preserving seasonal fruits and vegetables for thousands of years. Simple tarts and sweets have been put on Italian family tables for more years than any of us has been alive. Thankfully, this kind of hands-on food is making a big comeback these days. Highly technological cuisine may be fascinating, but food made by hand is what people are really excited about. American restaurants proudly serve house-cured meats and house-made breads. Every year, thousands more people turn to home canning, home brewing, home butchering, and making things like homemade pickles and home-cured bacon to save money and enjoy the satisfaction of doing things themselves.

You could chalk up the handcrafted food movement to tough economic times, but I think our interest in rustic food goes deeper. Breads, preserves, pies, roasted meats . . . these are the foods that cooks—especially Italian cooks—have been inspired by for centuries. These are the approachable foods that people everywhere feel comfortable preparing and eating. This is the cooking that I teach in *Rustic Italian Food*.

Here is my basic approach:

1. Cook and eat food that is as close to the earth as possible. The fresher and more local, the better.

2. Start with whole foods. They taste better than processed foods.

3. Keep it simple. A few high-quality ingredients make a bigger impact than a dozen cheap ones.

To help flesh out this philosophy, I don't just give you recipes here. I open each chapter with details about making satisfying Italian foods like home-made pasta, sausages, and vegetables. These introductions are like mini classes, explaining everything you need to know to get started. The recipes themselves also give you the ins and outs of rustic Italian food the way I cook it—with more than 120 of my favorite breads, pizzas, grilled meats, slow roasts, braises, pickles, preserves, and desserts. Some dishes, like Fusilli with Fava Beans and Pecorino (page 68), are perfect for off-the-cuff weeknight cooking. Others, like Chocolate Zabaione Tart (page 262), are more sophisticated and meant for special occasions. Still others, like Spit-Roasted Suckling Pig (page 192) and home-cured Soppressata Calabrese (page 149), require some serious time and attention but give you a huge payoff. Any time you cook a whole animal or serve home-cured salami, your guests will love you for it. Believe me. People appreciate the effort and care that goes into handmade food. This is the kind of rustic cooking that I am most excited to share with you.

BREAD AND PIZZA

I T SMELLED LIKE OLD BOOTS. I was cramped. Tired. And I could be caught and arrested at any moment. Luckily, the rumble of the train, chugging along the track, was putting me to sleep. This was in 1993, and I had left L.A. to go to Italy and learn everything I could about Italian food. For weeks, I had been staging at Taverna Colleoni dell'Angelo, a seminal Northern Italian restaurant in Bergamo, Lombardy. I finally felt like I'd found my roots in Italy. Yet, here I was on a train to France.

I usually don't tout the French for coming up with anything—except maybe béchamel—but I love French bread. It's amazing. In Italy, I was really underwhelmed by the bread, so I decided to spend my first *ferie* (vacation) in Paris. Of course, I was broke. *Stagiares* (culinary interns) don't make any money. So I stowed away on the train from Italy to France. The trains have luggage areas upstairs, and I hopped up into one of them and put luggage in front of me to hide. It was leather luggage and had that awesome smell of boots, somewhere between bread and sausage.

I was meeting my friend and mentor Joseph Manzare in Paris. He had just left Wolfgang Puck's Spago and come to France to work in a pastry shop. We met at his friend Larry's apartment and slept on Larry's floor for a week. Joseph and I rented bicycles and rode around the city all week eating whatever street food we could find. We walked in and out of all kinds of bakeries, sampling everything. I had made bread when I lived in L.A., but nothing like this. Different doughs and shapes were everywhere! From baguettes, batons and boules to ficelles, miches, fougasses, and épis.

I was on a quest to taste the best baguette ever. One day, Joseph and I rode away from the center of town onto a side street with a bakery on the corner. I don't remember the name of it. But they had a beautiful little food cart

out front that sold only one thing: sandwiches made of leg of lamb roasted with rosemary and garlic, on a baguette with tomatoes, lettuce, and horse-radish cream. We both got one. Of course, I'd had baguettes before. But this one was phenomenal. We were there in the morning, so the bread was probably right out of the oven. Crisp on the outside, marble-size air pockets on the inside . . . chewy . . . crunchy . . . sophisticated. I found myself taking one bite at a time, not to savor the filling, which was also amazing, but to really taste the bread! It was a life-changing moment. Unfortunately, this was France, and I was quickly reminded that I was not in Italy anymore.

Joseph and I were eating, and I was staring at something through the window of the antiques store next to the baguette shop. I must have leaned a little too close to the window, and a smudge of horseradish cream got on the glass. The store owner came out, furious, screaming at me in French. I said to the man, "I don't understand." He said in French-accented English, "Look at my window! You fucking Americans come to our country and you barely spend a fucking nickel!" But over the past week I'd spent every penny I had in search of the best baguette. And this guy was complaining about how I don't appreciate his country? I suppose my response was a bit excessive. I took the whole sandwich and rubbed it all over the window. Joseph and I took off on our bicycles as fast as we could!

I probably shouldn't have given up my perfect baguette that day. But I've never given up my love for great bread. I'm always working to make my bread better and better—a thicker crust, a loftier crumb, a deeper flavor. The French taught me a lot about these basics and helped hone my recipes for Ciabatta (page 28), Durum Focaccia (page 30), and other Italian breads. I'm starting this book off with bread because it is one of the world's most elemental foods. Only three ingredients—flour, water, and yeast—can produce thousands of different breads. But with so few ingredients, the techniques—from the measuring to the baking—become extremely important.

FLOUR

The French taught me quite a bit about flour. It is the cornerstone of any bread. What you need to know is that flours vary from region to region, brand to brand, type to type, and year to year. In baking, the type of wheat flour matters, because some wheat varieties are higher in protein, creating well-structured artisan breads, while others are low in protein and work better for cakes and pastries. Some fall in the middle.

I tried so many different flours to find the perfect one for pizza dough. I tried various combinations of tipo 00 (Italian finely ground all-purpose wheat flour), higher-protein bread flour, and durum flour. Then I started buying an Italian pizza flour from Naples that combined tipo 00 flour, soy flour, and a few others. It was good but expensive. And it was never consistent. So I tried using King Arthur Sir Galahad, the main all-purpose flour I keep around for most baking. It was ten times better and much more consistent.

Sir Galahad is a professional flour only available through food-service and bakery distributors. However, it is nearly identical to King Arthur Unbleached All-Purpose Flour, which is available in almost every grocery store. When I don't have Sir Galahad, I use K. A.'s Unbleached All-Purpose. That's the flour we recommend for all the baking recipes in this book. If you use another brand, look for flour milled from hard red winter wheat that has 11 to 12 percent protein. King Arthur Sir Galahad has 11.4 percent protein. K. A.'s Unbleached All-Purpose has 11.7 percent protein. You could also use

White Lily Bread Flour, another hard wheat flour with a similar protein content (11.7 percent). But be careful with other bread flours: some can have up to 13 percent protein, which will produce a denser loaf. Look for a bread flour with no more than 12 percent protein.

For very sturdy breads, I sometimes use durum flour. Durum is the hardest variety of wheat and has more protein than other varieties. When milled, durum flour has a pale yellow cast, while hard red winter wheats, if unbleached, are usually off-white in color. Durum is also where semolina comes from. The bright yellow endosperm of durum wheat (just under the seed coat) is coarsely ground into semolina, the key to great extruded pasta.

MEASURING

Technique in bread making is all about precision. In cooking, you'll hear me say, "a pinch of this, a pinch of that." Not in bread making. It needs to be exact. That's why I include both volume and weight measurements in all of the recipes in this chapter. For the most accuracy, use the weight measurements. Volumes change from brand to brand and day to day, depending on factors like humidity and how compacted the flour or yeast is. But weights always remain constant. Buy a decent gram scale (see Sources, page 279) and measure everything on it—especially the flour. If you measure by volume instead of weight, spoon the flour into the measuring cup, then level it off with something flat like a table knife.

YEAST

This magical microorganism, *Saccharomyces cerevisiae*, has been responsible for puffing up yeast breads for centuries. It feeds on sugars in the dough and gives off carbon dioxide, which makes its way into air pockets in the dough and inflates them when heated, raising the dough. I always use fresh yeast. It just seems to produce better results. In grocery stores, you'll find it in small cakes wrapped in foil, usually in the refrigerated dairy case. Supermarket brands of fresh yeast have a texture somewhere between stiff Play-Doh and a rubber eraser. It works fine, but remember: it's a living organism and is perishable. You must use fresh yeast within a week or two. If you bake bread often, I encourage you to use fresh yeast for the best-tasting breads and pizzas. If you don't bake as much, you can use active dry yeast or instant yeast. I have included measurements for both fresh and instant yeast in the recipes, but here are the equivalents: 2 tablespoons (18 g) fresh cake yeast equals about 2 1/4 teaspoons (8 g) instant yeast or active dry yeast. When measuring fresh yeast by volume, measure packed (the way it comes when you buy it), then crumbled to mix evenly with the other ingredients. When measuring instant yeast or active dry yeast, level off the tablespoon with the flat edge of a table knife.

WATER

Most bread recipes call for warm water to help activate the yeast, but I almost always use cold water. Keep in mind that mixing bread dough creates friction. If you knead in a stand mixer, which I always do, the paddle bangs the dough against the sides of the bowl, creating heat and activating the yeast. I like to knead dough in the mixer for at least 10 minutes—often more—which is plenty of time for the yeast to wake up and smell the coffee. Whenever I use warm water, the yeast wakes up too early, and the bread rises too fast. Then it ends up overrising and flattening out when I put it in the oven. I find that cold water keeps the dough cool enough throughout the mixing that the dough can rise gradually and continue to rise high in the oven. The only time I use warm water is when making a bread starter, which isn't kneaded but simply mixed up in a bowl. In that case, warm water (about 100 to 110°F) helps activate the yeast.

SALT

Salt can kill yeast. Understanding this is essential. If you put salt into bread dough before the yeast becomes incorporated and starts to activate, you may as well throw out the dough. This is why I mix the dough without salt first. It allows the yeast to get mixed in and start feeding on the flour. Then you add the salt and mix again. Now the yeast is spread throughout the dough, and the salt can't dehydrate it as easily, which can ruin the dough.

For baking, I usually use fine sea salt. I use kosher salt for most other cooking, but the two are drastically different. If you measure by weight, the weights will always be the same. But if you measure by tablespoons, as most

Americans do, the measurements can vary quite a bit. For instance, 10 grams of fine sea salt measures about 1 3/4 teaspoons, but 10 grams of Morton's kosher salt measures a little over 2 1/2 teaspoons, and 10 grams of Diamond Crystal kosher salt measures about 3 1/2 teaspoons. That's twice as much as fine sea salt. Now you see why bakers weigh everything!

To keep it straight, I've included both weights and volumes for salt in the baking recipes. When I call for kosher salt, measurements were taken using Diamond Crystal kosher.

STARTER

If you make a lot of bread and pizza, it makes sense to keep some starter on hand. It kick-starts the rising and gives bread and pizza crust a better texture. Starter also makes great yeast-raised waffles (my kids love them on Sundays!). To this day, I use a natural starter that I got going from wild yeasts back in 2001. It breathes life into most of my breads. What makes natural starter different from other starters is that no commercial yeast is actually stirred into the mixture. Natural starter begins with nothing but flour, water, and sugar or another sweetener (see the Natural Honey Starter on page 23 for an example). The sugar attracts wild yeasts from the air and gives the yeasts something to feed on. As the yeasts grow, they give off carbon dioxide and puff up the starter with hundreds of air pockets.

To make a more contemporary starter, mix together flour, commercial yeast, and water in a big container and let it sit out overnight to ferment (see page 22 for a few different ratios of these basic ingredients). After a day or so, the yeast will feed on the flour and the starter will bubble up and grow. When it puffs up with air pockets and smells nice and yeasty, it's ready to use. This is the type of starter I use for most of my breads, like Rustic Loaf (page 24) and Ciabatta (page 28). But natural starter made from wild yeasts has a sour edge that I like better in breads like Parmesan Bread (page 29) and Fig and Chestnut Bread (page 36).

Remember that yeast is a living organism. To keep a bread starter alive, you have to feed the yeast now and then. That just means you scoop out some of the starter and replace it with new flour and warm water. The temperature matters because warm environments help microorganisms like yeast grow. Cold water doesn't work as well here. That's why if you leave your starter out at room temperature, the warm temperature will cause it to grow faster and you'll need to feed it three times a day. Refrigerating the starter slows down the growth so you only need to feed it every other week. It's easier to chill the starter, but you do sacrifice some aroma in the finished bread that way. Either way, to feed it, remove half the starter (bake with it, give it away, or trash it) and replace what you removed with a 50-50 mixture of flour and warm water. If you refrigerate your starter, let it warm up at room temperature for 30 minutes before baking with it. And if you forget to feed your starter for several weeks, know that it may die (shame on you!). But it will usually come back if you feed it at room temperature once a day for a few days. You can tell it has come back if it smells alive, yeasty, a little sweet, and a little sour, and has lots of bubbles. If your starter looks flat or smells really funky, it's probably dead. Just toss it out and start a new one.

MIXING AND KNEADING

I always mix bread in a stand mixer. It makes it so much easier. Just keep in mind that you can't make the batch too big, or it will slow down the mixer and the dough won't mix right. The dough should take up only 25 to 35 percent of the mixer bowl. If you are serious about bread, you can buy a larger mixer. Anvil (Vollrath) makes a great 10-quart mixer that is perfect for the advanced home baker. Otherwise, the best you can do is a 5- or 6-quart KitchenAid. The recipes in this book were tested on a 6-quart KitchenAid, which works great as long as you don't overload it. Mix and knead in two batches if necessary.

Of course, if you don't have a stand mixer, you can knead the dough by hand on a lightly floured board. For most yeast breads, what you're looking for is a smooth, satiny texture. It usually takes a few more minutes to achieve this texture with hand-kneading than with mixer-kneading. But even when I'm mixer-kneading, I take the dough out and knead by hand a little to make sure the texture is right. The process requires some trial and error, because of all the variables like temperature, humidity, flour quality, yeast activity, and how dense you want the texture of the bread to be. Baking good bread isn't as simple as following a formula. You have to find out what works best for you, which is part of the fun of getting all floury in the first place.

PROOFING AND SHAPING

Proofing is the process of "proving" that the yeast is still alive and active. This typically happens when you set aside the dough and it bubbles up and rises. But if you use active dry yeast, which comes in large dry granules, you have to dissolve the yeast with water and a little sugar first. Dissolve about 1/2 teaspoon sugar in 1/2 cup of water from the recipe, then sprinkle the active dry yeast on top and let it sit for 5 minutes. If the yeast starts to bubble and grow, it's alive. If it doesn't, the yeast is proven dead. Check the expiration date of your yeast and try to use the freshest yeast possible. I usually crumble fresh yeast and mix it right into the flour and water in the mixing bowl. You can do the same thing with instant yeast, which dissolves faster than active dry yeast and doesn't need to be mixed with water first. As long as the fresh or instant yeast hasn't reached its expiration date, it should be active. I recommend using instant yeast such as SAF or Red Star.

To raise the dough, also called "proofing," professional bakers use temperature-controlled proofing boxes. These boxes are precise and constant because flavor develops in the bread dough as it gradually rises over a period of hours. If the temperature gets too hot, the yeast gets so active that the dough rises too rapidly and it doesn't have time to develop flavor. At home, just get creative. Most home bakers put the dough in an oiled bowl, cover it with plastic wrap, and let rise in a warm spot, about 90°F. The spot could be a gas oven with the pilot light on, or on a hot day, it could be outside. Some modern ovens have a proofing mode that sets a perfect temperature inside your oven. Either way, the temperature should be consistent and warm enough for the yeast to become active but not so hot that the heat overactivates the yeast or kills it (avoid going above 110°F). Even if it's a little cooler, it's okay. It'll just take a little longer for the dough to fully rise.

Once it's risen, you can shape the dough into nearly any shape you like, from large round or oval loaves to individual square or triangular rolls. Most of my recipes call for simple round or oval loaves, but feel free to experiment with shapes. Just be gentle when shaping the risen dough. You allow dough to rest and rise because you are creating air pockets. If you throw the dough around, you are going to flatten out all your hard work.

BAKING AND STEAMING

Brick-oven breads and pizzas are the best. The bricks stay incredibly hot, throwing the heat back onto the bread and absorbing some moisture to create a thick crust. The next best thing is a baking stone. That's what I use in my oven at home. Pick up a large stone about the size of your oven rack. You have to get it pretty hot, so preheat the stone in the oven for at least 30 minutes before putting bread dough on it. If you have convection, turn it on when baking pizza. It will blow hot air onto the top of the pizza to give you that charred and bubbly crust on top. If you don't have convection, you can heat a second stone on an upper rack above the stone you're baking on. The second stone will radiate heat down over the top of the pizza and help bubble up the crust.

For yeast breads, I like to add a blast of steam at the beginning of baking. The steam forms a layer of water on the dough that slows down the formation of the crust, allowing the dough to expand more and rise higher. Sugars on the surface of the dough also dissolve into the water, and when the water evaporates, the sugars melt and brown, creating a dark, delicious crust.

Some home ovens have a steaming option. If yours does, steam the bread for the first 20 minutes of baking. If not, the easiest way to get the steaming effect is to spritz the dough all over with water when it goes into the oven. Then spritz it again after about 10 minutes of baking. Another good method is to preheat a cast-iron pan in the oven. When the dough goes in, pour a cup of water into the hot pan and immediately close the door. After 15 to 20 minutes, take out the pan to stop the steaming so the dough can begin to dry out on the surface and develop a thick, browned crust.

As I said earlier, bread-baking is incredibly adaptable, which is why so many people around the world do it so many different ways. If you pay attention to all the little things like using cold water, adding salt after the yeast is mixed in, using a baking stone, and steaming during the early part of baking, you should be able to turn out awesome breads and pizzas in no time.

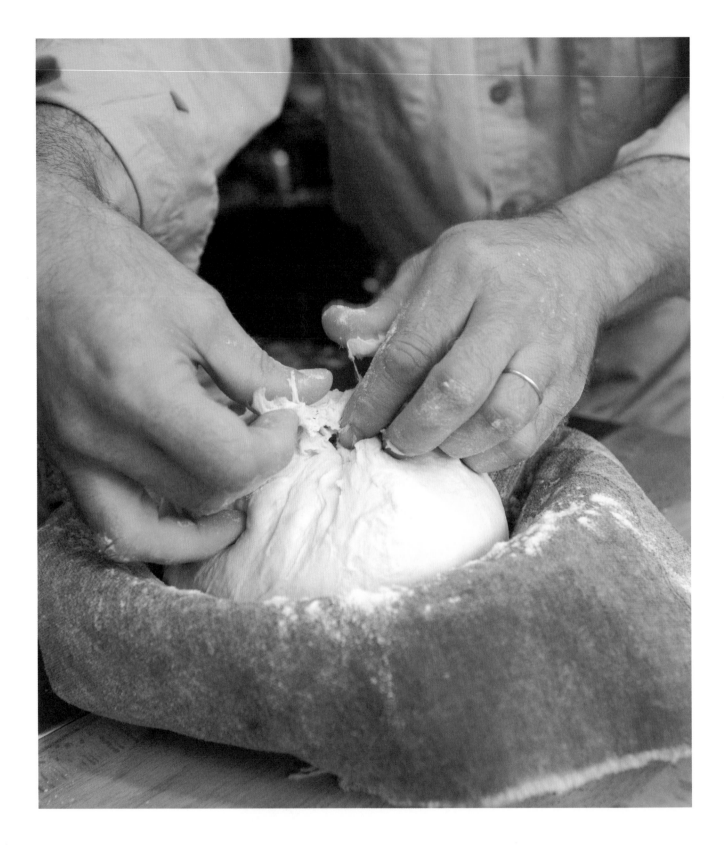

Biga STARTER

Biga is Italian for "chariot," referring to the way a bread starter drives the yeast throughout bread dough. Starter gives dough a better texture and allows it to stretch a little farther as it rises, keeping it from breaking too soon. I use this simple starter in all sorts of breads like Rustic Loaf (page 24) and Ciabatta (page 28). Different doughs call for different flours and different ratios of flour to water, so I always keep a few tubs of various starters on hand. But it's easy enough to make starter on the spot whenever you need it. Check out the variations below for a few of them.

Choose a large bowl that's about five times the volume of the ingredients. Mix the flour, yeast, and water in the bowl until well combined. Cover loosely with plastic wrap and let rise at room temperature for 12 hours, or until almost tripled in volume. Now, it's ready to use. (Keep the timing in mind. If you plan to bake bread in the morning, get the starter going early the night before.)

When making bread daily, store the starter at room temperature and feed three times a day. If baking less frequently, store it in the refrigerator and feed every other week. To feed the starter, scoop out 2 cups (bake with it, give it away, or trash it) and replace it with 2 cups high-protein flour and 2 cups warm water (100 to 110°F), stirring until blended. Most of the bread recipes in this book call for 1 to 2 cups of starter, so you can use that amount to bake with, then replace it with a 50-50 mix of flour and water.

MAKES ABOUT 5 CUPS (1 KG)

4 cups (500 g) high-protein flour, such as King Arthur Sir Galahad or Unbleached All-Purpose

1/2 teaspoon (2 g) packed fresh cake yeast, or 1/4 teaspoon (1 g) instant yeast

2 1/4 cups (500 g) warm water (100 to 110°F)

DURUM STARTER

Use 2 2/3 cups (335 g) durum flour, 1 tablespoon plus 2 teaspoons (15 g) packed then crumbled fresh cake yeast or 2 teaspoons (7 g) instant yeast, and 1 1/4 cups (280 g) warm water (100 to 110°F). To feed, scoop out 1 1/2 cups (300 g) and replace it with 1 cup (125 g) durum flour and 3/4 cup (160 g) warm water (100 to 110°F). Makes about 3 cups (about 600 g).

DURUM FOCACCIA STARTER

Use 3 1/2 cups (440 g) durum flour, 2 tablespoons (18 g) packed then crumbled fresh cake yeast or 2 1/4 teaspoons (8 g) instant yeast, and 2 cups (440 g) warm water (100 to 110°F). To feed, scoop out 1 cup (215 g) starter and replace it with 1 cup (125 g) durum flour and 3/4 cup plus 1 tablespoon (175 g) warm water (110 to 110°F). Makes about 4 1/4 cups (850 g).

NATURAL HONEY STARTER

Use 3/4 cup (220 g) whole wheat flour, 1 1/4 cups (275 g) warm water (100 to 110°F), and 1 tablespoon (21 g) honey. **DAY 1:** Mix the ingredients, cover loosely, and let sit in a warm spot (90°F) overnight. **DAY 2:** Take 1 cup (250 g) of starter and mix in 3/4 cup plus 2 tablespoons (110 g) whole wheat flour and 2/3 cup (140 g) warm water (100 to 110°F). Throw away the rest. Cover and let sit in a warm spot overnight. **DAY 3:** Mix 3/4 cup plus 1 tablespoon (100 g) high-protein flour, such as King Arthur Sir Galahad or Unbleached All-Purpose and 7 tablespoons (100 g) warm water (100 to 110°F) into all of the starter. Let sit in a warm spot overnight again. To feed, scoop out half of the starter and replace it with 3/4 cup plus 1 tablespoon (100 g) high-protein flour, such as King Arthur Sir Galahad or Unbleached All-Purpose, and 7 tablespoons (100 g) warm water (100 to 110°F). Makes about 3 cups (700 g).

NATURAL SOURDOUGH STARTER

Use 1 1/4 cups (160 g) high-protein flour, such as King Arthur Sir Galahad or Unbleached All-Purpose, 1/4 cup plus 1 1/2 tablespoons (40 g) whole wheat flour, and 7 tablespoons (100 g) warm water (100 to 110°F). **DAY 1:** Mix the ingredients, cover loosely, and let sit in a warm spot (90°F) overnight. **DAY 2:** Take all of the starter (about 1 1/3 cups or 300 g), and mix it with 1 3/4 cups (220 g) high-protein flour, 2/3 cup (80 g) whole wheat flour, and 2/3 cup plus 1 tablespoon (150 g) warm water (100 to 110°F). Cover and let sit in a warm spot overnight. **DAY 3:** Take all of the starter (about 3 1/3 cups or 750 g) and mix it with 4 3/4 cups (600 g) high-protein flour, 1 1/4 cups (150 g) whole wheat flour, and 1 2/3 cups (375 g) warm water (100 to 110°F). To feed, scoop out 2 1/4 cups (500 g) of the starter (use the rest or chuck it) and mix it with 3 cups plus 3 tablespoons (400 g) high-protein flour, 3/4 cup plus 1 1/2 tablespoons (100 g) whole wheat flour, and 1 1/8 cups (250 g) warm water (100 to 110°F). Makes about 5 2/3 cups (1.25 kg).

WAFFLE STARTER

Use 1 2/3 cups (250 g) tipo 00 or all-purpose flour, 1/4 teaspoon (1 g) packed then crumbled fresh cake yeast or 1/8 teaspoon (0.5 g) instant yeast, and 1 1/8 cups (250 g) warm water. To feed, scoop out 1 cup (215 g) starter and replace it with 3/4 cup (115 g) tipo 00 or unbleached all-purpose flour and 1 cup (220 g) warm water (100 to 110°F). Makes about 3 cups (700 g).

Biga starter

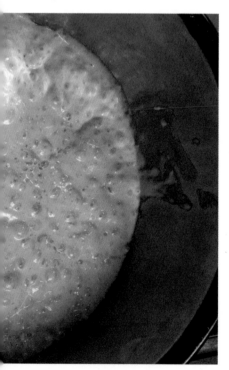

Rustic LOAF

Jeff Michaud came to work at Vetri in the fall of 2001. He had never really cooked Italian food, but he had a lot of skills and a lot of desire, which for me is the most important quality of a cook. Jeff would always tell me that we should make the bread for the restaurant. I had made bread for years, working in bakeries in Italy and Los Angeles; I had even taken a bread-baking class at the French Culinary Institute in New York. But I thought Vetri restaurant was too small to start making bread. Jeff was relentless, and we began making our own bread starters and experimented with various loaves, from ciabatta and focaccia to brioche and panettone.

We have been making bread at Vetri for over ten years now. The one that I remember most is the one that we started with: a simple, rustic, white, free-form loaf that we made from a natural starter in 2001. The starter is still living in the kitchen to this day. And we still bake this bread on a big stone that covers the whole oven. We severely brown the outside to give it a thick crust and deep flavor. It has always been my favorite bread.

Put the flour, water, and starter in the bowl of a stand mixer. Crumble in the yeast. Using the dough hook, mix on low speed until everything is moist, about 4 minutes, scraping the bowl as needed with a rubber spatula. Raise the mixer speed to medium and mix until the dough clings to the dough hook, about 6 minutes. Add the salt and mix at medium speed until the dough is slightly sticky and elastic, about 4 minutes.

Put the dough in an oiled bowl, turning to coat both sides with oil, cover with plastic wrap, and set in a warm spot (90°F) until doubled in size, about 1 hour. The shape can change with the proofing mold that you use.

Punch down the dough (one hard punch should do it), then shape into a ball. Place, seam side down, on a heavily floured rimless baking sheet, cover with a clean kitchen towel, and let rise in a warm spot until doubled in size, about 1 hour.

Meanwhile, remove all but the bottom rack in your oven and put a baking stone on the rack. Preheat the oven to 475°F for at least 30 minutes.

Slide the dough off the baking sheet onto the hot stone and slash a 4-inch X in the top of the dough. Immediately spritz the dough with a spray bottle of water until well coated, about 5 seconds. Bake for 10 minutes. Rotate the bread, spritz the dough again with water, and bake for another 10 minutes. Lower the oven temperature to 400°F and bake until the bread looks crusty and dark brown—about 50 minutes. Remove from the oven and let cool on a wire rack, but not too much. It's great warm.

PREP AHEAD

The starter can be made a day, a month—even years—ahead if you feed it and keep it alive.

MAKES ONE 10-INCH-DIAMETER ROUND LOAF

2 1/2 cups plus 1 tablespoon (650 g) high-protein flour, such as King Arthur Sir Galahad or Unbleached All-Purpose

1 cup (225 g) Biga Starter (page 22)

1 1/2 cups plus 1 1/2 tablespoons (350 g) cold water

2 tablespoons plus 2 1/2 teaspoons (25 g) packed fresh cake yeast, or 1 tablespoon (11 g) instant yeast

2 1/4 teaspoons (14 g) fine sea salt

I Want It Burnt!

In 1997, I was working as executive chef at Bella Blu in New York City. Alain Sailhac and his wife, Arlene, used to come into the restaurant. Alain was—and still is—executive vice president and dean of the French Culinary Institute (FCI) in New York. He and his wife ate at Bella Blu a lot because they lived right around the corner. I became good friends with them, and they invited me to become a judge of the FCI student graduations.

When I was planning to leave Bella Blu, I talked with Alain about opening my own restaurant. But first I wanted to go back to Italy and relearn some things, get back to basics. I wanted to know more about making sausage and bread. He mentioned that FCI was just starting a bread-baking class and invited me to attend. It was their first bread course ever, a monthlong one, all day, every day except Sunday. It was very intense. They planned to start with a French bread course and then offer an Italian bread course. I decided to take the French course.

It was one of the most eye-opening experiences I have ever had in a kitchen. We made so many styles and heard so many lectures on the science behind good bread. They even let us stay late and mess around with starters and doughs and shaping. It was a great opportunity for any chef. I remember we made a free-form rustic loaf almost every day for L'École, the restaurant downstairs from the school. Alain would come in when the bread was in the oven and tell everyone, "Darker, darker! It has to be burnt!" He loved it like that. The darker the color, the thicker the crust, and the play of flavors was incredible. When I started making rustic loaves at Vetri, I made them exactly the same way. It was the first bread we ever made at Vetri, and we still make more of that bread than any other. To this day, when I walk in the kitchen before service, I yell to everyone, "It's still not dark enough! I want it burnt!!"

Ciabatta

You find this bread everywhere now. The name means "slipper," and I make large ones for the restaurant. Sometimes at home, I'll shape it into smaller rolls to use as sandwich bread. It works great for slicing through the side and stuffing with whatever sandwich fillings you can dream up. Try thinly sliced Coppa (page 158), Beef Speck (157), Lamb Mortadella (page 142), and/or Rabbit Salami (page 144), paired with a gooey melting cheese like Bitto, buffalo mozzarella, or Crucolo. Then griddle the sandwich on a sandwich press. This bread is great for sandwiches because it has a lot of air holes inside—some about an inch in diameter—that can hold plenty of fillings like melted cheese and sliced meat.

Put the flour, water, and starter in the bowl of a stand mixer. Crumble in the yeast. Using the dough hook, mix on low speed until everything is moist, about 4 minutes, scraping the sides of the bowl as needed with a rubber spatula. Increase the mixer speed to medium and mix until the dough is smooth and clings to the dough hook, about 8 minutes. Add the salt and mix at medium speed until the dough is very smooth, about 4 minutes.

Put the dough in an oiled bowl, turning to coat it with oil, cover with plastic wrap, and set in a warm spot (90°F) until doubled in size, about 1 hour.

Using a bowl scraper or a large mixing spoon dipped in flour, scrape the dough onto a heavily floured surface. Pat the dough with floured hands into a 1/2-inch-thick rectangle and fold it into thirds as you would a letter.

If making rolls, cut into 12 equal pieces and shape into rough rectangles. If making a loaf, pat the dough into a rough rectangle. Put on a heavily floured rimless baking sheet and cover with a clean kitchen towel. Put in a warm place (90°F) and let rise until air bubbles form under the surface of the dough and the dough is light, airy, and almost doubled in size, about 1 hour.

Remove all but the bottom rack in your oven and put a baking stone on the rack. Preheat the oven to 475°F for at least 30 minutes.

Slide the dough off the baking sheet onto the hot stone and immediately spritz the dough with water until well coated, about 5 seconds. Bake for 10 minutes, then rotate the bread, spritz the dough again, and bake for another 10 minutes. The bread will be golden and crusty. Lower the oven temperature to 400°F and bake until dark brown, about 10 more minutes for rolls and 20 more minutes for a loaf. Remove from the oven and cool on a wire rack.

MAKES ONE 12 BY 6-INCH LOAF OR TWELVE 12 BY 6-INCH ROLLS

3 1/2 cups (500 g) high-protein flour, such as King Arthur Sir Galahad or Unbleached All-Purpose Flour

2 tablespoons (18 g) packed fresh cake yeast, or 2 1/4 teaspoons (8 g) instant yeast

1 cup (220 g) cold water

2 cups (450 g) Biga Starter (page 22)

1 tablespoon plus 1 3/4 teaspoons (28 g) fine sea salt

Parmesan BREAD

Whenever someone comes to my house—or my restaurants—I like to give them something to snack on right away, preferably bread. The Parmesan cheese in this one gives you an extra bite of salt, while the natural starter balances the salt with a light sourness. It also has a tight crumb (small air holes) that makes it perfect for soaking up olive oil when you dip it in.

MAKES ONE 12-INCH-DIAMETER ROUND LOAF

3 1/2 cups (500 g) high-protein flour, such as King Arthur Sir Galahad or Unbleached All-Purpose Flour

1 1/2 tablespoons (13 g) packed fresh cake yeast, or 1 3/4 teaspoons (6 g) instant yeast

1 1/3 cups (300 g) cold water

1/4 cup (50 g) extra-virgin olive oil

1 cup (240 g) Natural Honey Starter (page 23)

2 3/4 teaspoons (15 g) fine sea salt

1 cup (125 g) freshly grated Parmesan cheese

Put the flour, water, olive oil, and starter in the bowl of a stand mixer fitted with a dough hook. Crumble in the yeast. Mix on low speed until everything is moist and a rough dough forms, about 4 minutes, scraping the sides of the bowl as needed with a rubber spatula. Increase the mixer speed to medium and mix for 8 minutes; the dough will be very wet and elastic. Add the salt and cheese and mix on medium speed until the dough is smooth and clings to the dough hook, about 4 more minutes.

Put the dough in an oiled bowl, turn to coat it with oil, cover with plastic wrap, and set in a warm spot (90°F) until doubled in size, about 1 1/2 hours.

Punch down the dough and shape it into a ball on a floured surface. Place, seam side down, on a heavily floured rimless baking sheet, cover with a clean kitchen towel, and let rise in a warm place (90°F) until doubled in size, about 1 hour.

Meanwhile, remove all but the bottom rack in your oven and put a baking stone on the rack. Preheat the oven to 475°F for at least 30 minutes.

Slide the dough off the baking sheet onto the stone and immediately spritz the dough with a spray bottle of water until well coated, about 5 seconds. Bake until swollen and golden, about 20 minutes. Lower the oven temperature to 400°F, spritz the dough again, and bake until the bread is dark brown and crusty, about 20 more minutes. Remove from the oven and cool on a wire rack.

DURUM Focaccia

Who doesn't love focaccia? It's like a naked pizza, and it tastes even better made with durum flour. The durum gives it a more satisfying chew. The dough will be soft and loose when you mix it up, but don't worry, it'll crisp up nicely in the oven. For extra flavor, mix in some chopped fresh rosemary.

Put the flour, starter, and water in the bowl of a stand mixer. Crumble in the yeast. Using the dough hook, mix on low speed until everything is moist, about 4 minutes, scraping the bowl with a rubber spatula as needed. Increase the mixer speed to medium and mix until the dough clings to the dough hook, about 4 minutes. Add the salt and, if you like, 2 tablespoons (6 g) chopped fresh rosemary, and mix until the dough is smooth and elastic, about 2 minutes.

Shape the dough into a ball and put into an oiled bowl, turning it to coat with oil. Cover with plastic wrap and let rise in a warm spot (90°F) until doubled in size, about 1 1/2 hours.

Oil a large rimmed baking sheet (18 by 13 inches) or two smaller sheets with 2 tablespoons (30 g) of the oil. You can even use a large braising pan (as shown in the photos on page 32) or any pan with sides to give the focaccia a thick edge. Press the dough into the pans until it fills the pans to the rims and let rise for 30 minutes. Dimple the surface with your fingertips and let rise for another 30 minutes.

Preheat the oven to 475°F. Brush the top of the focaccia with the remaining 6 tablespoons (90 g) olive oil and sprinkle with some Maldon sea salt. Bake for 20 minutes(with the large in the center of the oven, the small ones on separate oven racks). Lower the oven temperature to 350°F, then bake until lightly browned on top, about 10 minutes.

Transfer to a wire rack and cool until warm. Cut into squares to serve.

MAKES ONE LARGE (18 BY 13 INCHES) OR TWO SMALL (13 BY 9 INCHES) FOCACCIAS

4 cups (680 g) durum flour

2 1/4 cups (480 g) Durum Focaccia Starter (page 23)

2 2/3 cups (580 g) cold water

2 tablespoons (18 g) packed fresh cake yeast, or 2 1/4 teaspoons (8 g) instant yeast

4 teaspoons (22 g) fine sea salt

8 tablespoons (120 g) olive oil

Maldon sea salt, for sprinkling

ROSEMARY Durum BREAD

Most all-purpose flour has about 8 to 11 percent protein, which is what determines how sturdy a bread will be when it comes out of the oven. Durum flour has up to 16 percent protein and gives this bread a nice, full body. It also gives the bread a chewy crust and deep, earthy flavor. It is one of the most flavorful breads I serve and one of the few that doesn't use a bread starter. Must be the durum. If you can't find durum flour in your local market, you can order it from King Arthur (see Sources, page 279).

MAKES ONE 10-INCH-DIAMETER ROUND LOAF

2 1/8 cups (300 g) durum flour

3/4 cup (105 g) high-protein flour, such as King Arthur Sir Galahad or Unbleached All-Purpose

1 tablespoon (9 g) packed fresh yeast, or 1 1/8 teaspoons (4 g) instant yeast

1 1/4 cups (275 g) cold water

1 1/2 teaspoons (8 g) fine sea salt

2 tablespoons (6 g) chopped fresh rosemary

Put the durum flour, and high-protein flour in the bowl of a stand mixer. Crumble in the yeast. Stir with a spoon to blend. Add the water, attach the dough hook, and mix on low speed until everything is moist, about 4 minutes. Increase the mixer speed to medium and mix until the dough is smooth, about 4 minutes. Add the salt and rosemary and mix until the dough is very smooth and silky, 1 to 2 minutes.

Put the dough in an oiled bowl, turning it to coat with oil. Cover with plastic wrap and set in a warm spot (90°F) until doubled in size, about 45 minutes. Punch down the dough, cover with plastic wrap, and let rise again in a warm spot until doubled in size, about 45 minutes.

Punch down the dough and shape into a ball. Put on a heavily floured rimless baking sheet. Cover with a clean kitchen towel and let rise in a warm spot until doubled in size, about 1 hour.

Meanwhile, remove all but the bottom rack in your oven and put a baking stone on the rack. Preheat the oven to 475°F for at least 30 minutes.

Slide the dough from the baking sheet onto the hot stone and immediately spritz the dough with a spray bottle of water until well coated, about 5 seconds. Bake until swollen and golden, about 20 minutes. Lower the oven temperature to 400°F, spritz the dough again, and bake until the bread is dark and very crusty, about 20 minutes more. Remove from the oven and let cool on a wire rack.

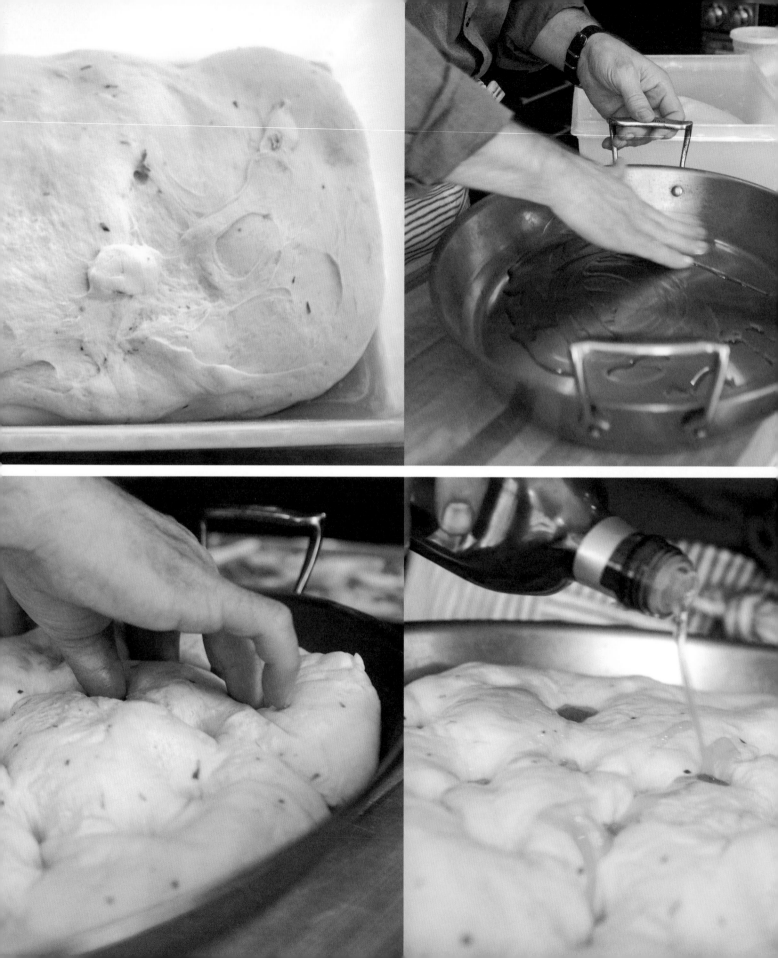

BLUEBERRY Schiacciata

About ten years ago, on one of my trips to Italy, I had a Concord grape schiacciata (skee-ah-chata). It was an eye-opening experience. This is what bread could taste like with a little sugar in it but not so much that it becomes a dessert. The only thing was, I kept crunching on the seeds of the grapes. In blueberry season, I thought, what a great substitute! Schiacciata means "pressed" or "flattened," referring to the way you press the fruit into this dough. It's usually made like focaccia with fruit pressed into the top, but I like to sandwich the fruit between layers of dough in little ring molds, then press more fruit on top. It makes a nice presentation. You could also skip the ring molds and roll the dough into a large round about 1/4 inch thick, put it on a baking sheet, and press the blueberries into the top. Note that this recipe uses a sponge, which is similar to a starter, except the mixture stands for just 30 minutes instead of the 12 hours required for a starter.

MAKES SIX 3-INCH ROUNDS

1 cup (220 g) warm (100 to 110°F) water

1 tablespoon plus 1 teaspoon (12 g) packed fresh cake yeast, or 1 1/2 teaspoons (5 g) instant yeast

1 1/3 cups (275 g) sugar

2 eggs (100 g)

3 1/2 cups (500 g) tipo 00 or all-purpose flour, plus more for rolling

2 tablespoons (30 g) lard or vegetable shortening

1 teaspoon (6 g) fine sea salt

4 tablespoons (62 g) unsalted butter, softened

2 cups (410 g) blueberries

Put the water in the bowl of a stand mixer. Stir in the yeast and 3 tablespoons (39 g) of the sugar and let stand until foamy, about 5 minutes.

Beat in the eggs with the paddle attachment on medium speed, then mix in 1 3/4 cups (250 g) of the flour on low speed until incorporated. Cover tightly with plastic wrap and let stand in a warm spot (90°F) until bubbly, about 30 minutes.

Beat the lard into the sponge with the paddle on medium speed. Mix in the remaining 1 3/4 cups (250 g) flour and the salt on low speed until the dough comes together. Mix in the butter.

Change to the dough hook and mix on medium speed for 3 minutes. The dough should be like stiff, sticky cake batter. Cover tightly with plastic wrap and let stand in a warm spot until doubled in size, another 30 minutes or so. At this point, the dough should be soft and pliable, yet rollable.

To roll and assemble: Lightly flour a work surface. Divide the dough in half and roll out each half into a 1/4-inch-thick round. Using a 3-inch ring mold or biscuit cutter, cut twelve 3-inch rounds out of the dough.

Preheat the oven to 400°F. Grease a baking sheet and the insides of six 3-inch ring molds. Put the molds on the sheet and place one circle of dough in each mold, pressing and stretching the dough to fit to the edges. Fill each mold halfway with a layer of blueberries. Sprinkle the blueberries with 2 tablespoons (26 g) of the sugar. Top with another piece of dough and press down gently, popping the blueberries a little bit. Press more blueberries into the top of the dough and sprinkle each schiacciata with 1 tablespoon (13 g) sugar.

Chocolate BREAD

I'm a chocolate freak. If there were no chocolate in this world, I would have no reason to live. So why not make bread with it? Whenever you need a midafternoon snack to go with espresso, here's your bread. I also use this once in a while to make a dessert sort of like chocolate French toast. Try it. Just make traditional French toast, but use this bread. With a few fresh strawberries and syrup, it's unbelievable.

MAKES ONE 12-INCH-DIAMETER ROUND LOAF

4¹/2 cups (600 g) high-protein flour, such as King Arthur Sir Galahad or Unbleached All-Purpose

¹/2 cup (60 g) unsweetened cocoa powder

¹/4 cup (60 g) sugar

2 tablespoons plus 1 teaspoon (21 g) packed fresh cake yeast, or 2³/4 teaspoons (10 g) instant yeast

1 cup (220 g) cold water

3 tablespoons (60 g) honey

¹/4 cup (50 g) grapeseed or olive oil

8 egg yolks (16 g), lightly beaten

1 teaspoon (6 g) fine sea salt

5 ounces (140 g) semisweet chocolate, chopped

²/3 cup (114 g) raisins

Put the flour, cocoa powder, and sugar in the bowl of a stand mixer. Crumble in the yeast. Mix with a spoon to combine. Add the water, honey, oil, and egg yolks and mix with the dough hook on low speed to moisten everything, about 4 minutes. Increase the mixer speed to medium and mix until the dough is stiff and clings to the dough hook, about 8 minutes. Add the salt, chocolate, and raisins and mix until incorporated, 1 to 2 minutes. You may have to knead the dough with your hands a little to get all the chocolate and raisins embedded into the dough.

Put the dough in an oiled bowl and turn it to coat with oil. Cover with plastic wrap and set in a warm spot (90°F) until doubled in size, about 1¹/2 hours.

Punch down the dough and shape into a ball. Put on a heavily floured rimless baking sheet. Cover with a clean kitchen towel and let rise in a warm spot until doubled in size, about 1 hour.

Meanwhile, remove all but the bottom rack in your oven and put a baking stone on the rack. Preheat the oven to 400°F for at least 30 minutes.

Slide the dough from the baking sheet onto the stone and immediately spritz the dough with a spray bottle of water until well coated, about 5 seconds. Bake for 20 minutes. Lower the oven temperature to 375°F, spritz the dough again, then bake until the bread is dark brown and crusty, about 30 minutes. Remove from the oven and let cool on a wire rack.

Fig and Chestnut BREAD

I'm always looking for new breads to serve with a cheese plate or salumi. I usually mix in some dried fruit, maybe some nuts. This is one of my favorite combinations, but feel free to swap out the figs for raisins, dates, dried apricots, or any other dried fruit. I usually slice the bread and warm it up a little in the oven or toast it on a grill.

Put the high-protein flour, chestnut flour, water, and starter in the bowl of a stand mixer. Crumble in the yeast. Using the dough hook, mix on low speed to moisten everything, about 4 minutes, scraping the sides of the bowl with a rubber spatula as needed. Increase the mixer speed to medium and mix until the dough is smooth and clings to the dough hook, 6 to 8 minutes. Add the salt and figs and mix on medium speed until the figs are well incorporated. If some of the figs don't play nice, flour your hands and push them into the dough with your fingers.

Put the dough in an oiled bowl, turning to coat it with oil. Cover with plastic wrap, and set in a warm spot (90°F) until doubled in size, about 1 hour.

Punch down the dough and shape into a ball. Put on a heavily floured rimless baking sheet. Cover with a clean kitchen towel and let rise in a warm spot until doubled in size, about 1 hour.

Meanwhile, remove all but the bottom rack in your oven and put a baking stone on the rack. Preheat the oven to 475°F for at least 30 minutes.

Slide the dough from the baking sheet onto the stone and immediately spritz the dough with a spray bottle of water until well coated, about 5 seconds. Bake until swollen and golden, about 20 minutes. Lower the oven temperature to 400°F, spritz the dough again, and bake until the bread looks dark brown and crusty, about 20 minutes. Remove from the oven and cool on a wire rack.

For the best flavor, slice and lightly toast the bread before serving.

PREP AHEAD

The starter must be made 3 days ahead but then will keep for months—even years—if you feed it and keep it alive.

MAKES ONE 10-INCH-DIAMETER ROUND LOAF

2 cups (280 g) high-protein flour, such as King Arthur Sir Galahad or Unbleached All-Purpose Flour

1/2 cup plus 1 tablespoon (80 g) chestnut flour

2 teaspoons (6 g) packed fresh cake yeast, or 3/4 teaspoon (3 g) instant yeast

1 cup (220 g) cold water

1 cup (287 g) Natural Sourdough Starter (page 23)

1 1/2 teaspoons (8 g) fine sea salt

4 to 5 dried figs (75 g), chopped

Brioche

I included a brioche recipe in my last book but I changed the recipe a little here. This one uses flour that's more widely available and a little lower in protein to make a softer brioche. The method is a little easier, too, because you don't have to fold the dough over as much. Sliced, toasted, and slathered with mostarda or marmalade, this brioche is hands-down my favorite bread to eat with cheese.

MAKES ONE 9 BY 5-INCH LOAF OR 13 BY 4-INCH PULLMAN LOAF

DOUGH

3 eggs (150 g), lightly beaten

2²/₃ cups plus 1¹/₂ tablespoons (370 g) high-protein flour, such as King Arthur Sir Galahad or Unbleached All-Purpose

1¹/₂ tablespoons (13.5 g) packed fresh cake yeast, or 1³/₄ teaspoons (6 g) instant yeast

1 tablespoon (15 g) sugar

¹/₃ cup (70 g) milk

1 cup (227 g) unsalted butter, cut into 8 pieces, softened

1¹/₂ teaspoons (8 g) fine sea salt

EGG WASH

2 tablespoons beaten egg (from above)

2 teaspoons milk

For the dough: Reserve 2 tablespoons of the beaten eggs. Put the high-protein flour, sugar, milk, and remaining beaten eggs in the bowl of a stand mixer. Crumble in the yeast. Using the paddle attachment, mix on low speed until everything is moistened and a rough dough starts to form, about 3 minutes.

Add the butter a few pieces at a time, waiting until one addition is incorporated before adding the next. When all of the butter has been incorporated, switch from the paddle attachment to the dough hook and add the salt. Increase the mixer speed to medium and mix until the dough is very satiny and smooth, about 15 minutes.

Put the dough in a buttered bowl, turning to coat it with butter. Cover with plastic wrap and set in a warm spot (90°F) until doubled in size, about 1 hour.

Meanwhile, butter a 9 by 5-inch loaf pan, or a 13 by 4-inch pullman (pain de mie) pan for small, square slices.

Punch down the dough and shape it into a rough rectangle long enough to fit comfortably into the loaf pan. Loosely roll the rectangle from one long side to the other to make a rounder log shape and place the log in the prepared pan, seam side down. Cover with a clean kitchen towel and set in a warm spot (90°F) until the dough is light, puffy, and nearly doubled in size, about 2 hours.

Preheat the oven to 375°F. Just before baking, make the egg wash: Whisk the reserved egg and the milk together and brush over the dough. Bake until golden brown and bulging from the top of the pan, about 40 minutes. Remove from the oven and let cool on a wire rack.

Romana PIZZA DOUGH

I first learned how to make pizza in 1991 when I was working for Wolfgang Puck at Granita. But it wasn't until 1997, when I met Matteo Puppilo at Bella Blu in New York City, that I really developed a love for pizza. He taught me with such passion about the dough and how crucial it is to great pizza. This is the thin-crust dough that Matteo taught me, and it remains the basic dough that I use for most of my pizzas. If you like a thicker, chewier dough, check out the Napoletana recipe on page 40. Oh, and by the way, this recipe makes enough for 6 or 7 pizzas, so you can freeze the extra dough and have it ready at a moment's notice.

MAKES SIX OR SEVEN 12-INCH-DIAMETER ROUNDS

6 cups (750 g) high-protein flour, such as King Arthur Sir Galahad or Unbleached All-Purpose

2 tablespoons (25 g) sugar

2³/₄ teaspoons (8 g) packed fresh cake yeast, or 1 teaspoon (3.5 g) instant yeast

1¹/₂ cups plus 2 tablespoons (355 g) cold water

¹/₄ cup (60 g) extra-virgin olive oil

2¹/₂ teaspoons (15 g) fine sea salt

Put the flour, sugar, water, and oil in the bowl of a stand mixer. Crumble in the yeast. Using the dough hook, mix on low speed until everything is moist, about 4 minutes, scraping the bowl as needed with a rubber spatula. Increase the mixer speed to medium and mix until the dough clings to the dough hook, about 4 minutes more. Add the salt and mix until the dough is very soft and stretchy, another 3 minutes.

Cut the dough into 6 or 7 equal pieces and roll into balls (about the size of a softball) on an unfloured board. Scatter on a little flour, cover with plastic wrap, and refrigerate overnight.

To roll out each ball of dough, remove the dough from the refrigerator and let stand at room temperature for 1 hour. It will stretch more easily when it's warm. Flatten the ball on a floured work surface, then hold the disk in your hands in the air and circle your fingers around the edge, pinching gently around the edge to make a border. It's easier to start stretching pizza dough in the air instead of on a work surface, because in the air gravity will pull down the dough, stretching it from where it's held in your fingers. Once it's stretched to about 8 inches in diameter, place the dough on the floured work surface and pat it out with your fingertips, from the center toward the edge, to fully stretch the round of dough. Gently push your palms into the center of the dough to gently stretch it away toward the edges. Pat and stretch to a round about 12 inches in diameter and ¹/₈ inch to ¹/₄ inch thick. Top and bake as you like.

PREP AHEAD

Cover and refrigerate the dough for up to 3 days or freeze in an airtight container for up to 1 month. Thaw and bring to room temperature before rolling out.

Napoletana PIZZA DOUGH

Naples dough is a little thicker than the pizza dough in Rome. It puffs up a little more and has a thicker rim. It's also made with a bread starter, but no oil and no sugar. It's more old-school. Chewier. I also use more dough per pizza to make it taste a little doughier. Learning this dough was a love affair. (It took me years to get it right.) You don't just get a recipe for this, then make thick-crust pizza. You need to nurture the dough. You need to get your hands into it and understand how thick the crust should be. I explain everything in the recipe below, but these details are why pizzaiolos are so admired around the world. In making a perfect crust, the ingredients are simple, but how you treat them is the most important thing.

MAKES FOUR OR FIVE 12-INCH-DIAMETER ROUNDS

4 cups (500 g) high-protein flour, such as King Arthur Sir Galahad or Unbleached All-Purpose

2¹/8 cups (500 g) Biga Starter (page 22)

1 cup minus 2 tablespoons (200 g) cold water

¹/2 teaspoon (1 g) packed fresh cake yeast, or ¹/8 teaspoon (0.5 g) instant yeast

2¹/2 teaspoons (15 g) fine sea salt

Put the flour, starter, and water in the bowl of a stand mixer. Crumble in the yeast. Using the dough hook, mix on low speed until everything is moist, about 4 minutes, scraping the bowl as needed with a rubber spatula. Increase the mixer speed to medium and mix until the dough clings to the dough hook, about 3 minutes more. Add the salt and mix until the dough is very soft and stretchy, another 3 minutes.

Put the dough in an oiled bowl, turning to coat it with oil. Cover with plastic wrap and set in a warm spot (90°F) until doubled in size, about 1 hour.

Cut the dough into 4 or 5 equal pieces and roll into balls (about the size of a small cantaloupe) on an unfloured board. Put the balls in an airtight container, cover, and refrigerate overnight.

To roll out each ball of dough, remove the dough from the refrigerator about 1 hour before using. It will stretch more easily when it's warm. Flatten the ball on a floured work surface, then hold the disk in your hands in the air and circle your fingers around the edge, pinching gently around the edge to make a border. It's easier to start stretching pizza dough in the air instead of on a work surface, because in the air gravity will pull down the dough, stretching it from where it's held in your fingers. Once it's stretched to about 8 inches in diameter, put the dough on the counter and pat it out with your fingertips from the center toward the edge to fully stretch the round of dough. Gently push your palms into the center of the dough to gently stretch it away toward to the edges. Pat and stretch to a round about 12 inches in diameter and a little more than a ¹/4 inch thick, with a thicker rim. Top and bake as you like.

PREP AHEAD

Cover and refrigerate the dough for up to 3 days or freeze for up to 1 month. Thaw and bring to room temperature before rolling out.

Think Outside the Wine Bottle

You will notice beverage pairings with the recipes throughout this book. I have been very careful to use the words *beverage* and *drink* here. It has become commonplace to think in terms of food and wine pairings. However, with all of the drink options available, wine alone can be extremely limiting for certain meals. The craft-brew movement has taken Italy by storm over the past decade and brought with it a fresh outlook on what to drink with what you eat. Plus, some people don't drink alcohol, yet they still want a beverage that helps them experience the full flavors of a meal.

I take a broad approach to beverage pairings, including wine, beer, specialty sodas, flavored teas, and fresh juices. Feel free to experiment with what you have around the house. Use what's available to you. If you think a certain wine works well because of the berry flavor it imparts, try other beverages that provide a similar flavor. What you drink with the dishes throughout this book is, of course, up to your personal preference. The pizzas are a case in point. How often do you swing by a pizzeria and just grab a soda with a slice? There's no need to limit yourself to wine. Something similar to American soda, like Italian Chinotto, will work equally well with pizza.

The same goes for desserts. I would hesitate to serve wine with Waffles with Nutella and Semifreddo (page 259), but a ginger beer float would be great—not to mention fun. The bottom line is that the drinks should enhance the meal. The ideal meal is one where you can relax and enjoy the company of those you've chosen to dine with. Stressing over the nuances of what you drink defeats the purpose. Loosen up and have fun with it!

Margherita PIZZA

Whenever I eat at a pizzeria, I always order the Margherita. It's the perfect combination: crust, sauce, and cheese. Nothing else. Maybe some fresh basil leaves if you have them. There are some combinations that you don't mess with, and this is one of them. Because the pizza toppings are so simple, I like to use a thinner, crispier Romana pizza dough. And it goes without saying that ingredients really matter here. There are only three in the topping. Make sure each ingredient is the best quality you can find.

Remove all but the bottom rack in your oven and put a baking stone on the rack. Preheat the oven to 500°F for at least 30 minutes. If you have convection, turn it on to help brown and blister the top of the pizza.

Place the dough round on a well-floured rimless baking sheet. Ladle the sauce into the center of the dough round, then spread from the center to the edges by moving the ladle in widening concentric circles. Break each slice of mozzarella into 2 pieces and scatter them over the sauce.

Slide the pizza off the baking sheet onto the hot stone and bake until the cheese melts and the crust is golden brown, 5 to 7 minutes.

Transfer to a cutting board and immediately scatter on the basil leaves. Cut into slices to serve.

MAKES ONE 12-INCH PIZZA

1 round Romana Pizza Dough (page 39)

About 2/3 cup Pizza Sauce (page 267)

2 slices fresh mozzarella, each about 1/2 inch thick

4 or 5 small fresh basil leaves

LOMBARDA PIZZA

Skip the mozzarella and basil. Instead, top the sauce with 1/2 cup grated Bitto cheese (or Italian fontina in a pinch), 1/2 cup cubed fresh mozzarella, and 1/3 cup crumbled cotechino sausage (or another cooked Italian sausage in a pinch). Crack an egg into the center of the pizza and bake. When the pizza is crisp, remove and scatter on 1/2 teaspoon mixed chopped fresh herbs like parsley, rosemary, and thyme.

PARMA PIZZA

Skip all the other toppings. Instead, scatter on 1/2 cup cubed fresh mozzarella and 1/2 cup cubed fontina cheese. Bake until crisp. Mix together 2 cups arugula, 1 tablespoon extra-virgin olive oil, 1 teaspoon sherry vinegar, and salt and pepper to taste. When the pizza comes out of the oven, put the arugula mixture on top and garnish with 4 thin slices of prosciutto.

TONNO

Skip the basil. Instead, spread on the pizza sauce and mozzarella as directed, then scatter on some dried oregano, 2 thin slices Vidalia onion broken into rings, and $1/3$ cup flaked Sicilian canned tuna.

ZUCCA

Skip all the other toppings. Instead, soak 2 tablespoons raisins in Marsala wine for 2 hours. Drain the raisins and mix them with 2 teaspoons pine nuts, a splash of extra-virgin olive oil, a spritz of sherry vinegar, and salt and pepper to taste. Spread a thin layer of Squash Crema (page 272) over the dough. Top with $1/2$ cup cubed fresh mozzarella and 2 tablespoons freshly grated Parmesan cheese. Bake until crisp. When the pizza comes out of the oven, scatter on the raisin mixture.

continued, page 46

BEVERAGE—Medici Ermete, Lambrusco di Salomino di Santa Croce 2009 "Concerto" (Emilia Romagna): Throughout Italy, Lambrusco is the wine to drink with Roman pizza. It's frothy, cold, inky purple in color, and loaded with tart berry fruit.

Part Skim Is Part Insane

The mozzarella we use on our pizza is very specific. It's usually aged for forty-eight hours before the cheese maker sends it to us. This makes all the difference in the world. We can tell when they are running behind and send us mozzarella that has been made the same day or only aged for twenty-four hours. It starts to break down when the pizza goes in the oven and it separates. Instead of creamy, it comes out grainy. It's important when making a simple pizza like Margherita to find handmade mozzarella from a reputable cheese maker. The store-bought vacuum-sealed stuff just will not do for this preparation. And please, if you are thinking of using part-skim mozzarella, stop thinking.

PANNOCCHIA PIZZA

Skip all the other toppings. Instead, sauté 2 tablespoons corn kernels and some snipped fresh chives in a little olive oil. Grill 1 trimmed scallion until it just starts to go limp, 1 minute per side, then coarsely chop it. Spread a thin layer of Rich Corn Crema (page 272) over the dough. Top with 1/2 cup cubed fresh mozzarella and bake until crisp. When the pizza comes out of the oven, spoon on the corn mixture, the grilled chopped scallion, and 1/3 cup diced buffalo mozzarella.

TRENTINO

Skip all the other toppings. Instead, cut 4 fresh figs in half lengthwise and grill, cut side down, over medium-high heat until browned, 1 to 2 minutes (or broil cut side up 4 to 6 inches from the heat until browned). Toss with 1 tablespoon extra-virgin olive oil, 1/2 teaspoon balsamic vinegar, and salt and pepper to taste. Arrange the figs, cut side down, on the dough round and scatter on 1/2 cup crumbled Gorgonzola and 1/3 cup diced fresh mozzarella. Bake until crisp, then top with 4 very thin slices of Beef Speck (page 157) or purchased pork speck.

SARDINIAN

Skip all the other toppings. Instead, slice half a small zucchini into thin rounds and bake on a baking sheet in a preheated 350°F oven until soft, 2 to 3 minutes. Mix together 2 tablespoons ricotta cheese, 1/8 teaspoon chopped fresh chives, and 1/8 teaspoon chopped fresh parsley. Layer the pizza with 1/4 cup diced fresh mozzarella, 2 tablespoons freshly grated Parmesan, the zucchini, and dollops of the ricotta. Bake until crisp, then top with 1 to 2 teaspoons very thinly sliced bottarga (Sardinian sun-dried fish roe).

NUTELLA

Skip all the other toppings. Stack two balls of Romana pizza dough directly on top of each other and roll out to a 12-inch diameter. Dimple the dough with a pizza dough docker (a roller with long spikes on it; see Sources on page 279). Bake the dough stack until it puffs but doesn't brown too much, 1 to 2 minutes. Remove from the oven and, using a long, serrated knife, cut the dough in half horizontally (essentially separating the two dough rounds). Scrape out the loose dough from the inside of each round with a spoon. You want to make it thinner, almost like a cracker. Spread the inside of one of the rounds with a layer of chocolate hazelnut spread such as Nutella. Put the other round back on top. Bake again until nicely browned, 1 to 2 minutes. Remove and dust with confectioners' sugar. Cut into wedges like a pizza.

Opposite: Pizza Lombarda

Mortadella PIZZA

I make all sorts of dishes with my homemade salumi. Pasta sauces, ravioli fillings, and pizzas top the list. When I make a pizza with sausage, I think about what's in the sausage and how to play off the flavors. Mortadella has pistachios, so I like to drizzle on some chopped pistachios and extra-virgin olive oil. When you buzz them together in a food processor, the oil picks up a beautiful green color. And because this pizza has a fair amount going on (the sausage, the cheese, the pistachios), I like to use the Naples dough, which holds all the ingredients a little better than the thinner Roman dough.

Remove all but the bottom rack in your oven and put a baking stone on the rack. Preheat the oven to 500°F for at least 30 minutes. If you have convection, turn it on to help brown and blister the top of the pizza.

Place the dough round on a well-floured rimless baking sheet. Arrange a few slices of mortadella over the dough. Scatter the Parmesan and mozzarella over the mortadella. Slide the pizza onto the hot stone and bake until the cheese melts and the crust is golden brown, 5 to 7 minutes.

Meanwhile, buzz the pistachios and oil in a food processor until the nuts are coarsely chopped, about a minute.

Transfer the pizza to a cutting board and drizzle with about 1¹/₂ tablespoons of the pistachio mixture (save the rest for another use). Cut into wedges.

continued, page 51

MAKES ONE 12-INCH PIZZA

1 round Napoletana Pizza Dough
(page 40)

¹/₄ cup grated Parmesan cheese

¹/₂ cup cubed fresh mozzarella

2 ounces thinly sliced Lamb
Mortadella (page 142) or purchased
pork mortadella

¹/₂ cup shelled pistachios

³/₄ cup extra-virgin olive oil

MARINARA PIZZA

Skip all the other toppings. Instead, thinly slice a clove of garlic and warm it up in a little olive oil in a pan, 2 to 3 minutes. Ladle $1/2$ cup of Hand-Crushed Marinara Sauce (page 266) over the dough round, then scatter on $1/4$ teaspoon dried oregano. Spoon the warm garlic and oil over the pizza and bake.

QUATTRO FORMAGGIO

Skip all the other toppings. Instead, top with $1/3$ cup each robiola cheese (or ricotta), goat cheese, diced fresh mozzarella, and grated Parmesan.

PESCA

Skip all the other toppings. Instead, cut a peach in half and grill one half, cut side down, over medium-high heat until lightly grill-marked, 1 to 2 minutes (or broil cut side up 4 to 6 inches from the heat until lightly browned). Then slice thinly and scatter over the dough round. Add 2 tablespoons chopped roasted mushrooms (see recipe for Roasted Mushrooms in Foil, page 227) and $1/2$ cup diced fresh mozzarella. Bake until crisp, then top with a few thin slices of Lardo (page 160) or purchased lardo.

PERA

Skip all the other toppings. Instead, scatter on a thinly sliced pear half, $1/2$ cup diced provolone, and $1/4$ cup finely chopped Shortcut Guanciale (page 162).

BEVERAGE—Mastroberardino Lacryma Christi 2008 (Campania): This regionally specific pairing perfectly matches the Naples dough. It's a plump, fresh, and fruity wine. But if you're craving a Coca-Cola here, don't fight it. Or put a spin on it with San Pellegrino Chinotto, a malty dark soda flavored with a small, bitter citrus fruit of the same name.

I**N THE SUMMER OF 2009,** I went on *Iron Chef* against Michael Symon. It was Battle Veal. We're not talking veal ribs or veal breast. No, this was a whole side of veal. One hundred and fifty pounds! It was as if someone handed you a calf and said, "Do something with it." I had my chefs Jeff Michaud and Brad Spence with me. I also brought a new pasta extruder that we got for Vetri restaurant. I've always had these monster pasta extruder machines that took up loads up precious kitchen space. We had just purchased a little tabletop model that you could plug into a regular outlet. It was small but really powerful, and I was excited to use it for cooking demonstrations. But we had just gotten it in and hadn't used it before. I remember talking the company, Arcobaleno, into giving us a great deal on it. We told them we were going to use it on *Iron Chef* and show the United States how great this pasta machine was.

PASTAS

After figuring out how to lift the side of veal to the table, we went at it. Jeff was set to make the pasta, and we started rolling. The thing is, all pasta machines are a little different, and if you're not used to how they work, a little too much water in the dough—or not enough—can be a real problem.

Anyway, I started butchering the veal, Brad was mixing up some sauces, and Jeff dove into making the extruded pasta. Fifteen minutes later, I heard Jeff yell, "Fuck!" I looked up from the veal and saw him banging the pasta machine with a big cleaver. I was like, "Dude, what's up?" "The machine is jammed up," he said. I started laughing. Brad was making his sauces, looking over his shoulder, saying, "You guys alright? You guys alright?" The cameras were rolling. Time was ticking away.

This happens now and again. If you don't have enough water in the pasta dough, the auger mixes the flour into cement. Not only will the dough not come out of the machine, but it will lock it up. The only way to get the machine going again is to open it up, take it apart and turn the auger in the opposite direction, picking out the hardened dough. That whole process was not going to happen in 60 minutes on *Iron Chef*. So I went over and tried to figure out how to fix the problem another way. I must have been there for 20 minutes. And there's Alton Brown on the microphone, saying, "They better stop messing with that pasta machine. They're not gonna make anything." His voice was piercing into my head like a bullet: "They're not gonna finish. They have to move on. I've never seen anything like this on *Iron Chef*, ladies and gentlemen." The whole time, I was thinking, "Will you shut the hell up already and let me work!" Finally, I said to Jeff, "Fuck it. Just make pappardelle." He did, we hauled ass, and needless to say, we finished—with seven minutes to spare—so early that Alton didn't know what to say. In the end, the judges gave us the nod. But later, when I heard back from Arcobaleno, I learned that pasta-extruder makers get pretty pissed off when you go on national television and bang their machine with a cleaver. Just sayin'!

FLOUR

Maybe it was all our sweat in the *Iron Chef* kitchen stadium that caused the pasta machine to lock up. Flour is very sensitive to moisture! Whether you're using high-protein flour or low-protein flour, it will inevitably absorb some of the moisture in the air. If it's really humid, it can make a big difference in how much water you add to your pasta.

That's especially true for extruded pasta dough, which only has two ingredients. Extruded pasta differs from fresh egg pasta in that it's made with only coarse semolina flour and water instead of fine all-purpose flour and eggs. The sandy-textured semolina dough is forced through an extruder that shapes it into long strands like spaghetti or short shapes like rigatoni.

Semolina is the endosperm of durum wheat, which means it's the part that takes up most of the grain's bulk. That part is bright yellow and usually coarsely ground, like cornmeal. Semolina is what gives extruded pastas like spaghetti and rigatoni that incomparable "al dente" chewiness. Water is the only other ingredient, so you have to carefully watch how much you add.

The dough for egg pastas that will be rolled into lasagna sheets and cut into fettuccine is a little more forgiving. And it uses different flour. For my basic egg pasta dough, I like to use tipo 00 flour as the primary flour.

Tipo 00 is Italy's all-purpose flour, and like American all-purpose flours, it is very finely milled. If you need to substitute, American all-purpose flours are the best stand-in because they have a similar protein content to tipo 00 flour (8 to 10 percent). For a little extra chew, I like to use a mixture of tipo 00 and durum flour in a ratio of about 3 to 1. Keep in mind that durum flour and semolina are a little different. They're both milled from durum wheat, but durum flour is finely ground and has a light tan color, while semolina is coarsely ground and has a bright yellow color.

EXTRUDED PASTA

When I cooked in Italy, I made extruded pasta in every shape imaginable, from short tubes to long strands. When I got back to Philadelphia, I made mostly rolled pastas like pappardelle and ravioli. But I missed the chewy texture of extruded pastas. So I started experimenting. I thought, there's gotta be something better than the boxed stuff, right? It's true that some boxed pasta extruded with bronze dies can have a great rough surface to it. But I found out that the most important thing wasn't the dough itself or the extruder but how to dry the pasta properly. Extruded pasta dough is nothing more than semolina and water mixed in a bowl. You add just enough water so the mixture looks like loose, damp sand. Then you knead it a little bit with your fingers until it clumps together and feels like wads of sandy, dry bubble gum when pinched between your fingertips. Depending on the humidity in the air, you add more or less water to get the consistency right. Too dry is better than too wet, because if it's too wet, it will gum up the extruder machine.

But making the dough isn't the really important part. The trick is drying it. At first, I just hung the pasta to dry on racks. This was in the middle of winter and I didn't take into account that the humidity was very low. The air was dry and when I came into the kitchen the next morning, all the pasta was cracked. After doing some more digging, I found out that the professional pasta makers, the artisan extruded-pasta makers, have extensive rooms that dry the pasta slowly in an environment with precisely controlled humidity and temperature. The big commercial pasta companies speed up the process by using high heat to dry the pasta faster.

But drying it slowly gives you much better texture, because it ends up with a higher moisture content than industrial boxed pasta. When cooked, you can tell the difference right away. Pasta that's dried slowly feels so much better between your teeth. It gives only gradually. It chews leisurely and never feels rubbery. During cooking, it also sloughs off a little more starch into the pasta water, which makes the pasta water better for thickening sauces.

That's the texture I was going for. I tried everything. After hanging the pasta at room temperature, I tried covering it in plastic wrap or with a kitchen towel at room temperature to trap some moisture. Then I put a humidifier in the room for extra moisture. Then I froze it both covered and uncovered. Nothing worked! I was baffled and frustrated and ended up leaving the pasta uncovered in the refrigerator one day by accident. The next day, it was perfect!

It turns out that refrigerator air has just the right temperature and humidity to slowly dry the pasta. You can leave it in the fridge for 4 to 5 days and it continues to dry out gradually but still holds enough moisture that it won't crack. Now, I adjust the cooking time based on how long the extruded pasta has been sitting in the fridge. If I make it in the morning, refrigerate it, and cook it that night, it's done in 2 minutes. If I leave it in the fridge uncovered for another day, it's done in 3 minutes. Another day, 4 minutes—and so on. It's a pretty basic way of thinking: for every day the pasta dries in the fridge, add 1 minute of cooking time. It's not a perfect system; you still need to watch the pasta as it cooks, checking its texture now and then, and adjusting the cooking time. But for making and cooking extruded pasta at home, it's the best method I've found.

Now I love making extruded pasta—especially with my kids. KitchenAid has a pasta press attachment, so you can make spaghetti, macaroni, bucatini, rigatoni, fusilli, and a few other shapes. I encourage you to give it a try. It's so easy. It helps to soak and clean the auger right after you use it. But if you're not able to, take apart the pasta press attachment and let it dry for a few hours or overnight. The dried pasta dough will crack right off.

If you're tempted to go for something premade instead of homemade, skip the extruded pasta in the refrigerated cases of supermarkets. Boxed dried artisan pasta from Italy is better—particularly if it's extruded with bronze dies and dried slowly. Setaro, Latini, and Rustichella d'Abruzzo are a few good brands.

ROLLED PASTA

The dough for fresh egg pasta is a little different. Instead of high-protein semolina, it uses lower-protein all-purpose flour and eggs. I also add a little durum flour for extra chew and use only egg yolks with a little olive oil for richness. You knead for a few minutes until the dough is smooth and silky. You should develop just enough gluten in the dough so that it pulls back gradually when you stretch the dough between your hands.

The best roller out there for home use is the KitchenAid attachment (no, I don't have an endorsement deal with them!). Forget the hand-crank rollers; they are just too much work and very inconsistent. To help the dough roll easier, bring it almost to room temperature before rolling and lightly dust it with flour as you go. Start on the widest roller setting, then gradually crank it down to a narrower setting each time, rolling the pasta once on each setting until you get to the narrowest setting. I always finish on the thinnest setting. Usually I roll each piece of dough 8 to 10 times. It may seem too thin, but it's not. You should be able to see your hand through the dough when you hold it up to the light like seeing someone through a shower curtain. Just go slowly and dust the dough with flour so it doesn't stick to the rollers. For each piece of dough, you should end up with a pasta sheet 4 to 5 feet long. Give yourself plenty of counter space to work on!

After rolling, switch to the cutting attachment and cut into whatever shape you like. All of the pastas in this book are made using common cutting attachments like fettuccine—or no cutting attachment at all. Most of the raviolis are cut old-school—by hand with a knife. Just try to work quickly. It helps to keep a spray bottle of water nearby. Spritz the dough every once in a while to keep it from drying out as you work.

If you're thinking of buying premade pasta sheets instead of making them yourself, don't do it. They're never as good, and in a dish like Mortadella Tortelli with Pistachio Pesto (page 89), there are so few ingredients that the quality of the pasta really makes a difference. Another tip for baking pastas like ravioli and lasagna: I always leave some of the ends hanging over the sides of the baking dish. When the dish goes in the oven, those overhanging edges get crispy and delicious. Then you have two great textures: the soft pasta and sauce and the crunchy outer edges of the pasta. If you have convection on your oven, turn it on for baked pasta to help crisp the edges.

HAND-ROLLED PASTA

In 1994, I was working at La Chiusa restaurant in the Tuscan town of Monte-follonica. It's about ten minutes from Montepulciano, basically in the middle of nowhere. Several elderly women rolled pici pasta by hand all day at the restaurant. Pici is a long, thin pasta like thick spaghetti but made with fresh egg yolk pasta. They would take a knob of dough and roll it back and forth under their palms on long wooden boards with just the right pressure until the dough stretched out into a long, thin strand. They made it look so easy. And the pici was perfect, as if it had come right out of a machine. I tried doing it over and over, but the pici never came out right. This experience is what got me so interested in hand-rolled pasta.

I started learning all the different shapes, like orecchiette and garganelli, and techniques to make the pasta easier to shape. For example, I usually flour the board when I'm handling dough. But with hand-rolled pasta, if you use too much flour, it slides around on the board, which makes it harder to shape. A light dusting on your hands is all you need. Then again, if the pasta is too wet, it will stick to the board. As I mentioned earlier, I keep a spray bottle of water handy. It's the easiest way to regulate the humidity without over- or under-watering. At different times of the year and in different places, the air simply has more or less water in it. Making pasta in the summer is not like making pasta in the winter and not like making it in the mountains or at sea level. Understanding the craft of rolling pasta means being aware of your environment so you can make pasta under any circumstances.

PASTA WATER

I've read all kinds of articles and heard from dozens of people about the different ways to boil pasta, the ratios of water to pasta and salt to water . . . the methods are endless. Here's how I do it at home. I put a large stockpot of water over high heat. I usually use about 5 quarts of water per pound of pasta. I use a lid to boil the water faster. Once it boils, I add salt. Salting the water is a matter of taste, but the water should taste seasoned, like a weak broth. I use about 1 tablespoon kosher salt per 8 cups water. Then I drop in the pasta with a little stir to keep it from sticking and put the lid back on to quickly return the water to a boil. You want to boil the pasta quickly so it doesn't get mushy on the outside and so it stays a little chewy in the middle. After a minute or so, the water should return to a boil; then you can remove the lid. If you get a little boil-over, don't worry, just take off the lid and stir it down. A little boil-over acts like an alarm clock. Just hang around the kitchen and keep an ear out for it!

As for doneness, the pasta should be tender yet firm, which usually only takes 30 to 90 seconds for fresh egg pasta sheets, 4 to 5 minutes for refrigerated extruded pasta, or 8 to 10 minutes for boxed dried pasta. But don't go by cooking times. Take a piece of pasta and bite into it. The pasta should feel firm at the center, almost chewy, a little less than "al dente." Instead of thinking of it as boiling pasta, think of it as blanching pasta. The pasta should be slightly underdone when it comes out of the water. Instead of just dumping the sauce over the top of the cooked pasta on a plate, you will finish cooking the pasta later in the sauce or in the oven, where it will meld with the liquid and absorb some of its flavor. That's how you marry pasta with sauce.

I always save the pasta water. It should be a little cloudy, which is the starch that has leached out from the pasta into the water. That starchy water is perfect for thickening sauces.

OPEN ←——→ CLOSE

EXTRUDED PASTA

BASIC Extruded PASTA DOUGH

This dough is less about the recipe and more what you do with it afterward. A refrigerator has the right humidity, and the pasta will dry nice and slow for almost a week before it starts to crack. Every day it just gets a little chewier. I like the texture best after 2 days of drying in the refrigerator. But try "aging" it for up to 5 days to see what texture you like best. Enjoy matching different shapes with different sauces, too. The recipes here offer only a few examples. Pastas and sauces are generally interchangeable, so find combinations to suit your taste.

Put the semolina in a bowl. Slowly stir in enough water until the mixture looks like damp sand. Knead it a little bit with your fingers in the bowl until it clumps together and feels like wads of sandy, dry bubble gum when pinched between your fingers. Depending on the humidity in the room, you may need to add more or less water to get the consistency right. It should feel like damp sand that sticks together when you pinch it. Too dry is better than too wet. Even though it appears as if it's not ready, the dough will come together when it is extruded through the machine.

If using a stand mixer attachment, fit the pasta extruder with the desired shape and attach it to the accessory hub. Set the mixer speed to medium and feed the dough into the extruder in golf-ball-size clumps, using the back of the pusher accessory to push the clumps into the extruder. When the first ones come out, get rid of them because they will be uneven. Continue gradually dropping in golf-ball-size clumps and pushing them through the machine, being careful not to overload it. As the pasta is extruded, cut it into the desired lengths as directed below.

To dry short pasta like rigatoni and macaroni, place it on wire racks that will fit in your refrigerator and refrigerate uncovered. For long pasta like spaghetti and bucatini, coil it into rounded "nests" so it takes up less room, then put the nests on the racks in the flat container. Refrigerate the pasta, uncovered, for at least 8 hours or up to 5 days.

To cook, adjust the total time according to how long the pasta has dried in the refrigerator. Cook 8-hour-old pasta for about 2 minutes, day-old pasta for 3 minutes, and 2-day-old pasta for 4 minutes (my favorite). Add a minute of cooking for every extra day of drying.

MAKES ABOUT 1 POUND

2 cups plus 2 tablespoons (500 g) semolina

About 1 cup (220 g) water

RIGATONI

Fit your pasta extruder with the rigatoni plate. If using a stand mixer attachment, set the mixer to medium speed and feed the dough into the extruder, cutting the rigatoni into 1½-inch lengths.

FUSILLI

Fit your pasta extruder with the fusilli plate. If using a stand mixer attachment, set the mixer to medium-low speed and feed the dough into the extruder, cutting the fusilli into 2½-inch lengths.

CANDELE

Fit your pasta extruder with the large macaroni plate. If using a stand mixer attachment, set the mixer to high speed and feed the dough into the extruder, cutting the candele into 6-inch lengths. Dry straight instead of forming into nests.

LARGE MACARONI

Fit your pasta extruder with the large macaroni plate. If using a stand mixer attachment, set the mixer to medium speed and feed the dough into the extruder, cutting the macaroni into 2-inch lengths.

BUCATINI

Fit your pasta extruder with the bucatini plate. If using a stand mixer attachment, set the mixer to high speed and feed the dough into the extruder, cutting the bucatini into 9-inch lengths.

SPAGHETTI

Fit your pasta extruder with the spaghetti plate. If using a stand mixer attachment, set the mixer to high speed and feed the dough into the extruder, cutting the bucatini into 9-inch lengths.

TONNARELLI

Fit your pasta extruder with the tonnarelli plate. If you don't have one, use the spaghetti plate. If using a stand mixer attachment, set the mixer to high speed and feed the dough into the extruder, cutting the tonnarelli into 9-inch lengths.

Rigatoni WITH SWORDFISH, TOMATO, AND EGGPLANT FRIES

The first time my wife, Megan, and I went to Rome together was in 2007. We ate pasta for three days straight. On our last night, we swore there would be no pasta. We went to a fish restaurant named Pierluigi to seal the deal. They had a beautiful display of fresh fish on ice, and we picked our fish for the mixed grill and waited. As we were talking at the table, the waiter brought over a pasta dish with swordfish and eggplant fries on top—still in the pan. He placed it in the middle of the table and gave us each a dish. "Excuse me, but we didn't order this," I said to him. He looked at us and said, "You need to start your meal with something. You can't just have the fish." So, we started eating the pasta anyway. We didn't stop eating it until we were fighting over the last bite. It was the best pasta dish of the entire trip. When I got home, I started experimenting immediately.

MAKES 4 SERVINGS

12 ounces refrigerated extruded Rigatoni (page 63), or 10 ounces boxed dried rigatoni

2 tablespoons olive oil

1/4 cup finely chopped onion

1 clove garlic, smashed

8 ounces grape tomatoes, halved lengthwise

Salt and freshly ground pepper

1 pound swordfish, cut into 3/4-inch cubes

Juice of 1/2 lemon

15 fresh basil leaves

Eggplant Fries (page 235)

Bring a large pot of salted water to a boil. Drop in the pasta, quickly return to a boil, and cook until the pasta is tender yet firm, 2 to 7 minutes, depending on how long it has been refrigerated (or 8 to 9 minutes for the boxed stuff). Drain the pasta, reserving the pasta water.

Meanwhile, heat the olive oil in a large sauté pan over medium heat. Add the onion and garlic and sauté until soft but not browned, about 3 minutes. Add the tomatoes and cook for 5 minutes. Season lightly with salt and pepper. Add the fish and cook until white all over but still translucent in the center, 2 to 3 minutes.

Add the drained rigatoni to the pan. Add a splash or two of pasta water and cook, tossing to coat, for about 2 minutes. Taste and season with lemon juice, salt, and pepper as needed.

Remove the garlic and divide among warm pasta bowls. Tear the basil into coarse pieces by hand and scatter over the pasta. Top with the eggplant fries.

BEVERAGE—Librandi, Ciro Rosso Classico 2008 (Calabria): Here's a classic regional pairing if there ever was one. The deep south of Italy is home to basil, tomatoes, eggplant, and simply prepared seafood, and this dish has it all. Countless Calabrese could be enjoying this same pairing as you read this sentence.

Rigatoni WITH CHICKEN LIVERS, CIPOLLINI ONIONS, AND SAGE

You go through phases in a kitchen. You get into making something like confit and then you end up trying to confit everything under the sun. A few months back, I was crazy about sausage. I put everything I could think of in the meat grinder to make sausage out of it. One day, I had some extra chicken livers, so I put those through the grinder and made a terrine. But it didn't come out right. Then, my chef Jeff Michaud had an idea to make a simple ragù with minced chicken livers and toss it with some pasta. It was amazing. That chicken liver pasta was on our menu at Osteria for two months. Then one day I walked into the restaurant and it wasn't on the menu anymore. I asked Jeff about it and he said he wanted to change things up. I screamed, "Are you out of your mind??!!!?? It is the perfect, most innovative, most unexpected dish. It should be on the menu forever!" That's an argument that I won pretty easily.

Bring a large pot of salted water to a boil. Drop in the pasta, quickly return to a boil, and cook until the pasta is tender yet firm, 2 to 7 minutes, depending on how long it has been refrigerated (or 8 to 9 minutes for the boxed stuff). Drain the pasta, reserving the pasta water.

Meanwhile, melt the 2 tablespoons butter in a large sauté pan over medium-high heat. Add the onions and sage and cook until lightly browned, 3 to 4 minutes. Season with salt and pepper to taste and add the chicken livers, cooking for 1 minute. Add a splash of pasta water, scraping the pan bottom.

Add the drained rigatoni to the pan. Toss with the 1/4 cup Parmesan cheese and additional butter and/or pasta water as needed to make a creamy sauce.

Divide among warm pasta bowls and garnish with Parmesan cheese.

PREP AHEAD

Make the rigatoni up to 5 days ahead of time and refrigerate uncovered.

BEVERAGE—Tramin, Gewürztraminer 2006 (Alto Adige): This wine is intensely tropical in aroma and flavor, and rich enough to match the chicken livers yet spicy enough to cleanse the palate. Or come at it from another angle with Corte Majoli, Valpolicella Ripasso 2006 (Veneto), which gives off rich dried fruit and chocolate aromas, but surprises you with a dash of acidity.

MAKES 4 SERVINGS

1 pound refrigerated extruded Rigatoni (page 63), or 14 ounces boxed dried rigatoni

2 tablespoons unsalted butter, plus more for sauce

8 small cipollini onions, peeled and thinly sliced into rings

12 fresh sage leaves

Salt and freshly ground pepper

8 ounces chicken livers, minced

1/4 cup grated Parmesan cheese, plus more for garnish

Candele WITH DUCK BOLOGNESE

Imagine a long macaroni that doesn't curve. That's candele, which means "candle," and of course resembles a tall, thin candle. This pasta shape is perfect for standing up to a thick ragù. You can break the candele into pieces, but I like to leave them long. They wrap around the ragù so nicely that way.

MAKES 6 TO 8 SERVINGS

DUCK BOLOGNESE

4 pounds skinless duck meat, cut into 1-inch chunks

1 pound pork fatback, cut into 1/2-inch chunks

1 large onion, halved and thinly sliced

1 large carrot, peeled and finely chopped

2 cups dry red wine

8 cups water

2 sprigs rosemary

1 clove garlic, smashed

6 sprigs thyme

1 bay leaf

1/4 cup (0.35 ounce) dried porcini mushrooms

1 cup Hand-Crushed Marinara Sauce (page 266)

Salt and freshly ground pepper

1 pound refrigerated extruded Candele (page 63), or 14 ounces boxed dried long ziti

6 tablespoons unsalted butter

1 1/2 cups freshly grated Parmesan cheese

For the bolognese: Spread the duck meat and fatback in a single layer on a baking sheet or other shallow pan that will fit in your freezer. Freeze until firm but not solid, about 1 hour. Freeze all the parts to the meat grinder, too. Grind the cold duck meat and fat with the meat grinder, using a large die. If you don't have a meat grinder, you can chop it in small batches in a food processor using 4-second pulses. Try not to chop it too finely; you don't want meat puree.

Preheat the oven to 325°F. Heat a large Dutch oven or heavy ovenproof casserole over medium-high heat. Add the ground meat mixture and cook until it is no longer red, stirring and scraping the pan, about 8 minutes. Add the onion and carrot and cook until barely tender, about 5 minutes. Add the wine, scraping up any browned bits from the pan bottom, and bring to a boil. Add the water and heat until simmering.

Meanwhile, tie the rosemary, garlic, thyme, and bay leaf in a square of cheesecloth and add to the pan. Add the mushrooms and marinara and season lightly with salt and pepper. Cover and cook in the oven until the flavors are rich and blended, 2 to 3 hours. Remove the cheesecloth sachet. Makes about 8 cups.

Bring a large pot of salted water to a boil. Drop in the pasta, return to a boil, and cook until tender yet firm, about 2 to 7 minutes, depending on how long it has been refrigerated (or 8 to 9 minutes for the boxed stuff). Drain the pasta, reserving the water.

Meanwhile, heat the bolognese in a large sauté pan until boiling. Add the butter and simmer until the sauce is creamy. Add the drained candele to the pan. Stir in a ladle of pasta water and 1 1/4 cups of the Parmesan and toss until the sauce is creamy. If the sauce gets too thick, add more pasta water.

Divide among warm pasta bowls and garnish with the remaining 1/4 cup Parmesan.

PREP AHEAD

The bolognese can be made ahead and refrigerated in an airtight container for up to 2 days or frozen for up to 3 months. Reheat it in a large sauté pan before adding the pasta.

BEVERAGE—Poggio alle Sughere, Morellino di Scansano 2006 (Tuscany): A coastal cousin to Chianti, this is a fantastic (albeit riper and juicier) alternative when you want something with decent structure, generous fruit, a touch of earth, and slightly rustic tannins.

Fusilli WITH FAVA BEANS AND PECORINO

I always look forward to the first young fava beans in the spring. They're small and sweet and taste delicious with some crusty bread and sharp pecorino. They're even better with fusilli pasta because the curves of the fusilli cradle the fava beans. There are so few ingredients here that quality really matters. Use the best pecorino you can find. And if your favas are old and tough, save them for another dish. Young favas fresh from the market are what make this dish great.

Bring a large pot of water to a boil. Add the whole fava pods and blanch for 1 minute. Transfer to a bowl of ice water. When cool, pluck the favas from the pods, then pinch open the pale green skin and pop out the bright green fava beans. You should have about 1 cup.

Bring a large pot of salted water to a boil (or salt the fava blanching water if you like). Drop in the pasta, quickly return to a boil, and cook until the pasta is tender yet firm, about 2 to 7 minutes, depending on how long it has been refrigerated (or 8 to 9 minutes for the boxed stuff). Drain the pasta, reserving the pasta water.

Meanwhile, heat 3/4 cup of the olive oil in a large sauté pan over medium heat. Add the onion and cook until soft but not browned, 3 to 4 minutes. Add the drained fusilli to the pan along with 1 1/2 cups of pasta water and the fava beans. Toss over medium-high heat until the water is reduced to almost nothing.

Cut the 1/4 cup mint leaves into thin strips (stack them, roll them like a cigar, then cut crosswise). Remove the pan from the heat and add the remaining 1/2 cup olive oil, 1 1/4 cups of the pecorino cheese, and the mint strips. Toss until the pasta and sauce become creamy and velvety. If it looks clumpy, add a small amount of pasta water to loosen the sauce. Taste and season with salt and pepper.

Divide among warm pasta bowls and garnish with the remaining 1/4 cup pecorino, a few grinds of fresh black pepper, and a few beautiful mint leaves.

PREP AHEAD

The favas can be blanched, peeled, covered, and refrigerated for up to 6 hours before you serve the pasta.

BEVERAGE—Tenuta Luisa, Cabernet Franc 2006 (Friuli): This is one of my favorite varietals to pair with green vegetables. Cabernet Franc harmonizes perfectly with the herbaceous aromas of the vegetables. Expect most Italian bottlings to follow with soft, chocolaty-strawberry fruit, medium body, and low tannins.

MAKES 4 SERVINGS

1 pound young fava beans in the pods

1 pound refrigerated extruded Fusilli (page 63), or 12 ounces boxed dried fusilli

1 1/4 cups extra-virgin olive oil

1/2 cup finely chopped onion

1/4 cup packed fresh mint leaves, plus a few for garnish

1 1/2 cups grated pecorino cheese

Salt and freshly ground pepper

Macaroni WITH BIGEYE TUNA BOLOGNESE

I am always trying new bolognese sauces. Some with beef. Some with veal. Some with lamb. Some with duck. Large, fatty fish also work remarkably well. My favorite is bigeye tuna. It has a brawny texture that pulls its own weight in a thick sauce like this. But you could substitute salmon or swordfish, if you like.

For the bolognese: Spread the tuna and fatback in a single layer on a baking sheet or another shallow pan that will fit into your freezer. Freeze all the parts to the meat grinder, too. Freeze the tuna and fat until firm but not solid, about 1 hour. Grind the cold tuna and fat in a meat grinder, using a large die. If you don't have a meat grinder, you can chop it in small batches in a food processor using 4-second pulses. Try not to chop it too finely; you don't want a fish puree.

Heat the olive oil in a large Dutch oven or heavy ovenproof casserole over medium-high heat. Add the ground tuna mixture and cook until the tuna is no longer red, stirring and scraping the pan, 10 to 12 minutes. Add the onion, carrot, and celery and cook until barely tender, about 5 minutes.

Add the garlic and tomatoes and cook for 5 minutes. Add the wine and bring to a boil. Add the rosemary, water, and Parmesan rind. Season lightly with salt and pepper and bring to a simmer. Cover and simmer until the sauce is creamy, about 1 hour. Remove the rosemary and Parmesan rind. Makes about 8 cups.

Bring a large pot of salted water to a boil. Drop in the pasta, quickly return to a boil, and cook until tender yet firm, 3 to 4 minutes (9 minutes for the boxed stuff). Drain the pasta, reserving the pasta water.

MAKES 8 SERVINGS

TUNA BOLOGNESE

1 3/4 pounds bigeye tuna, cut into 1-inch chunks

3/4 pound pork fatback, cut into 1/2-inch chunks

2 tablespoons olive oil

1 onion, finely chopped

1 carrot, peeled and finely chopped

1 rib celery, finely chopped

1 clove garlic, minced

4 canned San Marzano tomatoes, crushed by hand

1 cup dry white wine

1 sprig rosemary

3 cups water

1 piece Parmesan rind

Salt and freshly ground pepper

1¹/₂ pounds refrigerated extruded
Large Macaroni (page 63), or
1¹/₄ pounds boxed dried large
macaroni or penne

¹/₂ cup unsalted butter

1 cup extra-virgin olive oil

2 cups freshly grated Parmesan
cheese, plus more for garnish

¹/₂ cup chopped fresh flat-leaf
parsley, plus more for garnish

Meanwhile, heat the bolognese in a large sauté pan over high heat until boiling. Add the butter and olive oil and simmer over medium-low heat until the sauce is creamy.

Add the drained macaroni to the pan. Stir in a ladle of pasta water, the 1 cup Parmesan, and the ¹/₂ cup parsley, tossing until the sauce is creamy. If the sauce gets too thick, add more pasta water.

Divide among warm pasta bowls and garnish with Parmesan and parsley.

PREP AHEAD

The bolognese can be made ahead and refrigerated in an airtight container for up to 2 days or frozen for up to 3 months. Reheat it in a large sauté pan before adding the pasta.

BEVERAGE—Isole e Olena, Chianti Classico 2007 (Tuscany): This pairing is a take on a classic match: Chianti with bolognese. Here the tuna in the bolognese pushes me toward Paolo de Marchi's incredible all-Sangiovese entry-level Chianti. It has a delightful core of iron-rich minerality that supports abundant fruit and lively tannins.

Bucatini ALLA MATRICIANA

This is a very important dish in Italian cuisine. It gives you a taste of pork from the guanciale, a shot of salt from the pecorino, and a touch of acid from the tomato. It is the quintessential example of a perfect combination that should never be altered. And by the way, it is called bucatini alla matriciana, not bucatini al amatriciana. Americans butcher that all the time!

Bring a large pot of salted water to a boil. Drop in the pasta, quickly return to a boil, and cook until tender yet firm, 2 to 7 minutes, depending on how long it has been refrigerated (or 8 to 9 minutes for the boxed stuff). Drain the pasta, reserving the pasta water.

Meanwhile, heat 4 teaspoons of the oil in a large sauté pan over medium-high heat. Add the guanciale and cook until crispy and golden brown, about 5 minutes, stirring now and then. Add the tomatoes and pepper flakes and break up with tongs. Add the wine and 2 cups pasta water and boil until the sauce reduces in volume and thickens slightly, about 10 minutes.

Add the drained bucatini to the pan along with 1 cup of the pecorino, the parsley, and the remaining olive oil. Taste and season with salt and pepper, tossing until the sauce is creamy. If the sauce gets too thick, add more pasta water.

Divide among warm pasta bowls and garnish with the remaining 1 cup pecorino.

PREP AHEAD

Make the bucatini up to 5 days ahead of time and the guanciale up to a week ahead of time. Keep both refrigerated in airtight containers.

BEVERAGE—Masciarelli, Montepulciano d'Abruzzi 2008 (Abruzzo): A hint of heat in any dish is always one of the first things I'll consider when pairing a wine. This Roman classic always seems to demand a plush fruit-forward, low-tannin wine like Montepulciano, especially one with low alcohol.

MAKES 4 TO 6 SERVINGS

1 pound refrigerated extruded Bucatini (page 63), or 14 ounces boxed dried thick spaghetti

1/2 cup olive oil

8 ounces Shortcut Guanciale (page 162), cut into 1/2-inch cubes

4 peeled whole plum tomatoes, preferably San Marzano if canned

1/4 teaspoon red pepper flakes

1 cup dry white wine

2 cups grated pecorino cheese

4 teaspoons chopped fresh flat-leaf parsley

Salt and freshly ground pepper

Which Oil?

Do I always use extra-virgin olive oil when cooking? No! I try to match the oil to the dish. For drizzling on pasta and salads, I use *novello*, or first-cold-pressed olive oil, because it has a robust flavor and aroma. But when I make vinaigrette with a substantial amount of oil in it, I use half extra-virgin and half virgin olive oil. All extra-virgin would just be too intense, especially if it's a really strong-flavored oil. Or, let's say I'm making a dessert with olive oil like Olive Oil Cake (page 248), or drizzling the warm oil over solid chocolate. Then I'll use oil from Tuscany, because Tuscan oils are fruitier than oils from the south, which tend to taste more *piccante* in the back of the throat. The fruitier oil will pair better with the dessert. For dipping bread at the table, I usually make a 75 to 25 percent mix of strong-flavored extra-virgin olive oil and a milder virgin olive oil to keep the oil from overpowering the bread. If the extra-virgin is really strong, I'll use half and half. And for frying and grilling, I use grapeseed oil or canola oil because they have a higher smoking point than olive oil. The best thing to do is taste a lot of different oils, find your favorites, and experiment with them in the kitchen.

Tonnarelli CACIO E PEPE

Here's another example of how certain ingredients go perfectly together, like salt and pepper. In this elemental Roman pasta dish, cheese provides the salt. Cacio is a hard sheep's milk cheese similar to pecorino and just a little sharper than Parmesan. With the aroma of cracked black pepper and the chewy texture of the semolina pasta, it's a perfect three-way marriage. There's nothing you could add to make this dish any better.

MAKES 4 SERVINGS

1 pound refrigerated extruded Tonnarelli (page 63), or 14 ounces boxed dried spaghetti

1/2 cup unsalted butter, cut into 8 equal pieces

1/2 cup extra-virgin olive oil

1 teaspoon coarsely cracked black peppercorns

2 cups freshly grated cacio de Roma or pecorino cheese

Salt and freshly cracked pepper

Bring a large pot of salted water to a boil. Drop in the pasta, quickly return to a boil, and cook until tender yet firm, 2 to 7 minutes, depending on how long it has been refrigerated (or 8 to 9 minutes for the boxed stuff). Drain the pasta, reserving the pasta water.

Just before the pasta is ready, ladle about 2 cups pasta water into a large sauté pan. Add the butter, olive oil, and cracked pepper and bring to a simmer over medium-high heat.

Add the drained pasta to the pan. Simmer gently until the sauce is slightly creamy (most of the sauce will be absorbed by the pasta), about 2 minutes. Remove from the heat and stir in 1 cup of the cacio or pecorino cheese. Taste and season with salt and pepper.

Divide among warm pasta bowls and top with the remaining 1 cup cheese and a few grinds of black pepper.

PREP AHEAD

The tonnarelli can be made and refrigerated in an airtight container up to 5 days ahead. If you don't have a tonnarelli attachment (like a square spaghetti) on your pasta machine, make regular spaghetti instead, which will work just fine.

BEVERAGE—Germano Ettore, Langhe Nebbiolo 2007 (Piedmont): People sometimes skip this style in favor of its more esteemed (and pricier) older siblings, Barolo and Barbaresco. But Nebbiolo often delivers similar flavors in a fresher frame with noticeable but more manageable tannins. The result is a fresh, delicious, incredibly versatile wine with the ability to stand up to full-flavored salty cheeses like pecorino.

Spaghetti IN PARCHMENT WITH CLAMS AND SCALLIONS

The pasta in this dish cooks twice, so be sure to undercook it when you first boil it. Then when it bakes in the parchment, it will absorb all the briny, garlicky, wine-soaked, chile-flecked juices from the seafood. That's how you create flavor! It also helps to use fresh scallions from the farmers' market. Better yet, use ramps when they are in season. You can also replace the clams with cockles and serve this with grated Parmesan if you like.

Preheat the oven to 425°F. Bring a large pot of salted water to a boil. Drop in the pasta, quickly return to a boil, and cook until slightly underdone and chewy, 1 to 6 minutes, depending on how long it has been refrigerated (or 7 to 8 minutes for the boxed stuff). Drain the pasta, reserving the pasta water.

Meanwhile, heat 2 tablespoons of the oil in a large sauté pan over medium heat. Add the scallions and garlic and cook until soft but not browned, about 3 minutes. Add the clams, wine, pepper flakes, and water. Cover and simmer until the liquid reduces in volume by about half, 5 minutes. When the clams have opened, discard the garlic and any empty clam shells.

Add the drained pasta to the pan along with the remaining 6 tablespoons olive oil and the parsley. Cook over medium heat, tossing until the sauce gets a little creamy.

Tear 4 sheets of parchment paper, each about 2 feet long. Place one-fourth of the pasta mixture in the center of each sheet of parchment. Bring the long sides of the parchment up above the pasta so the edges meet. Fold the edges together and keep folding down until tight over the pasta. Flip over and pull each side of parchment over the center to make a tight packet. Flip back over so the folded seam side is up.

Transfer the packets to a baking sheet and bake until the paper browns lightly, 5 to 7 minutes. If you have convection, turn it on to help the paper brown. Transfer to plates and allow guests to slit open the packets lengthwise with a knife.

PREP AHEAD

The spaghetti can be made and refrigerated in an airtight container for up to 5 days ahead.

BEVERAGE—Scarpetta, Friulano Bianco 2007 (Friuli): This wine is crafted by our close friends Bobby and Lachlan of Frasca Food and Wine in Boulder, Colorado. It shows off everything that's great about the grape: mouthwatering acidity, pear and almond flavors, and cleansing minerality that makes it an ideal match for shellfish dishes spiked with garlic.

MAKES 4 SERVINGS

1 pound refrigerated extruded Spaghetti (page 63), or 12 ounces boxed dried spaghetti

8 tablespoons olive oil

4 scallions, trimmed and top quarter removed, sliced crosswise

4 cloves garlic, smashed

50 to 60 small clams, scrubbed

1/4 cup dry white wine

1/4 teaspoon red pepper flakes

1/4 cup water

1/2 cup finely chopped fresh flat-leaf parsley

Salt and freshly ground black pepper

ROLLED PASTA

BASIC Egg Pasta DOUGH

Here's my go-to dough for almost every ravioli, lasagna, fettuccine, and other flat pasta that I make. It's rich with egg yolks and satisfyingly chewy, thanks to high-protein durum flour. The amounts here are for 1 pound of dough, which is enough to make about 6 fully rolled pasta sheets, each 4 to 5 feet long. That will give you about 32 large (2-inch-square) ravioli or 46 small (1-inch-square) ravioli.

Put both flours in the bowl of a stand mixer. Using the paddle attachment, run the mixer on medium speed and add the egg yolks, water, and oil. Mix just until the ingredients come together into a dough, 2 to 3 minutes. Turn the dough out onto a lightly floured work surface and knead for about 5 minutes, or until silky and smooth, kneading in more flour if the dough is too sticky. The dough is ready if it gently pulls back into place when stretched with your hands. Shape the dough into a 6-inch-long log, wrap in plastic wrap, and refrigerate for at least 30 minutes or up to 3 days (it could get too soft and difficult to roll if left at room temperature).

Cut the dough into 6 equal pieces and let them return almost to room temperature. They should still feel a little chilly when you touch them. Position a stand mixer pasta roller or other pasta roller at the widest setting, and roll one piece of dough through the rollers, lightly dusting the dough with flour if necessary to prevent sticking. Reset the rollers to the next narrowest setting and again pass the dough through the rollers. Pass the dough once through each progressively narrower setting, concluding with the narrowest setting or as directed in the recipe you are making. Between rollings, continue to dust the dough lightly with flour if needed, always brushing off the excess. You should end up with a sheet 4 to 5 feet long and thin enough to see your hand through when the pasta is held up to the light.

Lay the pasta sheet on a lightly floured work surface and sprinkle lightly with flour. Use a knife or the cutter attachment on the pasta machine to create the pasta shape specified in the recipe you are making.

MAKES 1 POUND

1¼ cups (190 g) tipo 00 or all-purpose flour, plus more for dusting

½ cup plus 1 tablespoon (71 g) durum flour

9 egg yolks (150 g)

3 to 4 tablespoons (45 to 55 g) water

1 tablespoon (15 g) extra-virgin olive oil

BASIC FETTUCCINE

Cut the sheet into 9-inch lengths. Fit your stand mixer or pasta machine with the fettuccine roller and set to medium speed. Feed one length of dough at a time through the roller, dusting the dough lightly with flour as needed. Form the fettuccine into rounded nests and dry on a floured towel for 1 hour. Or dust with flour and freeze in an airtight container for up to 3 days. You can transfer the pasta right from the freezer to the boiling pasta water.

BASIC RAVIOLI

Lay a pasta sheet on a lightly floured work surface trim the edges so they are square, and notch the center of the sheet on the edge to mark the centerit. Spritz the pasta with a little water to keep it from drying out and to give you a little more time to work. Spoon $1/2$-inch-diameter balls of filling at 1-inch intervals in two rows down the length of the pasta sheet just to the center. Leave a 1-inch margin all the way around each ball of filling. Lift the opposite end of the sheet and lay it over the filling so the edges meet. Gently press the dough around each ball of filling to seal. Using a knife, cut into squares. Or use a $1^1/2$-inch fluted round cookie cutter and cut into rounds. Repeat with the remaining pasta and filling. Dust with flour, cover loosely, and freeze in an airtight container for up to 3 days. Take the pasta right from the freeze to the pasta water.

PREP AHEAD

The pasta dough can be wrapped in plastic wrap and refrigerated for up to 3 days or sealed in a ziplock freezer bag and frozen for up to 3 weeks. Bring the dough to room temperature before rolling and cutting. If you want to store it after rolling, sprinkle the cut or shaped rolled pasta with a little flour and freeze it in an airtight container for up to 3 days. That's usually what I do, then I take it right from the freezer to the pasta water.

Fettuccine WITH PORK RAGÙ AND STONE FRUITS

There is a lot of truth in the quote "Pork chops and applesauce—ain't that swell!" (Peter Brady of *The Brady Bunch*, imitating Humphrey Bogart). Pork marries well with other fruits too, especially plums, peaches, cherries, apricots, and nectarines. Try this dish in the late summer or early fall when peaches and plums are at peak flavor in the market. You won't be disappointed.

For the ragù: Spread the pork and fatback in a single layer on a baking sheet or another shallow pan that will fit into your freezer. Freeze until firm but not solid, about 1 hour. Freeze all the parts to the meat grinder, too. Grind the cold meat and fat using a meat grinder fitted with a large die. If you don't have a meat grinder, you can chop the mixture in small batches in a food processor using 4-second pulses. Try not to chop it too finely; you don't want meat puree. Stir in the sugar, salt, pepper, and garlic until very well mixed. Cover and refrigerate overnight.

Heat a large Dutch oven over medium heat. Add the ground meat mixture and cook, stirring and scraping the bottom of the pan, until the meat is no longer pink, about 10 minutes.

Add the onion, carrot, and celery and cook until barely tender, about 5 minutes. Add the tomatoes and cook until they start to break down, about 5 minutes. Increase the heat to medium-high and add the wine. Simmer until the alcohol aroma begins to fade, about 5 minutes. Add the water and Parmesan rind and reduce the heat to low. Cover and simmer until the sauce has a light, creamy consistency, about 1 hour. Remove the Parmesan rind. Makes about 4 cups.

Bring a large pot of salted water to a boil. Drop in the fettuccine, quickly return to a boil, and cook the pasta until tender yet firm, about 4 minutes (9 minutes for the boxed stuff). Drain the pasta, reserving the pasta water.

Meanwhile, heat the ragù in a large deep sauté pan over medium heat until simmering. Add a ladle of pasta water and the fruit. Simmer until creamy, 3 to 5 minutes.

Add the drained fettuccine to the sauce along with the butter, 1/4 cup Parmesan, and 2 tablespoons parsley. Toss. If the sauce gets too thick, add more pasta water.

Divide among warm pasta bowls and garnish with Parmesan and parsley.

PREP AHEAD

The ragù can be made ahead and refrigerated in an airtight container for up to 2 days or frozen for up to 3 months. Reheat it in a large deep sauté pan before adding the pasta.

BEVERAGE—Argiolas Cannonau 2008 "Costera" (Sardegna): Here's a pairing that mimics the key dynamic in the dish itself: a distinct fruit component supported by a savory backbone.

MAKES 6 SERVINGS

PORK RAGÙ

2 pounds boneless pork butt (shoulder), cut into 1-inch chunks

8 ounces pork fatback, cut into 1-inch chunks

1/2 teaspoon sugar

2 teaspoons kosher salt

1 teaspoon ground pepper

1 clove garlic, minced

1 onion, finely chopped

1/2 carrot, peeled and finely chopped

1 rib celery, finely chopped

4 canned San Marzano tomatoes, crushed by hand

3/4 cup dry white wine

3 cups water

1 piece Parmesan rind

1 pound fresh Fettuccine (page 81), or 14 ounces boxed dried fettuccine

2 plums or peeled peaches, pitted and cut into 1/4-inch chunks

2 tablespoons unsalted butter

1/4 cup freshly grated Parmesan cheese, plus a little for garnish

2 tablespoons chopped fresh flat-leaf parsley, plus some for garnish

Opposites Attract

When making food and beverage pairings, one approach I use is to highlight the opposites. If you like an overall balance, rather than pushing the extremes to the limits, you will most likely enjoy this approach. Let's say you are having a hot pastrami sandwich. The dominant flavors here are salt and pepper. To tame the extremes, try drinking a Bierre de Miel, a honeyed beer with a sweet, cool finish that balances out the briny salt and sharp pepper of the pastrami. Another example is the Bucatini alla Matriciana (page 72). As I mention in the notes, the chile in the dish calls for something with low alcohol and lush fruit like a Montepulciano wine. I recently had a chocolate bar with chile flakes in it and it gave me the same experience I had when I tasted the plush fruity Montepulciano with the peppery sauce on the bucatini. The opposite flavors played off each other perfectly. The Escarole Ravioli with Pine Nuts and Honey (page 94) illustrates the point even more. The escarole is bitter and the honey sauce is sweet—a great contrast on its own. But when you add some acidity in the wine, as with a crisp, tart Pinot Grigio, the three contrasting flavors make an even stronger statement.

Goat Cheese and Beet Plin WITH TARRAGON

When I opened Osteria in 2007, we started a garden the first year. We planted a few simple things, like lettuces, tomatoes, and beets. Everything came up, but the beets were outstanding and so plentiful that we had to use them in everything. One of the first things I experimented with was ravioli filling. I had just gotten some young goat cheese from our main farmer, Glenn Brendle, and with the beets, it was a match made in heaven. The filling has a gorgeous deep pink color offset by the sheer yellow of the egg yolk pasta. In Piemontese dialect, plin means "pinch," and to make this particular pasta, you pinch between each ball of filling to make small pillows. Plin are usually stuffed with meat, but I like to switch things up and use a colorful vegetable filling here.

For the filling: Preheat the oven to 425°F. Wrap the beet in heavy-duty aluminum foil, place in a shallow pan, and roast until fork-tender, 50 to 60 minutes. Remove and let cool enough to handle. Peel the beet, cut it into small chunks, and puree along with the goat cheese, egg, and Parmesan in a food processor or with a handheld immersion blender. Season with salt and pepper to taste and spoon the filling into a pastry bag or ziplock plastic bag with one corner cut to make a small piping hole.

Lay a pasta sheet on a lightly floured work surface, one long side parallel to the edge of the counter. Trim the short sides so the edges are straight. Cut the dough in half lengthwise, preferably with a fluted pasta cutting wheel, to make 2 long sheets. Lightly mist the dough with water.

Pipe teaspoon-size rounds of filling along the bottom half of each pasta sheet, right along the bottom edge, leaving 3/4 inch between the rounds.

Pick up the dough beneath the filling on the long side of the pasta sheet and fold the pasta and the filling over, working your way down the pasta sheet so the entire bottom edge of the pasta and the filling is folded over once (see the photos on page 85). Repeat, folding the entire bottom edge of the pasta and the filling over once more. You should be left with one long strip of naked pasta above the folded part. Using both hands, gently pinch your fingertips and thumb together on the pasta between each round of filling to create a pillow of filling that stands a bit more upright. Use the pasta wheel or a knife to trim the entire length of excess pasta to within 1/2 inch of the pillows. Cut between each pillow to create individual pastas, being careful to leave an even, sealed edge on each side. Repeat with the remaining pasta dough and filling. Toss with a little flour and set aside. Makes about 48.

continued, page 87

MAKES 8 SERVINGS

BEET FILLING

1 large red beet (6 to 8 ounces), scrubbed

1/4 cup fresh white goat cheese

1 small egg, lightly beaten (2 1/2 tablespoons)

1 tablespoon freshly grated Parmesan cheese

Salt and freshly ground pepper

1 pound Basic Egg Pasta Dough (page 80), rolled into sheets

1/3 cup fresh tarragon leaves, coarsely chopped, plus some whole leaves for garnish

1/2 cup unsalted butter, cut into 8 equal pieces

1/2 cup freshly grated Parmesan cheese

Freshly ground pepper (optional)

Goat Cheese and Beet Plin with Tarragon, *continued*

Bring a large pot of salted water to a boil. Drop in the plin, quickly return to a boil, and cook until tender yet firm, 3 to 4 minutes. Drain the pasta, reserving the pasta water.

Just before the pasta is done, ladle 1 cup pasta water into a large sauté pan. Add the chopped tarragon and bring to a boil over medium-high heat. Add the butter, one piece at a time, whisking until melted before adding the next piece. Continue until the butter is incorporated and the sauce is creamy.

Slide the drained plin into the warm sauce. Toss gently until the sauce is creamy, adding more pasta water as needed.

Divide among warm pasta bowls and garnish with Parmesan and tarragon. Add a few grindings of black pepper if you like.

PREP AHEAD

The plin can be assembled, tossed with flour, and frozen in an airtight container for up to 3 days before cooking. Take the plin right from the freezer to the pasta water.

BEVERAGE—Coppo, Chardonnay 2008 "Costebianche" (Piedmont): On the whole, piemontese Chardonnay is cleaner and crisper than this rounder version from Coppo, which has enough richness to play off the sweetness of the beets. But it also gives a nod to the region's stylistic preference with a dose of acidity and minerality on the finish, bringing balance to the wine and complementing the tanginess of the goat cheese.

Robiola Francobolli
WITH CHANTERELLE MUSHROOMS AND THYME

You don't see too much robiola cheese in America. But you should. It's like an Italian version of cream cheese, but lighter and much more flavorful. Oselli is the best brand of robiola I've found, and it works in tons of preparations, but it's best as a ravioli filling. It's so creamy and so good. It makes the perfect backdrop for a sauce of woodsy chanterelle mushrooms. If you can't find robiola, try mascarpone. And if you're wondering, francobolli means "postage stamps," which is exactly how these small ravioli look when you cut them with a fluted pasta wheel.

For the filling: Mix the cheeses and egg until smooth, then season with salt and pepper.

Lay a pasta sheet on a lightly floured work surface and dust with flour. Trim the ends to make them square, then fold the dough in half lengthwise and make a small notch at the center to mark it. Open the sheet so it lies flat again and spritz with water. Beginning at the left-hand side, place 2 rows of $1/8$-teaspoon-size balls of filling the length of the pasta, leaving a $1/2$-inch margin around each ball and stopping at the center of the sheet. Lift up the right-hand side of the pasta sheet and fold it over to cover the balls of filling. Gently press the pasta around each ball of filling to seal. With a knife or fluted pasta wheel, cut into 1-inch squares, trimming off any excess. Repeat with the remaining pasta dough and filling. Makes about 46.

Bring a large pot of salted water to a boil. Drop in the francobolli, return to a boil, and cook until tender yet firm, 3 to 4 minutes. Drain the pasta, reserving the water.

Meanwhile, melt $1/4$ cup of the butter in a large sauté pan over medium heat. Add the mushrooms and thyme sprigs and sauté until the mushrooms are tender, about 4 minutes. Ladle $1^1/2$ cups of pasta water into the pan and boil over medium-high heat until the sauce is creamy. Stir in the remaining $1/2$ cup butter and remove the thyme.

Slide the drained francobolli into the warm sauce. Toss gently until the sauce is creamy, adding more pasta water as needed.

Divide among warm pasta bowls and garnish with Parmesan and thyme leaves.

PREP AHEAD

The francobolli can be assembled, tossed with flour, and frozen in an airtight container for up to 3 days before cooking. Take them right from the freezer to the pasta water.

BEVERAGE—Monzio Compagnoni, Curtefranca Rosso 2005 (Lombardia): The wine (a unique blend of Cabernet, Merlot, Barbera, and Nebbiolo) gives off a distinct mushroom aroma to resonate with the chanterelles.

MAKES ABOUT 6 SERVINGS

ROBIOLA FILLING

$1/2$ cup robiola cheese

$1/2$ cup freshly grated Parmesan cheese

2 tablespoons lightly beaten egg

Salt and freshly ground pepper

1 pound Basic Egg Pasta Dough (page 80), rolled into sheets

8 tablespoons unsalted butter

3 ounces chanterelle mushrooms, cleaned, trimmed, and sliced

4 sprigs thyme, tied together, plus thyme leaves for garnish

$1/2$ cup freshly grated Parmesan cheese

Mortadella Tortelli WITH PISTACHIO PESTO

Can you tell that I love mortadella? It shows up in a lot of my stuffings, stocks, pizza toppings, and fish and meat dishes. I make spreads out of it. I eat it with bread. I started to make mortadella myself a couple years ago. With a little ricotta and egg, mortadella can stand on its own as a ravioli filling. Definitely one of my favorites.

MAKES ABOUT 6 SERVINGS

MORTADELLA FILLING

6 ounces Lamb Mortadella (page 142) or purchased pork mortadella, finely chopped

1/4 cup whole-milk ricotta cheese

1 egg

Salt and freshly ground pepper

8 ounces Basic Egg Pasta Dough (page 80), rolled into sheets

2 1/2 cups Pistachio Pesto (page 269)

1/3 cup freshly grated Parmesan cheese

For the filling: Put the mortadella, ricotta, and egg in a food processor and puree until smooth and fluffy, scraping the sides of the bowl as needed. Season with salt and pepper.

Lay a pasta sheet on a lightly floured work surface, one long side parallel to the edge of the counter. Trim the sides and ends so they are straight, then cut the pasta into 3-inch squares. Spritz lightly with water to keep it from drying out.

Put teaspoon-size spoonfuls of filling on each square, then bring the opposite corners together over the filling to make a triangle. Press gently on the edges to seal. Makes about 36.

Bring a large pot of salted water to a boil. Drop in the tortelli, quickly return to a boil, and cook until tender yet firm, 3 to 4 minutes. Drain the pasta, reserving the pasta water.

Just before the pasta is done, ladle 3 cups of the pasta water into a large sauté pan. Add the pesto and bring to a boil over medium-high heat. Boil until the sauce is creamy, about 2 minutes.

Slide the drained tortelli into the warm sauce. Toss gently until the sauce is creamy, adding more pasta water as needed.

Divide among warm pasta bowls and garnish with the Parmesan.

PREP AHEAD

The tortelli can be assembled, tossed with flour, and frozen in an airtight container for up to 3 days before cooking. take the tortelli right from the freezer to the pasta water.

BEVERAGE—Matjaz Cetrtic, Ferdinand, Ribolla Gialla 2008 (Brda, Slovenia): Although this is technically not Italian, it feels too right to pass up. Ribolla is a grape typically found only in the northernmost corner of Italy and across the border into Slovenia. It makes a fantastic pairing with the pistachio-studded lamb in this pasta stuffing.

Caramelle di Zucca Ravioli WITH AMARETTI

Mostarda, the Italian preserves of fruit in mustard syrup, usually make their way to the table as a condiments served with salumi. But here they give ravioli filling just the right kick, balancing out the sweetness of crushed amaretti cookies. This particular pasta is classic Italian. With the amber-colored squash filling and the pasta twisted around it on either side, the ravioli ends up looking like a caramel candy wrapped in tan waxed paper.

For the squash filling: Melt the butter in a large saucepan over medium-low heat. Add the onion and cook until soft but not browned, about 5 minutes. Add the garlic and squash, cover, and cook until the squash is soft, about 15 minutes, stirring now and then. Let cool until barely warm. Transfer to a food processor along with the Parmesan, egg, amaretti, mostarda, oil of mustard, and nutmeg. Puree using 5-second pulses, scraping down the bowl as needed, until the mixture is smooth. Season with salt and pepper to taste and spoon the filling into a pastry bag or ziplock plastic bag with one corner cut to make a small piping hole. Makes about 2 cups.

Lay a pasta sheet on a lightly floured work surface, one long side parallel to the edge of the counter. Trim the short ends so the edges are square. Lightly mist the dough with water.

Pipe teaspoon-size rounds of filling in a single row down the length of the pasta right in the center of the sheet, leaving a 2-inch margin around each round of filling.

Pick up the top half of the dough and fold it over the filling so the top and bottom sides of the pasta meet. Using both hands, gently press down the dough around each ball of filling to enclose the filling. Using a 2 1/2-inch round cutter, cut out individual pastas; each will be shaped like a three-quarter moon. Fold each three-quarter moon up on the curved edge of the pasta so that the filling rests in the center with a "wing" of dough on either side of the filling. To shape the caramelle-like candies with twisted wrappers, pick up each filled pasta, holding it with the fingers of each hand, and lightly twist the "wings" of dough in opposite directions around the filling. Repeat with the remaining pasta. Toss with a little flour and set aside. Makes about 36.

Bring a large pot of salted water to a boil. Drop in the caramelle, quickly return to a boil, and cook until tender yet firm, 3 to 4 minutes.

Just before the pasta is done, melt the butter in a large sauté pan over medium heat. Add the 6 to 8 sage leaves, amaretti, and a ladle of pasta water. Boil until the sauce is creamy, about 2 minutes.

MAKES 6 SERVINGS

SQUASH FILLING

1 tablespoon unsalted butter

1/2 onion, finely chopped

1/2 clove garlic, minced

1 butternut squash (about 3 pounds), peeled, seeded, and chopped

3 tablespoons freshly grated Parmesan cheese

2 tablespoons lightly beaten egg

2 tablespoons ground amaretti cookies

1 tablespoon Squash Mostarda (page 172)

1 drop essential oil of mustard, or 1 teaspoon mustard powder or pure mustard oil

Grating of nutmeg

Salt and freshly ground pepper

1 pound Basic Egg Pasta Dough (page 80), rolled into sheets

6 tablespoons unsalted butter

6 to 8 fresh sage leaves, plus a few beautiful leaves for garnish

2 tablespoons ground amaretti cookies

3 tablespoons freshly grated Parmesan cheese

Drain the pasta, reserving a little pasta water, and slide the caramelle into the warm sauce. Toss gently until the sauce is creamy, adding more pasta water as needed.

Divide among warm pasta bowls and garnish with the Parmesan and a few sage leaves.

PREP AHEAD

The caramelle can be assembled, tossed with flour, and refrigerated in an airtight container for up to 3 days before cooking. Take the caramelle right from the freezer to the pasta water. To peel the squash easily, stab it all over with a knife and microwave it on a plate on high for 2 to 3 minutes (little beads of juice will seep out the stab wounds). Cut off the top and bottom and peel the squash with a sharp vegetable peeler or paring knife.

BEVERAGE—Paitin, Dolcetto d'Alba 2008 "Sori Paitin" (Piedmont): Gewürztraminer would play nicely on the squash's inherent sweetness, but a soft, plush, medium-bodied red like Sori Paitin envelops the breadth of the flavors even better, simultaneously countering them with a note of bitter almond on the finish.

Salt Cod Ravioli WITH MARJORAM

Baccalà is one of my comfort foods. My grandmother Jenny always served it at Christmas, and we usually had it on the menu at Taverna Colleoni dell'Angelo in Bergamo. At the Taverna, we used to serve baccalà dell'Angelo, a salt cod casserole with anchovies and onions. Rich, creamy, and white, it always looked like ravioli filling to me. So when I came back to Philadelphia, I made this pasta dish with it. Marjoram helps soften the one-two punch of salt from the cod and anchovies. Look for whole anchovies packed in salt. For this recipe, separate one anchovy into two fillets, lift out the backbone, and soak the fillets in cold water for 20 minutes to cut the saltiness. Use one of the fillets in the recipe.

For the filling: Soak the salt cod in cold water in the refrigerator for 24 hours, changing the water 3 times (this helps remove the excess salt). Cut the soaked cod into small pieces and set aside.

Melt the butter with the oil in a medium skillet over medium heat. Add the onion and cook until soft but not browned, about 3 minutes. Add the anchovy, pepper flakes, and salt cod, then sprinkle the flour into the pan. Sauté until the flour browns a little and begins to stick to the pan, stirring often. Stir in the milk and reduce the heat to low. Stir in the garlic and bay leaf, cover, and simmer until very soft and thickened, about 30 minutes. Remove the bay leaf and puree the mixture in a food processor until smooth. Season with pepper to taste. Makes about 1 cup.

Lay a pasta sheet on a lightly floured work surface and dust with flour. Using a 2- to 2¹⁄₂-inch round cutter, punch out rounds of dough from the pasta sheet. Repeat with the remaining pasta dough.

Spritz the rounds of dough lightly with water and place a rounded ¹⁄₄ teaspoon filling in the center of each round. Fold the pasta rounds in half, forming half-moons that encase the filling. Gently press down the dough around each ball of filling to seal the edges. Makes about 64 half-moon-shaped raviolis.

Bring a large pot of salted water to a boil. Drop in the ravioli, quickly return to a boil, and cook until tender yet firm, 3 to 4 minutes. Drain the pasta, reserving the pasta water.

Meanwhile, melt the butter in a large sauté pan over medium-high heat. As soon as the butter melts, ladle in 2 cups of pasta water, add the 2 tablespoons marjoram, and boil over medium-high heat until the sauce is creamy, about 3 minutes.

Slide the drained ravioli into the warm sauce. Toss gently until the sauce is creamy, adding more pasta water as needed.

Divide among warm pasta bowls and garnish with marjoram leaves.

MAKES 8 SERVINGS

SALT COD FILLING

8 ounces salt cod

1 tablespoon unsalted butter

1 tablespoon olive oil

¹⁄₄ onion, finely chopped

1 salted anchovy fillet, minced

Pinch red pepper flakes

1 tablespoon tipo 00 or all-purpose flour

¹⁄₂ cup milk

¹⁄₂ clove garlic, minced

1 small bay leaf

Freshly ground black pepper to taste

8 ounces Basic Egg Pasta Dough (page 80), rolled into sheets

³⁄₄ cup unsalted butter

2 tablespoons fresh marjoram leaves (roughly chopped if large), plus more for garnish

The ravioli can be assembled, tossed with flour, and frozen in an airtight container for up to 3 days before cooking. Take the ravioli right from the freezer to the pasta water.

BEVERAGE—Vallerosa Bonci, Verdicchio dei Castelli di Jesi 2008 "Carpaneto Vineyard" (Marche): Baccalà is enjoyed all over Italy with various wines, but it's at its best alongside the crisp whites of the Marche on the Adriatic coast. Bonci's simple but gutsy Verdicchio is all unexpected flavors and all sensational: green olive, honeydew melon, unripe peach, a hint of almond, and mineral-to-the-point-of-briny packed into a lean, tidy package.

Getting Floury with the Kids

On Sunday mornings, my oldest son, Maurice, loves to help make pasta or bread. He likes to toss flour onto the dough as I roll it through the machine. He squirts water onto the dough and plays with the water bottle like it's a squirt gun, shooting me in the chest. We make ravioli. We roll out bread sticks. He loves it. The more I cook at home, the more great memories I have of hanging out in the kitchen with my family. Most of the recipes in this book are fun to make with your little ones, so don't forget to get them involved in the action.

Escarole Ravioli WITH PINE NUTS AND HONEY

One of the joys of cooking at home is that you can switch up your menu every night. You can't always do that in a restaurant. If a customer loves a certain dish, he or she usually orders it over and over. However, we do serve specials on a regular basis. It's one of the things I love most about Vetri restaurant. Last year, we had a bumper crop of delicious escarole in the garden, but I was traveling for a week. I told my chefs to start using the escarole—to make something with it and put it on the menu. When I came back, I was happy to see this ravioli dish on the menu. But when I went to the garden, it was still full of escarole. I was stumped, but then I heard that my chefs had ordered the escarole from our vegetable farmer. I was pissed. Why would you pay to get escarole trucked into the city when you had perfectly great escarole growing out the back door in our own garden? I mean, c'mon! From now on, the chefs always check the garden first.

MAKES 6 SERVINGS

ESCAROLE FILLING

Leaves from 1 head escarole (about 1½ pounds), rinsed and coarsely chopped

1 tablespoon olive oil

½ onion, chopped

¾ cup ricotta impastata or drained whole-milk ricotta cheese

2 tablespoons lightly beaten egg

Salt and freshly ground pepper

1 pound Basic Egg Pasta Dough (page 80), rolled into sheets

3 tablespoons pine nuts

6 tablespoons unsalted butter

1 teaspoon honey

¼ cup freshly grated Parmesan cheese

For the filling: Dry the escarole thoroughly in a salad spinner or with paper towels. Heat the olive oil in a large sauté pan over medium heat. Add the onion and cook until soft but not browned, 3 to 4 minutes. Add the escarole and cook until tender, about 5 minutes. Puree the mixture in a food processor and transfer to a large double-layered square of cheesecloth. Tie it tightly with kitchen twine and put the bag in a strainer over a bowl. Let drain until most of the liquid drips out, at least 2 hours, or overnight in the refrigerator.

Put the drained escarole in a bowl and mix in the ricotta and egg. Season with salt and pepper to taste.

Lay a pasta sheet on a lightly floured work surface and dust with flour. Trim so the edges are square, then fold the dough in half lengthwise and make a small notch at the center. Open the sheet so it lies flat again and spritz with water. Starting at the left-hand side, place 2 lengthwise rows of ¾-inch-diameter balls of filling on the pasta, leaving a ¾-inch margin around each ball and stopping at the center of the sheet. Lift the right-hand side of the pasta sheet and fold it over to cover the balls of filling. Gently press on the dough around each ball of filling to seal. With a knife or pasta cutter, cut into 2-inch squares. Repeat with the remaining pasta dough and filling. Makes about 36 ravioli.

Bring a large pot of salted water to a boil. Drop in the ravioli and cook until tender yet firm, 3 to 4 minutes. Drain, reserving the pasta water.

Meanwhile, toast the pine nuts in a large dry skillet over medium heat until lightly browned and fragrant, 3 to 4 minutes, shaking the pan often. Add the butter and cook, stirring occasionally, until the butter melts and turns deeply golden, 4 to 5 minutes. Add the honey and a ladle of pasta water and boil until creamy, about 2 minutes.

Slide the drained ravioli into the warm sauce. Toss gently until the sauce is creamy, adding more pasta water as needed.

Divide among warm pasta bowls and garnish with the Parmesan.

PREP AHEAD

The ravioli can be assembled, tossed wtih flour, and frozen in an airtight container for up to 3 days. Take the ravioli right from the freezer to the pasta water.

If you can't find ricotta impastata, drain whole-mik ricotta instead. Line a sieve with cheesecloth or paper towels and place over a bowl. Put the ricotta in the sieve, cover, and let drain in the refrigerator for at least 8 hours or up to 24 hours.

BEVERAGE—Cantina Terlano, Pinot Grigio 2008 (Alto Adige): This dish is both sweet and savory, so approaching it with contrast makes sense. Terlano's Pinot Grigio is dry, slightly floral, crisp, and very minerally, but with enough weight to keep up with the escarole. It even displays a mild, honeyed, caramelized pineapple aroma that echoes the sauce.

BAKED PASTA

Veal Cannelloni WITH PORCINI BÉCHAMEL

I opened Amis, a casual Roman trattoria, around the corner from Vetri restaurant on January 15, 2010. A few months before opening, I was testing lots of baked pastas like lasagna. I started messing with cannelloni, which usually has a lighter filling. But it was the middle of winter, and we needed something hearty. I loved this veal stuffing in ravioli, so I decided to try it in cannelloni. It was perfect. All it needed was a flavored béchamel to go over the top. Porcini mushrooms were the way to go. When we opened the restaurant, this dish was an instant hit. As with most filled pastas, this one takes a bit of time to complete, but you can make the pasta, filling, and béchamel up to 3 days ahead of time, so all you have to do is assemble the cannelloni before baking it.

For the filling: Season the veal with salt and pepper. Heat a large sauté pan over medium-high heat, then sear the veal in the dry pan, turning occasionally, until all the moisture is gone and a dark brown film glazes the pan bottom, about 10 minutes.

Lower the heat to medium and add the onion and celery to the pan. Cook until the vegetables are tender, about 5 minutes. Stir in the water, scraping the pan bottom and simmering to dissolve the browned bits. Remove from the heat and cool the pan by dipping the bottom in ice water. Cover the cool pan and freeze until the contents are firm but not frozen solid, about 1 hour. At the same time, freeze all the parts of a meat grinder. Or if you're making the filling ahead, refrigerate the filling for up to 1 day, then freeze everything until firm but not frozen solid, about 30 minutes.

Grind the cold meat mixture using a meat grinder fitted with a large die. If you don't have a meat grinder, you can chop it in small batches in a food processor using 4-second pulses. Try not to chop it too finely; you don't want meat puree. Weigh the mixture (it should be about $1^1/4$ pounds), then add an equal weight of ricotta cheese. Stir in the egg and season lightly with salt and pepper. Spoon the mixture into a pastry bag fitted with a $^1/2$-inch plain tip or into a ziplock plastic bag with one corner cut to make a small piping hole. Seal and refrigerate for at least 20 minutes.

Lay a pasta sheet on a lightly floured work surface and cut into 4-inch squares. You should get 10 to 12 squares from the sheet. Repeat with the remaining pasta until you have a total of about 24 squares. Spritz the pasta lightly with water as you work to keep it from drying out. Refrigerate any remaining pasta for another use.

Bring a large pot of salted water to a boil. Drop in the pasta squares, quickly return to a boil, and cook for 15 to 20 seconds. Immediately transfer the squares to ice water to stop the cooking. Lay the pasta squares flat on kitchen towels and pat dry.

MAKES 8 TO 10 SERVINGS

FILLING

$1^1/4$ pounds boneless veal breast, coarsely chopped

Salt and freshly ground pepper

1 cup finely chopped onion

1 cup finely chopped celery

$^1/4$ cup water

$1^1/4$ pounds ricotta impastata or drained whole-milk ricotta cheese

1 egg, beaten

8 ounces Basic Egg Pasta Dough (page 80), rolled into sheets

2 cups Porcini Béchamel (page 268)

$^1/4$ cup freshly grated Parmesan cheese

1 tablespoon chopped mixed fresh herbs (rosemary, thyme, chives, and flat-leaf parsley)

Preheat the oven to 500°F. If you have convection, turn it on to help brown the top of the pasta.

Pipe a 1-inch-thick line of the cold filling along one edge of each pasta square. Starting at the filled side, roll the pasta to the edge of the unfilled side to enclose the filling (see photos on page 96).

Spread a thin layer of the béchamel over the bottom of a large baking dish. Place the cannelloni, seam side down, in the dish and top with the remaining béchamel. Sprinkle with the Parmesan and bake until the cheese melts and browns on top, 8 to 10 minutes. Garnish with the herbs before serving.

PREP AHEAD

The pasta, sauce, and filling can all be made ahead and refrigerated in airtight containers for 3 days. Reheat the sauce in a saucepan over low heat before assembling the dish.

If you can't find ricotta impastata, drain whole-mik ricotta instead. Line a sieve with cheesecloth or paper towels and place over a bowl. Put the ricotta in the sieve, cover, and let drain in the refrigerator for at least 8 hours or up to 24 hours.

BEVERAGE—Andrea Oberto, Barbera d'Alba 2007 (Piedmont): True, Barbera goes with everything, but this plump, juicy, blackberry-driven example from Oberto becomes something new when the porcini béchamel summons an earthy, truffled note in the wine.

Fazzoletti WITH SWISS CHARD AND SHEEP'S MILK RICOTTA

Here's one of the simplest rolled pastas to make: just squares of pasta. Fazzoletti means "handker-chiefs" and refers to the way the squares fold over themselves naturally when you toss the pasta with the sauce. I decided to doctor these up a little bit by stuffing them. You put a little filling on a square, fold the square into a triangle, then put on a little more filling and fold it again into a smaller triangle. When you bite into the pasta you get a cascading effect of pasta, filling, pasta, filling.

For the filling: Heat the oil in a large sauté pan over medium heat. Add the chard and toss with tongs to coat with the oil. Cover the pan and cook, tossing occasionally, until the chard is tender, about 8 minutes. Cool briefly and chop into bite-size pieces. Mix with the ricotta, egg, nutmeg, Parmesan, and salt and pepper to taste. Set aside.

For the sauce: Melt the butter in a medium saucepan over medium heat. Add the onion and cook until soft but not browned, about 3 minutes. Stir in the flour until the mixture is bubbling, about 2 minutes. Whisk in the hot milk in 3 additions, stirring until smooth and bubbling between each addition. Remove from the heat and season with salt and pepper to taste. Strain the sauce and set aside to cool.

Lay a pasta sheet on a lightly floured work surface, one long side parallel to the edge of the counter. Trim the short ends so they are straight and cut the sheet into 4-inch squares. Repeat with the remaining pasta, lightly spritzing the pasta with water as you go to keep it from drying out. You should have at least 16 pasta squares.

Preheat the oven to 400°F.

Put $1/2$-tablespoon mounds of filling in the center of each square and sprinkle with about $1/2$ teaspoon of the Parmesan. Fold each square in half again by bringing the opposite corners together over the filling to make a triangle and gently spreading out the filling as you fold, pressing the edges together to seal them. Spoon another $1/2$-tablespoon mound of filling onto the center of the triangle. Sprinkle the filling with another $1/2$ teaspoon Parmesan, then fold in half again into a smaller triangle, gently spreading out the filling and pressing the edges to seal. Put the folded fazzoletti on a lightly oiled baking sheet while you fill and fold the rest of the pasta sheets.

MAKES 4 SERVINGS

FILLING

1 tablespoon olive oil

12 ounces Swiss chard leaves (stems removed)

2 cups sheep's milk ricotta cheese or drained whole-milk ricotta

1 egg, beaten

Generous grating of nutmeg

6 tablespoons freshly grated Parmesan cheese

Salt and freshly ground pepper

SAUCE

2 tablespoons unsalted butter

1/4 cup finely chopped onion

2 tablespoons tipo 00 or all-purpose flour

2 cups whole milk, heated

Salt and freshly ground pepper

8 ounces Basic Egg Pasta Dough
(page 80), rolled into sheets

6 tablespoons freshly grated
Parmesan cheese

18 fresh sage leaves

Freshly cracked pepper, for garnish

Top each filled pasta with 1 tablespoon of the sauce, a sprinkling of Parmesan, and a sage leaf. Bake until heated through, about 10 minutes.

Using a spatula, divide the pasta among warm pasta bowls, allowing 3 or 4 squares per person. Garnish with cracked black pepper.

PREP AHEAD

If you can't find sheep's milk ricotta, drain whole-mik ricotta instead. Line a sieve with cheesecloth or paper towels and place over a bowl. Put the ricotta in the sieve, cover, and let drain in the refrigerator for at least 8 hours or up to 24 hours.

BEVERAGE—Burlotto Pelaverga 2008 (Piedmont): It's always fun to step out of your comfort zone when pairing. Although you might instinctively lean toward a white with this dish, a super fruity, fresh, tart light red from Piedmont will do more to pick up the bitterness of the chard while maintaining the delicate balance of the dish.

Semolina Gnocchi WITH OXTAIL RAGÙ

Most people think of gnocchi and picture little flattened balls of pasta, usually made with potato. But gnocchi just means "dumplings," and these are made with a rich semolina dough, similar to polenta. The dough is poured onto a board, rolled out like pie dough, then stamped out in rounds. I like to top the rounds with a rich oxtail ragù, then bake them with some Parmesan until golden brown. You could use almost any thick meat sauce here, like Duck Bolognese (page 67) or Pork Ragù (page 82).

For the ragù: Preheat the oven to 325°F. Season the oxtail with salt and pepper, then dust with flour. Heat the oil in a large roasting pan over medium-high heat. Add the oxtail and sear until browned all over, 10 to 15 minutes.

Remove the meat from the pan and add the onion, carrot, and celery. Cook until lightly browned, 5 to 10 minutes. Add the tomatoes and cook for 2 to 3 minutes. Add the wine, stirring to dissolve the browned bits on the pan bottom. Return the meat to the pan and cook until the liquid reduces in volume by about half, 5 minutes. Add enough stock to come two-thirds of the way up the meat. Sink the sachet into the pan, cover, and cook in the oven until the meat pulls off the bone easily, 2¹/₂ to 3 hours.

Remove the meat and sachet from the pan, then pass the sauce through a food mill or blend briefly in a food processor.

Pick all the meat from the bones (discarding any large chunks of fat) and return the meat to the sauce. Taste and season with salt and pepper.

MAKES 6 SERVINGS

OXTAIL RAGÙ

2¹/₂ pounds oxtail, trimmed of fat

Salt and freshly ground pepper

Tipo 00 or all-purpose flour for dusting

2 tablespoons grapeseed oil or olive oil

¹/₂ onion, coarsely chopped

1 carrot, peeled and coarsely chopped

2 large ribs celery, coarsely chopped

3 peeled plum tomatoes (canned are fine, preferably San Marzano)

1 cup dry red wine

3 to 4 cups beef stock or water

Sachet: 1 rosemary sprig, 5 flat-leaf parsley sprigs, 5 black peppercorns, 1 bay leaf, 1 smashed clove garlic, tied in a cheesecloth square

GNOCCHI

3 cups milk

1/2 cup unsalted butter

11/2 teaspoons salt

1 cup semolina

4 egg yolks

1 cup freshly grated Parmesan
cheese

GARNISH

1/2 cup freshly grated Parmesan
cheese

1 tablespoon mixed finely chopped
fresh herbs (flat-leaf parsley, rosemary, thyme)

For the gnocchi: Put the milk, butter, and salt in a medium saucepan and bring to a boil over medium heat. Gradually whisk in the semolina, then use a wooden spoon to stir the blobby mass until thick, 3 to 5 minutes.

Remove from the heat and stir in the egg yolks 1 at a time, stirring until smooth after each addition. Return the pan to low heat, stir in the Parmesan, and cook for 3 to 4 minutes more.

Spread the mixture on a rimmed baking sheet into a 1/2-inch-thick circle. Let cool until firm, 10 to 15 minutes.

Increase the oven temperature to 475°F. Cut the gnocchi into 2- to 3-inch rounds with a biscuit cutter or drinking glass and arrange the rounds in the bottom of a casserole dish (you can add the scraps, too). Top with the ragù and sprinkle with the 1/2 cup Parmesan.

Bake until the cheese melts and browns lightly, 3 to 5 minutes. If you have convection, turn it on to help the cheese brown.

Divide among warm plates and top with the mixed herbs.

PREP AHEAD

The gnocchi and ragù can be made up to 2 days ahead and refrigerated separately. Reheat the ragù before assembling and baking.

BEVERAGE—Feudi di San Gregorio, Aglianico 2006 "Rubrato" (Campania): Oxtail is full of rich, beefy flavor that not every wine can match. But this Aglianico's fresh, dark fruit and black earth flavors bring the long-cooking ragù alive.

Lasagna WITH ZUCCHINI AND STRACCIATELLA

I usually make this dish as individual lasagnas (see note on page 105), but here it's made in one big baking dish. The taste is the same both ways. Great cheese is the key. Stracciatella is the soft, stretchy, inner part of burrata cheese. If you can't find it, burrata will do. Either way, it's the perfect cheese for an early summer vegetable lasagna when the zucchini are small and garlic chives are available at the farmers' market.

Lay a pasta sheet on a lightly floured work surface and cut into lengths that will fit a 1¹/₂-quart (6-cup) baking dish. Spritz the pasta lightly with water as you work to keep it from drying out. Refrigerate any remaining pasta for another use.

Bring a medium pot of salted water to a boil. Drop in the pasta, quickly return to a boil, and blanch for 15 to 20 seconds. Transfer the pasta to a bowl of ice water to stop the cooking. Lay the pasta flat on kitchen towels and pat dry.

Meanwhile, preheat the oven to 425°F. Heat the oil in a medium sauté pan over medium heat. Add the squashes, garlic, and thyme and cook until soft but not mushy, 3 to 4 minutes. Remove from the heat and let cool.

Mix the ricotta and stracciatella in a small bowl and season with salt and pepper to taste.

Butter a 1¹/₂-quart baking dish and line the bottom with pasta, leaving some hanging over the edges. Spread on the cheese mixture, squash, and Parmesan, spreading each almost to the edge of the pasta. Repeat with one layer each of pasta, cheese mixture, squash, and Parmesan. Top with pasta and butter (if you have any cheese or squash left over, arrange it decoratively on top).

Bake until lightly browned on the edges, 10 to 12 minutes. If you have convection, turn it on to help crisp the edges of the overhanging pasta.

Divide among warm plates and drizzle each serving with some of the chive oil. Garnish with Parmesan.

MAKES 6 SERVINGS

8 ounces Basic Egg Pasta Dough (page 80), rolled into sheets

2 tablespoons extra-virgin olive oil

1 yellow squash, julienned (about 1 cup)

1 green squash, julienned (about 1 cup)

1 clove garlic, minced

Leaves from 3 to 4 sprigs thyme

³/₄ cup ricotta impastata or drained whole-milk ricotta cheese

6 ounces stracciatella or burrata cheese

Salt and freshly ground pepper

²/₃ cup freshly grated Parmesan cheese, plus more for garnish

8 teaspoons unsalted butter, cut into teaspoon-size slices

³/₄ cup Garlic Chive Oil (page 269)

If using pasta squares, they can be made up to 2 days ahead, lightly floured, stacked in an airtight container, and refrigerated.

If you can't find ricotta impastata, drain whole-mik ricotta instead. Line a sieve with cheesecloth or paper towels and place over a bowl. Put the ricotta in the sieve, cover, and let drain in the refrigerator for at least 8 hours or up to 24 hours.

LASAGNETTE

To make individual lasagnas, cut the rolled pasta sheets into 4-inch squares to make 27 squares. Blanch as directed in the main recipe, then arrange 9 squares on a buttered rimmed baking sheet and layer each with a layer of cheese, squash, Parmesan, and pasta. Repeat, ending with a pasta square. Top each lasagnetta with 2 pats of butter. Bake as directed. Makes 9 individual lasagnas.

BEVERAGE—Tramin, Sauvignon 2009 (Alto Adige): One of the top whites in its price range, this laser-sharp Sauvignon Blanc from the pre-Alps is all grapefruit up front and all green grass and herbs on the finish. Those aromas coax out the green snap of the zucchini in the dish.

Eggplant Lasagnette ALLA PARMIGIANA

I've served eggplant Parmesan dozens of different ways over the years: grilled giant slabs of eggplant and tomatoes, roasted whole tomatoes and eggplant, ravioli stuffed with eggplant and tomatoes. Here, the eggplant is sautéed, pureed with ricotta, and layered on pasta squares with Parmesan. The tomatoes are oven-dried with garlic and olive oil, then draped over the top of each individual lasagna. It's still classic, just tweaked a bit.

For the eggplant filling: Heat the oil in a large skillet over medium-high heat. Add the eggplant and sauté until tender and golden brown on the edges, about 10 minutes.

Let cool slightly, then transfer to a food processor. Puree until smooth, then add the ricotta, Parmesan, egg, and bread crumbs. Season with salt and pepper and pulse briefly until mixed. Set aside. Makes about 2 1/4 cups.

Lay a pasta sheet on a lightly floured work surface, trim the edges so they are straight, and cut the sheet into 4-inch squares. You should get 10 to 12 squares from the sheet. Repeat with the remaining pasta until you have a total of 27 squares. Spritz the pasta lightly with water as you work to keep it from drying out. Refrigerate any remaining pasta for another use.

Bring a large pot of salted water to a boil. Drop in the pasta squares, quickly return to a boil, and blanch for 20 seconds. Transfer the squares to a bowl of ice water to stop the cooking. Lay the pasta squares flat on kitchen towels and pat dry.

Preheat the oven to 400°F. Coat one large or two small baking sheets with a little butter.

Arrange 9 of the pasta squares on the buttered sheets, leaving a little space between each square. Spread 2 tablespoons eggplant filling over each pasta square and sprinkle each with 1 teaspoon Parmesan. Top each with another pasta square, another layer of eggplant filling, and another sprinkling of Parmesan. Top each with a third pasta square and sprinkle the tops with the remaining Parmesan. Bake until golden and crispy on the edges, about 10 minutes.

Using a wide spatula, transfer each lasagna to a warm plate and spoon 1/4 cup tomato conserva over each. Serve immediately.

PREP AHEAD

The pasta squares can be made up to 1 day ahead, sprinkled with flour, stacked, and refrigerated in an airtight container. The eggplant filling and tomato conserva can also be made up to 1 day ahead and refrigerated. Return all to room temperature before assembling and baking.

MAKES 9 INDIVIDUAL LASAGNAS

EGGPLANT FILLING

2 tablespoons grapeseed oil

1 Italian globe eggplant, peeled and chopped (about 3 cups)

3/4 cup ricotta impastata or drained whole-milk ricotta cheese

2 tablespoons freshly grated Parmesan cheese

1 egg

2 tablespoons dried bread crumbs

Salt and freshly ground pepper

8 ounces Basic Egg Pasta Dough (page 80), rolled into sheets

9 tablespoons freshly grated Parmesan cheese

2 1/4 cups Tomato Conserva (page 268)

If you can't find ricotta impastata, drain whole-mik ricotta instead. Line a sieve with cheesecloth or paper towels and place over a bowl. Put the ricotta in the sieve, cover, and let drain in the refrigerator for at least 8 hours or up to 24 hours.

BEVERAGE—Bisson's Ciliegiolo Rosato 2008 (Liguria): Eggplant is a fun food to match. You can get away with much more tannin than you'd expect, and this rosato provides freshness and lively fruit for the tomatoes, along with spice and sharp tannin for the eggplant.

Parmigiano

In Italy, Parmigiano-Reggiano cheese is called Parmesan. But in America, Parmesan and Parmigiano-Reggiano are not always the same thing. If you say "Parmesan" in America, it could refer to some kind of processed cheese food product that comes in a green can. But in Italy, Parmesan always comes from a wheel of quality-controlled Parmigiano-Reggiano cheese. When I say Parmesan, what I mean is Parmigiano-Reggiano. That's what I always use. With my restaurants, I spend more money on Reggiano in a year than many people spend on a down payment for a house! In the end, it's worth it. Reggiano is the king of Italian cheeses. It is the most regulated and the most flavorful. But if you don't want to pay so much for cheese, grana padano is second best. Grana is made in a similar way to Reggiano, but it's not as widely regulated and it doesn't have to be aged as long. Stick with the oldest grana you can find, aged about twenty months (vecchio). It will have a nice sharp flavor and similar texture to a mid-vecchio (middle-aged) Reggiano. Just remember: there is only one king!

HAND-ROLLED PASTA

Orrechiette WITH VEAL RAGÙ AND BITTER GREENS

People tell me it's a pain in the ass to make pasta. For me, there is nothing more relaxing. If you're the sort who likes to keep your hands busy, shaping little pastas gives you something to do while hanging out in the kitchen and talking about your day. Kids love it. What better way to spend time with your family doing something you can all take part in and feel proud of? The best part is, you get to eat everything you make!

For the ragù: Spread the veal and fatback in a single layer on a baking sheet or other shallow pan that will fit into your freezer. Freeze until firm but not solid, about 1 hour. At the same time freeze all the parts of a meat grinder. Grind the cold meat mixture with a meat grinder using a large die. If you don't have a meat grinder, you can chop the mixture in small batches in a food processor using 4-second pulses. Try not to chop it too finely; you don't want meat puree.

Heat a Dutch oven or large sauté pan over medium heat. Add the ground mixture and cook, stirring and scraping the pan bottom, until no longer pink, about 10 minutes.

Add the onion and carrot and cook until soft but not browned, about 5 minutes. Add the Parmesan rind and enough wine to cover the mixture. Reduce the heat to low, cover and simmer until the sauce has a light, creamy consistency, about 1 hour. Remove the Parmesan rind. Makes about 2 1/2 cups.

For the pasta: Put the semolina in a bowl. Slowly stir in enough of the water until the mixture looks loose in the bowl like damp sand. Knead it a little bit with your fingers in the bowl until it clumps together and feels like wads of sandy, dry bubble gum when pinched between your fingers. Depending on the humidity in the room, you may need to add more or less water to get the consistency right. It should feel like damp sand that sticks together when you pinch it. Knead the dough into a ball with your hands. It should be stiff but rollable.

Divide the dough into 4 pieces and wrap 3 of them in plastic to keep them from drying out. On an unfloured board, roll the remaining piece into a long rope about 3/8 inch thick (a little thicker than a pencil). Cut crosswise into 3/8-inch-thick pieces; each piece will look like a little pillow.

To form each orrechiette, put the edge of a butter knife onto one of the pasta pillows (see the photos on page 108). Drag the knife down across the dough, using medium pressure. The dough will roll around the knife blade into an oval shape. Remove the dough from the knife and place it, seam side up, on the tip of your pinky.

MAKES 4 SERVINGS

VEAL RAGÙ

1 1/4 pounds boneless veal leg or chuck, cut into 1-inch chunks

5 ounces pork fatback, cut into 1/2-inch chunks

1/2 cup onion cut into thin strips

1/4 cup peeled and finely chopped carrot

1 piece Parmesan rind

About 1 cup dry white wine

ORRECHIETTE

2 cups semolina

3/4 cup water

2 teaspoons olive oil

8 ounces escarole, trimmed and chopped

1/2 clove garlic, smashed

Salt and freshly ground pepper

1/4 cup freshly grated Parmesan cheese, plus more for garnish

continued, page 112

Orrechiette with *Veal Ragù* and *Bitter Greens*, continued

Securing the dough with your other hand, push your pinky into the smooth side of the dough, turning the dough inside out so the rough side is facing out. Each orecchiette should resemble a small, roughly shaped ear. Repeat with the remaining dough. Toss the finished orrechiette in a little semolina to keep them from sticking together. Lay the orrechiette in one layer in a large, flat container and refrigerate, uncovered, for at least 8 hours or up to 24 hours.

To cook, bring a large pot of salted water to a boil. Drop in the orrechiette, quickly return to a boil, and cook until tender yet firm, 3 to 4 minutes. Drain the pasta, reserving the pasta water.

Meanwhile, heat the olive oil in a large skillet over medium-high heat. Add the escarole and garlic and sauté until the greens are tender, about 4 minutes. Taste and season with salt and pepper. Remove the garlic and add the veal ragù and 2 ladles of pasta water to the greens. Simmer until the sauce is creamy, about 2 minutes.

Slide the drained orrechiette into the warm sauce. Add the 1/4 cup Parmesan and gently toss until the sauce is creamy, adding pasta water as needed.

Divide among warm pasta bowls and garnish with Parmesan.

PREP AHEAD

You can make the ragù up to 2 days ahead. Refrigerate it in an airtight container and reheat in a sauté pan before using. The orrechiette can be made up to 1 day ahead, sprinkled with a little flour, and refrigerated in an uncovered container.

BEVERAGE—Allegrini, La Grola IGT (Veneto): Allegrini's La Grola blends classic Amarone grape varietals with Syrah and Sangiovese. The result is a dark, luxurious wine with fig, black plum, and warm spice flavors, along with ripe tannin.

SPINACH AND RICOTTA Gnudi

The spinach gnocchi I serve at Vetri restaurant have become such a staple that they will never come off the menu. And I never wanted to put anything similar on the menu. I worked so hard to get those dumplings just right, it seemed pointless to reinvent the wheel. Then Jeff Michaud made these light, pillowy dumplings at Osteria. When I tasted them, they were so perfect that I knew they had to go on the menu. Gnudi are dumplings that are very similar to gnocchi, but this recipe is different enough from my spinach gnocchi that I wanted to share it with you here.

Bring a large pot of water to a boil. Add the spinach leaves and blanch for 1 minute. Remove, let cool, squeeze dry, and finely chop. Measure out 7 ounces spinach (about $3/4$ cup packed) and put it in a mixing bowl. Mix in the ricotta, egg, the $1^{1}/3$ cups flour, and the nutmeg. Season with salt and pepper to taste and mix thoroughly but gently.

Put 1 to 2 cups more flour in a pie pan or shallow bowl. Put the gnudi mixture in a pastry bag fitted with a $1/2$-inch plain tip or a ziplock bag with a $1/2$-inch hole snipped from a corner. Pipe $1/2$-inch-diameter balls of the dough into the flour a few at a time. Gently roll into dumplings in the flour and transfer to a baking sheet coated generously with flour.

Bring a large pot of salted water to a boil. Drop in the gnudi, quickly return to a boil, and cook until the gnudi float, about 2 minutes, then cook 20 seconds longer. Each dumpling should feel soft, delicate, and slightly springy when pressed with a fingertip, and have a creamy center when bitten. Drain the pasta.

Meanwhile, melt the butter in a medium sauté pan over medium-low heat until hazelnut brown, 6 to 8 minutes, stirring now and then.

Divide the drained pasta among warm pasta bowls. Drizzle with the brown butter and garnish with the Parmesan.

PREP AHEAD

If you can't find ricotta impastata, drain whole-mik ricotta instead. Line a sieve with cheesecloth or paper towels and place over a bowl. Put the ricotta in the sieve, cover, and let drain in the refrigerator for at least 8 hours or up to 24 hours.

BEVERAGE—Terre di Sole, Sangiovese 2008 (Sicily): Sangiovese is a great food wine, with enough acidity to cut through rich dishes, yet enough dark cherry fruit and herbal, earthy flavors to keep the acidity in check. It works wonders with the spinach dumplings.

MAKES 6 SERVINGS

10 ounces spinach leaves (no stems), stemmed and rinsed

4 cups ricotta impastata or drained whole-milk ricotta

1 egg, lightly beaten

$1^{1}/3$ cups tipo 00 or all-purpose flour, plus more for tossing gnudi

Grating of nutmeg

Salt and freshly ground pepper

6 tablespoons unsalted butter

$1/4$ cup freshly grated Parmesan cheese

Garganelli WITH GORGONZOLA, RADICCHIO, AND WALNUTS

Here's a nifty little pasta rolled on a comb. You can buy a special garganelli board or comb (pettine) with little ridges cut into it especially for this pasta (see Sources, page 279). But in a pinch, any large, clean comb will do the trick. To make garganelli, you roll squares of pasta around a pencil-thick dowel over the comb and end up with little tubular pastas that resemble penne with cross-wise ridges. Garganelli means "esophagus" in Italian, and that's exactly what these little things are: tiny esophagi that suck up sauce and melt away in your mouth. With the ruddy color of radicchio, this is the perfect pasta for a cool fall day. Be sure to use Gorgonzola dolce for the best taste. It's firmer, yellower, sweeter, and less pungent than regular Gorgonzola.

Lay a pasta sheet on a lightly floured work surface and dust with flour. Trim the ends so they are straight and cut the sheet into 2-inch squares. Place a garganelli comb or board on your work surface, or securely tape a large, clean, fine-toothed pocket comb to the surface. Flour it lightly. To form each garganello, place a square of pasta on the comb so one of the corners is pointing in the same direction as the teeth of the comb. Lightly flour a 1/4-inch wooden dowel or a clean pencil and lay it over the pasta perpendicular to the teeth of the comb.

Fold the bottom corner of the pasta over the dowel or pencil, then roll the pasta loosely onto the dowel. Roll back and forth on the comb a couple of times, pressing gently into the ridges of the comb to seal the edges of the pasta and create a ridged quill shape similar to penne. Slide the pasta off the dowel or pencil and set aside. Repeat with the remaining pasta squares, spritzing the shaped garganelli with a little water and covering them to keep them from drying out. To hold it longer, sprinkle the shaped garganelli with a little flour and freeze them in an airtight container for up to 3 days (no need to thaw before cooking).

Bring a large pot of salted water to a bowl. Drop in the garnanelli, quickly return to a boil, and cook until tender yet firm, about 1 minute. Drain the pasta, reserving the pasta water.

MAKES 4 SERVINGS

1 pound Basic Egg Pasta Dough (page 80), rolled into sheets

1/2 cup olive oil

1/4 cup chopped onion

6 ounces radicchio, cut into thin strips

12 large walnuts, coarsely chopped

Salt and freshly ground pepper

4 teaspoons chopped fresh flat-leaf parsley

6 ounces Gorgonzola dolce, broken into pieces

Meanwhile, heat the olive oil in a large sauté pan over medium heat. Add the onion and radicchio and cook until wilted, about 1 minute. Ladle in about $^1/_2$ cup of pasta water. Add the walnuts and cook until there is only a little liquid left.

Slide the drained garganelli into the pan. Toss gently until the sauce is creamy, adding pasta water as needed. Taste and season with salt and pepper. Remove from the heat and gently stir in the parsley and Gorgonzola just until the cheese is slightly melted.

Divide among warmed pasta bowls and enjoy.

PREP AHEAD

You can make the garganelli up to 3 days ahead. Toss with a little flour, seal in an airtight container, and freeze. Then take it straight from the freezer to boiling pasta water. If you're feeling lazy, you can replace the garganelli with 12 ounces boxed dried penne pasta, but it won't be nearly as good because penne is made with a semolina dough (just semolina and water), while garganelli is made with a richer, softer egg pasta dough.

BEVERAGE—Allegrini, Valpolicella 2008 (Veneto): Here is a great example of watching a wine transform into something entirely different as you drink it with a meal. The pungency of the Gorgonzola in this dish brings out a sweetness in the wine that you might miss otherwise, while the radicchio and walnuts amplify the wine's menthol aroma.

SALUMI

THE BOX WAS MARKED "LINENS FROM ITALY." It must have weighed twenty pounds—obviously too heavy for linens. This was back in 2003 on the cusp of the Spanish chefs movement. A few months before my box of "linens" arrived, I happened to be up in New York for a weekend and decided to go to Babbo for dinner. Mario Batali was there, and after a few courses he came over to my table and we started talking. He told me about Casa Mono, the Spanish tapas place he was planning to open later that year. He was really excited about the ingredients: the Spanish olive oils, the bacalao, the Iberico ham, the perfectly aged Manchego, the chorizo. "I'm taking a bunch of chefs to Barcelona in a couple of weeks," he said, "to do research." It sounded good, and I happened to mention how unimpressed I'd been with most of the chorizo I'd tasted so far in my life. "Dude, you should come with us," he said. "You can see what it's supposed to taste like."

It took me all of a micro-second to say, "Sounds awesome!" A week and half later, I was on a plane to Barcelona. I toured around with Mario and his chefs for a few days, tasting everything in sight. When we hit La Boqueria, the big public market, I found it: that perfect chorizo with just the right spice. Mario looked at me, but he didn't say anything. He just watched me eat and smiled. I savored that chorizo bite by bite so my mouth would remember what it tasted like when I got back home. I was going to make a chorizo just like it.

Mario opened Casa Mono later in the fall of that year. To mark the occasion, I decided to smuggle a whole Iberico ham into the United States for the opening. This was before it was legal to buy jamón ibérico de bellota in the States. I told my friend Marco Rossi in Italy about the plan and he said, "I have just the right guy. He raises some of the best Iberico pigs free-range on a small farm in Spain. They eat acorns by the bushel and get nice and plump." I was sold. "You have to FedEx it to me," I told him. "But how?" he shot back. "Isn't it illegal?" I thought for a moment. "I don't know," I said, "You'll figure something out. Just FedEx it to me and send me the bill."

My twenty-pound box of "linens" from Italy arrived a few days later. The contents cost $800. The FedEx charge was another $800. But I didn't care. I took my linens up to New York for the Casa Mono opening. I handed the box to the chef, Andy Nusser, and said, "Here." He nearly dropped it because it was so heavy. "What is this?" he asked. I looked at him and said, "Open it."

Andy and Mario were blown away. Especially on opening night of Casa Mono. I mean, a whole pata negra? The real deal, shipped from Spain? Illegally? Who does that?

Some things are worth taking a risk for, and great food is one of them. I had finally tasted a great chorizo, and the ham was simply a way of saying thanks.

TYPES OF SALUMI

Iberico ham is a dry-cured ham similar to prosciutto. Preserved and cured meats like these fall under the umbrella term salumi, which is the Italian equivalent of charcuterie. I like to make four basic types of salumi: terrines, cooked sausage, dry-cured salami, and whole-muscle salumi. Prosciutto and Iberico are whole-muscle salumi. A few quick definitions: A terrine is like a coarse-textured pâté. It's made with seasoned ground meat that's packed into a loaf-shaped mold or baking dish and then baked in a water bath. After cooking, a terrine is usually chilled, unmolded, then cut crosswise into slices like bread. It's an old-school salumi that makes a big impression on a modern menu. The type of salumi that's probably most familiar to home cooks is cooked sausage. Think bologna, mortadella, or anything else called a "cold cut" in the States. Cooked sausage is ground meat stuffed into a casing—usually a large casing—poached until the meat is cooked, then chilled and sliced as needed. A cold cut. Cooked sausage is similar to a terrine, except that it's tubular in shape and poached on the stove top instead of baked in a water bath. So what's the difference between cooked sausage (salami cotto) like bologna and dry-cured salami like Spanish chorizo? Both are made with ground meat stuffed into tubular casings. But dry-cured salami like Spanish chorizo and Italian soppressatta are not cooked. Instead, they are fermented for several hours to create good bacteria and then hung in a cool, moist environment to air-dry and cure over a period of several weeks. Curing salt and gradual dehydration help prevent the meat from spoiling, or "cure" it, so that the dry-cured salami will keep for a month or more under normal refrigeration. That dry-curing environment is the same for whole-muscle salumi, the last type of salumi I like to make. Whole-muscle salumi refers not to ground meat but to whole pieces of meat like pork shoulder, pork belly, or pork leg (ham) rubbed with seasonings and hung in a cool, moist environment to air-dry and cure over a period of several months. Whole pieces of meat take longer to dry-cure than ground meat sausage because the muscle fibers remain intact and hold on to their moisture longer. Whole-muscle salumi includes things like Italian pancetta and American bacon (cured whole pork belly), ham and prosciutto (cured whole pork leg), coppa (cured whole pork shoulder), guanciale (cured whole pork jowl), and lardo (cured whole pork fatback).

Why do I make all these different forms of salumi when it's easy enough to buy them in a store? Because they taste better when you make them yourself. The satisfaction of dry-curing a piece of meat over several weeks in your home, then serving it to friends and family, is enormous. It's like growing your own tomatoes. Once they're ready, you're so proud, you just can't wait to eat them, cook with them, and share them with everyone you know. Guests never fail to be impressed by home-cured salami. Get ready for eager friends to rub their hands together and ask, "Are they ready yet?" Imagine shaving off a thin slice of your own homemade Soppressata Calabrese (page 149) or Fennel Salami (page 152) to begin a meal. It's unlike any other form of cooking because it isn't cooking. It's curing. There's something magical about taking a piece of raw meat, salting it, then serving it with full confidence three months later. It's something you have to experience for yourself.

SANITATION

Sausage making isn't hard, but you have to be diligent in how you handle the meat. You want to minimize any bacterial contamination. Use clean and sanitized equipment and utensils. To make sanitizer, mix a capful of full-strength chlorine bleach with a gallon of water, then scrub or soak anything that will come into contact with the meat. Simply put, keep your work area sanitized, wear gloves, and handle the meat as little as possible. Any time you take another step with the meat, you are introducing new bacteria. Work quickly in a small area, and try not to touch the meat too much.

FREEZING

It takes longer for bacteria to grow in cold temperatures, so try to keep everything as cold as possible—from the meat to whatever's holding the meat to whatever's grinding the meat. A good rule of thumb is to keep everything

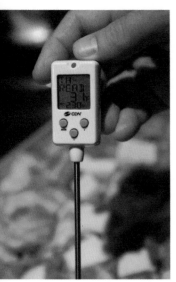

below 41°F (refrigerator temperature) the entire time you're working with it. Working in a cold room helps, too.

Most of my ground sausage has a ratio of about 80 percent meat to 20 percent fat. I usually cut both the meat and the fat into 1-inch cubes, then freeze them in a single layer on metal baking sheets until partially frozen. After about an hour in the freezer, they should be the right texture—firm but not frozen solid. Put all your meat grinding and mixing parts in the freezer, too, from the grinder auger and cutting die to the mixing bowls, paddles, and trays. Keeping everything cold serves two purposes. First, it reduces bacterial activity, and second, it makes it easier to grind the fat into those nice, juicy white pieces you see in a cross-section of salami. If the fat warms up too much as you work, it will soften and smear in the grinder instead of getting cut into nice little pieces. Again, don't handle the meat and fat too much, because the heat from your 98.6°F body will transfer to the meat, which you want to keep below 41°F throughout the process. Before you start making salumi, wash your hands in hot soapy water, put on gloves, and stick your hands in a bowl of ice until they are very cold, almost painful. Remember, everything should stay cold.

SEASONING

I like to season the meat and fat right when I take it out of the freezer—before grinding. This is an old method I learned in Italy, and when you are making smaller artisan-style batches, the sausage gets more consistently seasoned this way. Just scatter all of the dry seasonings over the partially frozen chunks of meat/fat and mix it thoroughly, wearing rubber gloves (on your cold hands).

When adding spices and herbs, I tend to season my sausage lightly to let the taste of the meat shine through. If you want to test the seasoning of the raw sausage, fry some and taste it before stuffing it into casings. Just pinch up a large piece of the seasoned ground meat, form it into a little patty between your gloved palms, and cook it over medium heat in a skillet until browned on both sides. Then taste it. If you want to taste more of any single seasoning like black pepper or ground coriander, mix a little more into the raw meat. Jot down your changes so you know how you like it next time. But don't go overboard with seasoning. Dry-cured sausage tends to lose about 30 percent of its weight when fully dry-cured, a dehydration process that concentrates all the flavors. I under-season to make sure the fully cured meat isn't overwhelmed by spice flavors.

SALT AND SUGAR

When adding salt and sugar to ground sausage, I usually calculate the amount as a percentage of the total weight of the meat and fat. I add 2 to 4 percent salt and 0.5 to 1 percent sugar by weight. For instance, in my Soppressata Calabrese (page 149) and Fennel Salami (page 152), the total weight of the meat and fat in each recipe is 5 pounds (2.5 kg). In each recipe, I add 2.8 percent salt and 0.5 percent sugar by weight, which works out to 70 grams ($1/2$ cup plus $1 1/2$ teaspoons) Diamond Crystal kosher salt and 12.5 grams ($5 1/4$ teaspoons) dextrose powder or 10.5 g (4 teaspoons) superfine sugar.

It might sound like a lot of salt, but salt does the hard work of curing sausage by dehydrating the meat and making it less hospitable to bad bacteria. I use kosher salt for curing salumi and measure it by weight because this is more accurate than volume measurements. Here's the reason: salt is the main ingredient that cures the meat, and different salts vary dramatically in their weight-to-volume ratios. See for yourself. Weigh out the same weight of three different salts—fine sea salt, Morton's kosher salt, and Diamond Crystal kosher salt. Say, 10 grams each. Then use level tablespoons to measure the volume of each little pile of salt. You'll see that Morton's measures about one and a half times more than fine sea salt, and Diamond Crystal about twice as much as fine sea salt. That's a big difference, especially when you're scaling up salumi recipes from 1 pound of meat to 10 pounds or more. But I know that most American cooks measure by volume, so I tested all the salumi recipes with both volume and weight measurements to make sure they work. For accuracy's sake, you should know that the volume measurements in my salumi recipes are based on Diamond Crystal kosher. That's the salt I use for curing meat. If you use a different brand, go by the gram amounts in the recipes, and weigh your salt for an accurate measurement.

The other salt in cured sausage is, you guessed it, curing salt. There are two types: curing salt No. 1 and curing salt No. 2. Simple, right? Both are formulated so that 1 level teaspoon cures 5 pounds of meat. Cure No. 1, also known as pink salt, Tinted Cure Mix (TCM), Insta Cure No. 1, and DQ Curing Salt No. 1, is tinted pink so it's easy to recognize. It contains 6.25 percent sodium nitrite and 93.75 percent salt. Use Cure No. 1 for fresh and cooked sausages like mortadella, terrines, and fresh link sausage. Cure No. 2 (aka Insta Cure No. 2 and DQ Curing Salt No. 2) is white, like regular kosher salt, and it's used for uncooked dry-cured salumi like soppressata, chorizo, pancetta, and coppa that will be dried for weeks. Cure No. 2 also contains 6.25 percent sodium nitrite, but with 4 percent sodium nitrate and 89.75 percent salt. That small amount of nitrate is what helps control the growth of harmful bacteria over weeks and months of curing in the open air.

Sugar has the opposite effect of salt. Instead of slowing down the growth of bacteria, it speeds it up. Sugar gives the bacteria something to feed on. By adding sugar to the cure, you're trying to feed the good bacteria early on in the process, so it will develop during the initial fermentation of the salumi. This good bacteria helps fight off the bad bacteria as the salumi dries and cures.

It's important to add something sweet to the mix, and I use powdered dextrose. It has a fine texture that distributes very evenly throughout the sausage, much more evenly than granulated sugar. I typically use 0.5 percent dextrose for soppressatta and other dry-cured sausages that will be fermented. You can find dextrose powder in most natural foods stores and nutrition stores like GNC. Fitness buffs use it in smoothies and such, and

most of them probably have no clue that it's perfect for making salumi, too. If you can't find dextrose, you can substitute superfine granulated sugar, but the measurements aren't one to one. Dextrose is made from corn, and superfine sugar (aka castor sugar or bar sugar) is usually made from cane. Dextrose is about 25 percent less sweet than cane sugar. That means you need to use about 25 percent less superfine sugar than dextrose. Essentially, substitute 1 cup dextrose with ³/₄ cup plus 2¹/₂ teaspoons superfine sugar. Or, replace 100 grams of dextrose with 80 grams of superfine sugar. I wrote the salumi recipes to list both dextrose and superfine sugar. And what if you can't find superfine sugar? Just make it at home. Take regular granulated sugar, put it in a clean spice grinder or coffee mill, and process until very finely ground.

GRINDING

There's a nice segue! Once your meat and fat are seasoned with sugar, salt, curing salt, and whatever other seasonings you like, you'll need a meat grinder to get the texture right. If you have a KitchenAid stand mixer, you're all set. Every sausage recipe in the book was tested on a 6-quart KitchenAid with the sausage grinder attachment. The key is grinding the meat quickly so it

doesn't have time to warm up and smear. Attach your cold grinder parts to the machine, then set it to high speed. I grind most sausage with a large cutting die for a coarse texture, and I usually grind twice. But for smoother sausages, like mortadella, I grind the meat and fat together five times using a small die. Big die for coarse sausage. Small die for smooth sausage. Give yourself a couple of hours for grinding, especially if you're making smooth sausages like mortadella that must be put through the grinder at least five times to get the texture right. That gives you enough time to grind the meat and put it back in the freezer between grindings to get it cold and firm again so it won't smear. When grinding more than once, it also helps to grind the meat into a bowl set in a larger bowl of ice.

MIXING

After you grind, it's important to mix everything into a sort of paste. If you grind into the bowl of the stand mixer, you just put the bowl in the machine and mix with the paddle attachment on low speed. Most sausages include some kind of cold liquid like ice water or wine, and this is the time to add it. Sausage makers often use garlic powder or onion powder, but I can't stand that stuff. I like to soak the smashed whole cloves of fresh garlic in wine for 30 minutes or so, then toss the garlic and use the wine. You get a nice, light garlic scent that way. Either way, mix everything on low speed until it looks dense and sticky, kind of like wet bread dough. It takes only a minute or two.

STUFFING

For cooked sausage and dry-cured salami, the next step is stuffing the meat mixture into casings. I use three types of casing, all of them natural: hog casings, beef middles, and beef bungs. These come from the intestines of pigs and cows and have been the perfect casings for handmade artisanal sausage for centuries. Hog casings are the smallest (think link sausage), beef middles are the next biggest (think soppressatta), and beef bungs are the largest (think mortadella and bologna). The larger the casing, the longer the sausage will take to dry-cure. Sausages in hog casings dry in a matter of weeks, while those in beef bungs can take months. I like the beef middles because the sausages seem to age best in them.

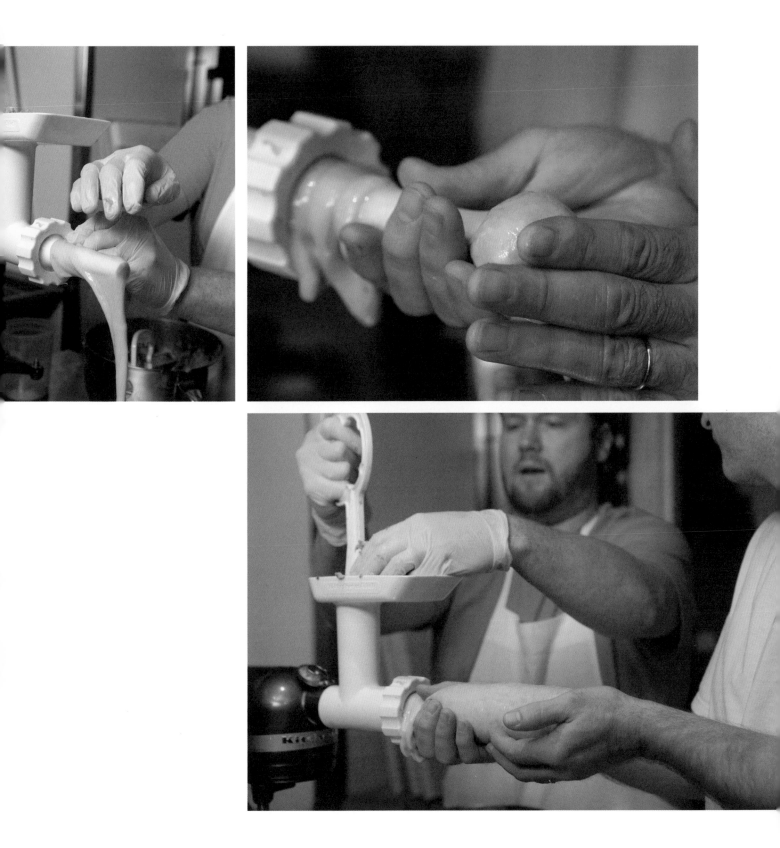

The casings will come packed in salt and should be soaked and rinsed to remove the salt. After soaking them in cold water in the refrigerator for about an hour, I usually tie one end closed with butcher's string (tie it extra tight!), then fill it with water like a water balloon. That helps me see the shape the final sausage will take once it's stuffed. As for sausage length, it's up to you. You can fill an entire casing at once and twist it into links, or cut the casing into lengths a little longer than the final sausage length you want. If you want links, just feed the meat into the casing until you reach a link length, then twirl the sausage a couple of times to form the link. Keep stuffing until you reach another link length, then twist the sausage in the opposite direction from the first time. That keeps the links from unraveling as you go. The first time you make sausage, you might find it easier to just cut the casings into 1¹/₂-foot lengths and tie them off. That will give you sausages that are about a foot long—a very manageable size. Or make them longer, if you like. Sausage is one of those great arts that is totally open to your personal preference!

I will say that stuffing is the only time it's hard to use gloves. With gloves on, you just can't hold the casing tightly enough against the sausage stuffer without it slipping away. Stuffing is the time to invite a friend over. Believe me, the process is much, much easier with two people: one person feeds the meat into the stuffer (wearing gloves) and the other handles and shapes the sausage (without gloves).

Start by feeding some of the meat mixture into the feed tube until it just starts to poke out of the end of the sausage stuffer. That way, there is no air in the system. Then you grease the stuffer tube with a little meat mixture and slip the casing onto the stuffer. Slip it all the way to the end of the stuffer tube, like putting a sock on your foot. Once it's on there, it helps to put pressure on the tied end of the casing so it's gently pressed against the stuffer. When the meat comes through the machine, a little pressure helps the meat pack tight into the middle of the casing with fewer chances of air getting in. You want a nice tight sausage with no air in it. If you have any air bubbles, mold will grow inside of them during dry-curing and ruin the sausage. The worst thing is getting halfway through the weeks and weeks of dry-curing and anticipation to find out that you've got air bubbles in your sausage. As the meat gets stuffed into the casing, constantly check for air bubbles, working them out the open end of the casing as needed. You can also prick the casing wherever there is a bubble to let out the air.

Remove the stuffed casing from the stuffer, grab the open end, and squeeze it down tightly against the meat to pack it down. Twist the open end several times against the meat until the sausage is sealed. Then tie off that twisted end with butcher's string. Be sure to leave enough extra string for hanging the sausage in your curing room, which can be as simple as an empty basement closet with a humidifier and air conditioner or heater in it.

COOKING

The hardest thing about cooked sausage is poaching it at the right temperature. If the poaching liquid is too hot, the fat in the sausage will melt. If it's too cold, the meat won't cook properly. The temperature also can't fluctuate too much. I like to use a big pot of water on the stove so the temperature doesn't change too drastically when the cold sausage goes in. Use a thermometer and adjust the burner to maintain the poaching water at a constant temperature. That temperature could be anywhere from 145°F to 165°F, depending on what kind of meat is in the sausage. Fish and rabbit should poach on the lower end of that range to keep them tender, while lamb and pork should poach at the upper end.

Cooked sausages often include internal "garnishes" like cubed pork fat and pistachios. To keep fat garnishes from melting when the sausage is cooked, I like to blanch the fat first to render it a little. It's a simple step that makes a big difference.

I also like to sear my cooked sausages. Once poached, you could slice and eat Rabbit Salami (page 144) or Swordfish Sausage (page 146) as is. But they taste even better if you slice them lengthwise or into rounds, then sear them in a hot skillet until brown. It puts a nice crispy crust on the outside of the tender sausage.

As I mentioned earlier, terrines are another type of cooked sausage. Sausage just means "ground meat," which certainly applies to a terrine. The difference is that the meat for a terrine is packed into a terrine mold instead of being stuffed into a soft casing. Then it's cooked, usually in a water bath (bain marie). The cooking is very similar to poaching a stuffed sausage except that the terrine isn't completely submerged in the water. Either way, the water helps cook the ground meat slowly and gently so it stays moist and rich when it's done. Terrines are a great place to start in this chapter because they are easy and impressive. The cooked sausages like Lamb Mortadella (page 142) and Swordfish Sausage are good starting places, too, because you don't have to deal with the issues of fermentation and controlling humidity and air temperature as you do with dry-cured sausages.

FERMENTATION

Ground-meat dry-cured sausage is by far the most complicated type to make. It takes dedication, precision, and a lot of patience. Don't be surprised if it doesn't work out the first time you try it. There are so many variables to control! You could do everything right and it still won't work. I still get failed batches now and then. Don't worry; it's not you. It's just a very complex process! The most important variables are sanitation, temperature, and humidity. Learn as much as you can about these factors, be diligent about them, and you'll have the best shot at success.

The bottom line for all dry-cured salami is the drying itself. You basically need to dry the salami so it has a very low "water activity" level, which is expressed numerically by scientists as "aw." When the salami has an aw of 0.85 or lower, it is considered microbiologically stable. But how do you get there without creating a petri dish of bacteria inside the salami? That is the dilemma. The solution is to slow down the growth of bad bacteria with an initial fermentation step. This step creates good lactic bacteria that holds off the unwanted bad bacteria. It's that simple. Create good bacteria and it will deter bad bacteria. Commercial sausage makers in America create the good lactic bacteria by adding a starter culture like Bactoferm. But that chemical fermenter can bring the pH up so high that it gives the finished salami a metallic taste. The pH should range between 4.6 and 5.3. But if it's too high, it can make the salami texture too rubbery, which is how you end up with horrible rubbery pepperoni.

The artisan sausage makers in Italy create good bacteria the old-school way—by letting it grow naturally. They put the sausage in a warm, humid environment to ferment, encouraging good bacteria like *Staphylococcus carnosus* and *Kocuria* to grow right away. Increasing the number of these bacteria helps develop good color and flavor in the finished salami. Fermentation also increases the number of good lactic acid–producing bacteria like *Lactobacillus* and *Pediococcus*. These beneficial bacteria keep the harmful bacteria at bay, and they continue to multiply during the weeks or months of dry-curing.

That's the trick: keeping the beneficial bacteria multiplying and keeping the harmful bacteria at bay. I have found that the best way to initiate this fermentation process is with an exact temperature, humidity, and length of time. I ferment my salami at 90°F and 100 percent humidity for 36 hours. I do it in an oven that has a steaming function. If you have an oven with steam, set it for 100 percent humidity and 90°F, put the salami inside (preferably hung so each one is separate) and close the door for 36 hours.

If you don't have a steam oven, create one using a regular oven and a small humidifier. This method will work for most home cooks and it's how we tested all the fermented sausage recipes in this book. You can use a gas oven with the pilot light on, or if your oven has a bread-proofing or warming mode, set the oven to 90°F. Take out all the oven racks and put a small humidifier right inside the oven on the oven floor. Run the cord out the oven door, plug it in, and set the humidifier to high. To monitor the temperature and humidity, put a thermometer and hygrometer inside the oven, and close the oven door. A remote thermometer/hygrometer is really convenient because the sensor stays inside the oven and sends a wireless signal to a receiver that automatically displays the temperature and humidity. It allows you to easily monitor the salami without opening the oven. Then, you simply adjust the oven temperature or the humidifier to maintain 90°F and 100 percent humidity inside the oven for 36 hours. You may have to replenish the water in the humidifier once or twice, and I highly recommend using distilled water to keep the humidifier from getting gummed up by any minerals in hard water. Plus, it will get pretty wet in there, just like a steam room, so put a large drip pan or rimmed sheet pan on the oven floor to catch some of the water. If you have enough room at the top of the oven, keep one oven rack in place so you can hang the salami from it.

Either way, you can see that the most important factors to regulate are the heat and the humidity. To make it easy, pick up an inexpensive remote thermometer/hygrometer. As for timing, I've found that 36 hours is the sweet spot, but if your temperature and/or humidity is over or under 90°F and 100 percent, you may have to adjust the total time. You can tell that the salami is done fermenting when it starts to turn reddish and the casing begins to get tight, as if the meat has plumped up a bit. At that point, it is ready to be put into the curing room.

CURING

To slow down the bacterial activity, you need to move the salami to a cooler and less humid environment. I hang my dry-cured salumi at 50°F to 55°F and 75 percent humidity for anywhere from 4 weeks to 6 months, depending on the size of the casing and whether they are ground-meat sausages or whole-muscle salumi. Here is where the salumi gets gradually drier, firmer, and more flavorful.

Pick a small area so it's easier to regulate the key environmental factors of temperature and humidity. It should also be dark to prevent light from discoloring the salumi. A wine cellar or root cellar is traditional, but an uninsulated basement closet works great, too. The area should be clean, with at least a little air circulation. Here are a few options I've tried successfully:

Basement closet: For most home sausage makers, an uninsulated basement closet will be the way to go. As long as your basement is underground, the temperature should stay at or close to 55°F. Temperatures do fluctuate at different times of the day and different times of the year, so it's safest to set a small window-style air conditioner in the closet to adjust the temperature if it gets too hot. You can also put a small space heater in there if it gets too cold. To regulate the humidity, put a small cool-mist humidifer in the closet (use a standard cool-air humidifier, the kind used to relieve congestion in kids). To monitor everything, hang a remote thermometer/hygrometer in the closet. They only cost around fifty bucks. Get the room set up a few hours ahead of time, so you've got the environmental factors stabilized before you put the salumi in the room. Then, if the temperature gets too high, turn up the air conditioner. If the humidity falls too low, turn up the humidifier. To make it even easier, you can buy an in-line thermostat and hydrostat for each appliance and set the thermostat to 55°F and the hydrostat to 75 percent humidity. They cost a hundred dollars or so each, but they do the real work of sensing the temperature and humidity and automatically turn the air conditioner or humidifier on or off whenever necessary. When testing this method, I simply cranked the humidifier and air conditioner to high and plugged them into the thermostat and hydrostat. The in-line thermostat and hydrostat did the rest of the work. It was by far the easiest method for home use.

Wine refrigerator: Here's another nifty option. It is a little more expensive than a basement closet, but wine refrigerators are designed to replicate a cave or cellar environment, and they are generally adjustable to 55°F and 75 percent humidity. Just be sure to buy a wine refrigerator with adjustable temperature and humidity controls and adjustable racks so you can fit the salumi inside. Bonus: When you're not curing salumi, you can age wine in the fridge!

Converted freezer: I haven't tried this method myself, but dedicated home sausage makers swear by it. Buy a small freezer and plug it into an in-line thermostat to bypass the freezer control. A freezer has its own internal thermostat that powers the cooling mechanism to drive the temperature down to around 0°F. With an in-line thermostat, you can bypass the internal thermostat, set the temperature to 55°F, and the freezer's cooling mechanism won't power on until that temperature is exceeded. Humidity is the other factor to control and placing a cool-mist humidifier in the freezer is the best way do it, just as described above for a basement closet. If you plug the humidifier into an in-line hydrostat, then both the thermostat and the hydrostat will automatically regulate the temperature and humidity. Simple! The only other thing to keep in mind is the defroster, which is designed to cycle on periodically to eliminate moisture in the freezer—basically, all the humidity you've worked so hard to get in there! If you have a frost-free unit, find and disconnect the wire to the defroster, which usually runs beneath the main cooling coils of the freezer. The advantage to this converted freezer method is that when you're not curing salumi, you have an extra freezer on hand.

EQUIPMENT AND DONENESS

So where do you buy all this sausage making equipment? And the ingredients? Most of the ingredients like curing salt and sausage casings you can order from the Sausage Maker (see Sources, page 279). As for equipment, if you don't have a KitchenAid sausage grinder and stuffer attachment, you can order those through KitchenAid. Or go to the Sausage Maker for a separate meat grinder, plus other equipment like a gram scale, thermometers, etc. You can get cool-mist humidifiers, small window air conditioners, and space heaters at most home stores. For the humidifier, Crane makes a one-gallon model that fits nicely into small spaces. Just be sure to use distilled water and be prepared to replenish it every couple of days, which isn't a big deal because that's how often you should check on your dry-cured salumi anyway.

Curing salumi is like growing a garden. It requires some advance planning and careful tending, but the rewards are well worth it when you reap the harvest. It's easy to tell when vegetables are ready to pick because they are so heavy they weigh down the entire plant. With salumi, it's the opposite. They should actually lose weight. A good rule of thumb is that dry-cured salami like soppressata and chorizo should lose 25 to 30 percent of their initial weight. Whole-muscle salumi like coppa and speck should lose 20 to 25 percent of their weight. To keep track, weigh each string of salami before dry-curing. Jot down the name of the salami, the weight, the starting hang date, and the expected doneness date in a notebook or on masking tape taped to the hanging string of the salami. When you think the salami are done, weigh them. They should weigh 20 to 30 percent less than what you initially jotted down, depending on the type of salami. For instance, 5 pounds of coppa should weigh about 4 pounds when cured. Five pounds of soppressata should weigh about 3$^1/_2$ pounds when cured.

The size of the casing determines the aging time. I usually make soppressata, chorizo, and other salamis in beef middles and age them for 6 to 8 weeks. But if you use smaller hog casings, figure on 4 to 6 weeks. At that point, the salami should be firm yet pliable, not quite as dry as the pepperoni you're probably familiar with. I like my sausage young.

The other thing to keep track of is the look and feel of the salami. When you touch the casing after a week or so, it should start to feel a little tacky, almost sticky, just like your own skin would feel if you were in 75 percent humidity for a week. When the casing feels a little tacky, the moisture is right on. If the casing feels smooth and tight, as if it's wrapped in plastic wrap, the humidity is too low and the salami is drying too fast. If it goes the other way and the casing feels really sticky, the humidity is too high. Don't worry about a little white mold on the surface. That is normal. But a thick covering of mold or off-colored mold usually means the humidity is too high. If you find a salami that looks bad and isn't getting any better, remove it so it doesn't contaminate the whole batch.

Touch and feel the salami with gloves every couple of days. When fully cured, the salami should feel firm but slightly pliable when you try to bend one. As for looks, the meat should get a deeper and deeper red as it ages. So deep that you just want to cut it open right there and bite into it. After you do bite into it, or slice it, or devour it in a single sitting, store any leftover salami in the refrigerator. It should keep for a month or more and continue to slowly age and dry.

Both whole-muscle salumi and ground-meat sausage can be dry-cured as described here. Whole-muscle salumi is a great way to learn the process. There is minimal chance to mess things up, so I highly recommend it. Instead of dealing with grinding and stuffing, you simply soak the meat in a tub of dry cure in the refrigerator for a week or two, turn it over every day or so, then hang the meat at 50°F to 55°F and 75 percent humidity for several weeks or a few months. This is how Pancetta (page 159), Coppa (page 158), and Beef Speck (page 157) are made. Starting with this whole-muscle salumi will give you confidence and time to get your curing environment dialed. Then when you move on to ground-meat sausages like Soppressata Calabrese (page 149), Fennel Salami (page 152), and Chorizo (page 154), you'll be ready to fully enjoy the craft of making artisanal salumi in your own home with little more than meat, fat, salt, and your own two hands.

TERRINES

Potted Trout TERRINE

Fish may not be the first thing that comes to mind for a terrine, but it's delicious. I like to use trout because it has a lot of natural gelatin that enriches the terrine. I usually grill the fillets for a little smoke flavor, but if you like it more plain Jane, just sear the fillets in a pan. This terrine is so easy because there is no exact cooking process, no precise poaching temperature, and no terrine mold! I spoon the mixture into tiny glass mason jars, which makes an awesome presentation at the table. With a few crackers on the side, some sliced Pickled Eggs (page 169) and a dollop of Horseradish Crème Fraîche (page 273), it makes a really impressive appetizer. Or you can just serve the trout with Rustic Loaf (page 24). Or tie a ribbon around the jars and give them away as gifts!

MAKES ABOUT 1½ PINTS TOTAL, OR 6 HALF-PINT JARS FILLED HALFWAY

1¾ pounds boneless trout fillets (9 or 10 fillets)

2 tablespoons grapeseed oil

Salt and freshly ground black pepper

3 tablespoons plus 1 teaspoon unsalted butter

3 tablespoons plus 1 teaspoon olive oil

¼ cup minced shallot

2 to 4 teaspoons fresh lemon juice

2 tablespoons chopped fresh flat-leaf parsley

Light a grill for medium-high heat. Scrape the grill clean and oil it with a wad of paper towels dipped in oil. Place the trout on a foil-lined baking sheet, skin side up. Oil the skin with grapeseed oil, then flip and oil the flesh. Season the flesh with salt and pepper.

Grill the trout directly on the grill grate, flesh side down, for 2 to 3 minutes. Flip and cook just until the trout is cooked through, 1 to 2 minutes more. Transfer the grilled trout to a baking sheet to cool.

Meanwhile, melt the butter with the olive oil in a small sauté pan over medium heat. Add the shallot and cook until soft and barely browned, 2 to 3 minutes. Remove from the heat and let cool.

Working over a large bowl, use your hands to peel off and discard the trout skin, dropping the flesh into the bowl. Mix in the lemon juice, shallot mixture, and parsley. Season with salt and pepper. Mix with your hands, breaking up the flesh, but not too much. Taste and season with lemon juice, salt, and pepper as needed.

Spoon the terrine into half-pint mason jars until half full, then seal and refrigerate.

PREP AHEAD

Make the terrine up to 5 days ahead and keep it sealed in the refrigerator.

BEVERAGE—Cantina Ferentana, Pecorino 2009 (Abruzzo): Recently rediscovered, the Pecorino grape is being brought back into production, and its round, balanced flavors of stone fruit, honey, and citrus are propelling it into the mainstream.

Duck TERRINE

Here's a terrine with a little flair. When you slice it, you see three layers: ground meat on top and bottom with a strip of whole duck breast pieces in the center. I make this with whole ducks and remove all the fat, skin, and bones. It's always better (and less expensive!) to start with the whole food and break it down yourself. But you could also start with 4 pounds of skinless, boneless duck meat instead. You'll need about 1¼ pounds breasts and 2¾ pounds thigh and leg meat. Sprinkle the finished sliced terrine with some Maldon sea salt and serve with bread and savory preserves like Artichoke Mostarda (page 174) or Pickled Mustard Seeds (page 170).

Separate the breasts from the rest of the duck meat and cut the breasts into cubes. Combine the sugar, the ½ cup salt, and the thyme in a medium bowl. Add the cubed breasts, tossing to coat. Cover and refrigerate for 1 hour.

Cut the remaining meat into cubes and freeze in a single layer on a baking sheet that will fit in your freezer until firm but not solid, about 1 hour. At the same time, freeze all the parts to a meat grinder.

Fit the meat grinder with the small die, then put on plastic gloves and stick your hands in a bowl of ice until very cold, almost painful. Set the grinder to high speed and grind the partially frozen meat through the small die into the bowl of a stand mixer. Add the flour, the remaining 2½ teaspoons salt, the curing salt, black pepper, cream, egg, egg yolk, and Madeira. Using the paddle attachment, mix on low speed for 1 to 2 minutes.

Rinse the salt mixture off the duck breasts and preheat the oven to 300°F.

Line an 8-cup terrine mold with heavy-duty heatproof plastic wrap, leaving enough extra plastic hanging over the sides to cover the mold when it is filled. To get 3-inch rectangular slices, use a 15½ by 3¼ by 3-inch terrine or pullman loaf pan (pain de mie; 8-cup capacity). Or use 4 mini-loaf pans (each 5½ by 3 by 2 inches) for a similar shape. Gently pack half of the meat mixture into an even layer in the plastic-lined mold. Lay the duck breasts over the meat. Gently pack the remaining meat mixture around and over the breasts to create three layers. Securely pack in the meat to eliminate all air pockets. It's important to press out all the air to help keep the terrine from spoiling. Smooth the top and fold the plastic over the meat, covering it completely and gently pressing it onto the meat.

MAKES 10 TO 12 SERVINGS

2 whole ducks (about 3¾ pounds each), fat, skin, and bones removed (about 4 pounds meat)

½ cup sugar

½ cup plus 2½ teaspoons kosher salt

2 to 3 tablespoons fresh thyme leaves

1½ tablespoons tipo 00 or all-purpose flour

½ teaspoon curing salt No. 1 (pink salt)

½ teaspoon ground pepper

⅓ cup heavy cream

1 egg

1 egg yolk

½ teaspoon Madeira wine

Maldon sea salt, for garnish

Set the mold in a larger, deep roasting pan and put on the center oven rack. Pour enough hot water into the larger pan to come at least $1/2$ inch up the sides of the mold. Bake in the water bath to an internal temperature of 145°F, 1 to $1^1/2$ hours for a single large mold or 45 to 55 minutes for several small molds.

Remove the terrine from the oven and compact it: cut a piece of cardboard to fit inside the terrine mold; put a heavy weight over the cardboard, and let cool to room temperature. When cool, remove the weight, cover with plastic wrap, and refrigerate until cold.

Unmold the terrine and slice about $1/2$ inch to 1 inch thick. Sprinkle each slice with Maldon sea salt. Refrigerate any remaining terrine for up to 1 week.

PREP AHEAD

You can bone the ducks, removing all fat and skin, up to a day ahead of time and refrigerate the meat in an airtight container.

BEVERAGE—Scarbolo, Merlot 2006 "Campo del Viotto" (Friuli): Made in the Amarone style, this Merlot exhibits rich, dried fruit flavors and spice but also feels fresh. It displays much of that weighty mouthfeel that Amarone has while retaining a velvety texture that complements the smoothness of the terrine.

Pork Liver TERRINE

This is by far my favorite terrine. Brad Spence, my chef at Amis, came up with it, and I love its sage and coriander flavors. It's also firm enough to slice yet soft enough to spread on bread. I like to serve it with toasted Brioche (page 37) and Shallot Marmalade (page 171). If you can't find pork liver, you can use the same amount of chicken liver instead. But the pork liver is much, much better.

Freeze the pork liver and pork butt in a single layer on a baking sheet until firm but not solid, about 1 hour. At the same time, freeze all the parts to a meat grinder.

Meanwhile, heat the oil in a small sauté pan over medium heat. Add the onion and sage and cook until soft but not browned, about 5 minutes. Let cool.

Fit the meat grinder with the small die, then put on plastic gloves and stick your hands in a bowl of ice until cold, almost painful. Set the grinder to high speed and grind the cold liver, shoulder, and onion mixture into the bowl of a stand mixer. Add the salt, sugar, pepper, coriander, curing salt, cream, and egg. Mix on low speed with the flat beater until sticky like wet bread dough, about $1^1/2$ minutes.

Preheat the oven to 300°F. Line a 6-cup terrine mold with heavy-duty heatproof plastic wrap, leaving enough extra plastic hanging over the sides to cover the mold when it is filled. To get $2^1/2$-inch rectangular slices, use an 8-cup terrine or pullman loaf pan (pain de mie). Or use 3 mini-loaf pans (each $5^1/2$ by 3 by 2 inches) for a similar shape. Gently pack the meat mixture into the mold, pressing to eliminate all air pockets. Smooth the top and fold the plastic over the meat, covering it completely and gently pressing it onto the meat.

Set the mold in a larger, deep roasting pan or baking sheet and place on the center oven rack. Pour enough hot water into the large pan to come at least $^1/2$ inch up the sides of the mold. Bake in the water bath to an internal temperature of 145°F, 40 to 50 minutes for a single large mold or 30 to 40 minutes for small molds.

Remove the terrine from the oven and compact it by cutting a piece of cardboard to fit inside the terrine mold; put a heavy weight on top of the cardboard and let cool to room temperature. Remove the weight, cover with plastic wrap, and refrigerate until cold.

Unmold the terrine and slice $^1/2$ inch to 1 inch thick. Sprinkle each slice with Maldon sea salt. Refrigerate any terrine for up to 1 week.

BEVERAGE—Birrificio Italiano, Scires NV (Lombardia): This beautiful sour ale brewed with cherries has a sweet/tart flavor that exemplifies Italy's thriving craft beer culture: exciting, original, often with a nod to Belgium, and sometimes incorporating herbs, fruit, nuts, spices, and tea.

MAKES 6 TO 8 SERVINGS

$1^1/4$ pounds pork liver, cut into 1-inch cubes

$1^1/4$ pounds boneless pork butt (shoulder), cut into 1-inch cubes

$1^1/2$ teaspoons grapeseed oil or olive oil

1 cup finely chopped onion

1 tablespoon chopped fresh sage

$5^1/2$ teaspoons kosher salt

1 teaspoon sugar

1 teaspoon ground pepper

1 teaspoon ground coriander

$^1/2$ teaspoon curing salt No. 1 (pink salt)

$6^1/2$ tablespoons heavy cream

1 egg

Maldon sea salt, for garnish

COOKED SAUSAGE

Lamb MORTADELLA

Whenever I can, I go to Vinitaly, the wine show held every year in Verona. It is the largest wine show in the world, taking up ten airplane hangars. If you go, you'll find little mortadella panini everywhere at the show. Mortadella is the classic Italian pork salami made with cubes of pork fat. At Vinitaly, you can't miss the mortadella. It's usually sitting on a table, and it's almost as big as one of the mini cars you'll see on the city streets. You'll find a big knife like a machete on the table. Just slice off hunks of the mortadella, put them on one of the small rolls on the table, and slather on some mayonnaise. I once spent a whole day at the wine show eating those little sandwiches. But when it came time to make it myself, I thought, "You always see pork mortadella. Let's try something different!" In the summer of 2010, my chef Brad Spence tried it with lamb and it was fantastic. The key here, as with all mortadella, is the grinding. I like to grind it five times, but if you do more, it won't hurt. The more you grind the meat, the creamier the mortadella will become. Once it's cured, try it in sandwiches, in Mortadella Tortelli with Pistachio Pesto (page 89), or on Mortadella Pizza (page 48).

Freeze the lamb and 1 pound cubed fatback in a single layer on a baking sheet until firm but not solid, about 1 hour. At the same time, freeze all the parts to a meat grinder.

Meanwhile, blanch the 8 ounces 1/2-inch-diced fatback by immersing it in boiling water for 30 seconds, then immersing it in ice water until cold. Refrigerate until needed. Soak the garlic in the wine for 30 minutes, then discard the garlic and keep the wine.

Fit the meat grinder with the large die. Put on plastic gloves and stick your hands in a large bowl of ice until very cold, almost painful. Place the bowl of a stand mixer in the large bowl of ice, then set the grinder to high speed. Grind the cold lamb and fat into the mixer bowl. Cover the bowl and freeze for 10 minutes. Switch to the small die in the grinder, then uncover the meat and grind with the small die 4 more times, covering and freezing the bowl for 10 minutes between each grinding. You can also work in batches, dividing the ground mixture between two small baking sheets and keeping one batch in the freezer while grinding the other batch. Just be sure to grind at least 5 times so the mixture is very smooth.

Add the ice water, dry milk, kosher salt, dextrose, gelatin, curing salt, ground pepper, ground coriander, and nutmeg to the lamb mixture. Mix with the paddle attachment (or the dough hook if your mixer seems to be working too hard) on medium speed for a minute or so. Add the wine, blanched fatback, and pistachios and mix until the meat is sticky, like wet bread dough, another minute or so.

MAKES ONE 5-POUND SAUSAGE

4 pounds (1.8 kg) lean lamb leg meat, cubed

1 pound (450 g) pork fatback, cubed, plus 8 ounces fatback (225 g), cut into 1/2-inch dice

1 clove garlic (4 g), smashed

1 tablespoon (15 g) dry white wine

1 cup (224 g) crushed ice with water

2/3 cup (89 g) dry milk

1/4 cup plus 1 tablespoon (44 g) kosher salt

3 tablespoons (22 g) dextrose powder, or 2 tablespoons (16 g) superfine sugar

1 3/4 teaspoons (8 g) unflavored powdered gelatin

1 teaspoon (6 g) curing salt No. 1
(pink salt)

1 teaspoon (3.5 g) whole black peppercorns, ground

1 teaspoon (3 g) whole coriander
seeds, ground

1/8 teaspoon (0.5 g) ground nutmeg

2/3 cup pistachios (70 g)

1 beef bung, soaked in cold water for
1 hour, then rinsed inside and out

Attach a large sausage stuffer tube to the grinder. You may need to leave off the retainer bar so the pistachios will fit through the tube. Grease the stuffer tube with some of the meat mixture. The next step of stuffing the sausage is much easier with two people: if you can, have one person feed in the meat and the other person handle the casing as it fills up. Feed some of the meat into the feed tube on high speed until it just starts to poke out the end of the sausage stuffer. Turn off the machine. Slip the open end of the beef bung (casing) onto the stuffer all the way to the end, like putting a sock on your foot. Put pressure on the end of the casing so it's gently pressed against the stuffer. Turn the machine to high speed and feed in the meat. Keep gentle pressure on the casing so the meat packs into the middle of the casing as tightly as possible. You want no air in there. As the meat gets stuffed into the casing, it should surround at least 1 inch of the end of the stuffer tube to prevent air from getting into the sausage. While stuffing, constantly check the sausage for air bubbles, working them out the open end of the casing as necessary. Continue stuffing the meat into the casing until you have a tight sausage about 1 foot long.

Remove the stuffed casing from the stuffer, grab the open end, and squeeze it down tightly against the meat to pack it down. Twist the open end several times against the meat until the sausage is firm and sealed. Tie off the twisted end with butcher's string. If necessary, tie the mortadella in several places to make it tight.

Put the mortadella in a large, deep roasting pan and cover with cold water. Put the pan over medium-high heat and bring the water to 160°F. Adjust the heat to maintain that temperature until the mortadella reaches an internal temperature of 150°F, 2 to 3 hours. Remove from the water and immerse in a large bowl of ice water (or the emptied roasting pan) until the mortadella is cool.

Store in the refrigerator for up to 2 weeks.

BEVERAGE—Monzio Compagnoni, Saten 2002 (Lombardy): This beautiful, richly flavored sparkler is my go-to alternative to Champagne. The quality will surprise you. Bottled at a lower atmospheric pressure near the lake district in Lombardy, Saten exhibits a soft, sparkling character with flavors of apple, pear, and spice. The mortadella, with its silky texture and pistachios, benefits from this wine's supple mouthfeel.

Rabbit SALAMI

Salami requires a careful balance of lean meat and fat, and rabbit has very little fat, so you need to add a little more fat than usual here or the sausage won't be tender. I like to serve this sliced and seared with some crusty bread (try the Rustic Loaf on page 24) and dried fruit. My favorite is prunes soaked in Armagnac.

Freeze the rabbit and 1 pound cubed fatback in a single layer on a baking sheet until firm but not solid, about 1 hour. At the same time, freeze all the parts to a meat grinder.

Meanwhile, blanch the 4 ounces $1/2$-inch-cubed fatback pieces in boiling water for 30 seconds, then immerse in ice water until cold. Refrigerate until needed. Soak the garlic in the wine for 30 minutes, then discard the garlic and keep the wine.

Fit the meat grinder with the large die, then scatter the kosher salt, dextrose, mustard powder, curing salt, black pepper, sage, and ground juniper berries over the cold meat and fat. Put on plastic gloves, then stick your hands in a large bowl of ice until very cold, almost painful. Place the bowl of a stand mixer in the large bowl of ice. Mix together the meat and seasonings with your hands, then set the grinder on high speed. Grind the meat, the 1 pound fatback, and the seasonings into the mixer bowl. Dump the mixture back onto the baking sheet and grind it a second time. Add the wine, the blanched diced fatback, and the pistachios to the bowl.

Mix with the paddle attachment (or the dough hook if your mixer seems to be working too hard) on medium speed until the mixture is sticky, like wet bread dough, about 2 minutes.

Cut the beef middles into $1^1/2$-foot lengths and tie one end tight with butcher's string. Attach a large sausage stuffer tube to the food grinder. You may need to leave off the retainer bar so the pistachios will fit through the tube. Grease the stuffer tube with some of the meat mixture. The next step of stuffing the sausage is much easier with two people. If you can, have one person feed in the meat and the other person handle the casing as it fills up. Feed some of the meat mixture into the feed tube on high speed until it just starts to poke out the end of the sausage stuffer. Turn off the machine. Slip the open end of a beef middle (casing) onto the stuffer all the way to the end, like putting a sock on your foot. Put pressure on the end of the casing so it's gently pressed against the stuffer. Turn the machine on high speed and feed in the meat. Keep gentle pressure on the casing so the meat packs into the middle of the casing as tightly as possible. You want no air in there. As the meat gets stuffed into the casing, the meat should surround at least 1 inch of the end of the stuffer tube to prevent air from getting into the sausage. Constantly check the sausage for air bubbles,

MAKES ABOUT 5 POUNDS

4 pounds (1.8 kg) boneless lean rabbit meat, cubed

1 pound (450 g) pork fatback, cubed, plus 4 ounces (125 g) pork fatback, cut into $1/2$-inch dice

1 small clove garlic (2.5 g), smashed

4 tablespoons plus $1^1/4$ teaspoons (62.5 g) dry white wine

$1/3$ cup plus $3/4$ teaspoon (50 g) kosher salt

$5^1/4$ teaspoons (12.5 g) dextrose powder, or 4 teaspoons (10 g) superfine sugar

1 tablespoon (6 g) mustard powder

1 teaspoon (6 g) curing salt No. 1 (pink salt)

1 teaspoon (3.5 g) cracked pepper

1 teaspoon (2 g) chopped fresh sage

$1/4$ teaspoon (1 g) ground juniper berries

1 cup (125 g) pistachios

Beef middles, soaked in cold water for 1 hour, then rinsed inside and out

working them out the open end of the casing as necessary. Continue stuffing the meat into the casing until you have a tight sausage about 1 foot long.

Remove the stuffed casing from the stuffer, grab the open end, and squeeze it down tightly against the meat to pack it down firmly. Twist the open end several times against the meat until the sausage is tight and sealed. Tie off the twisted end with butcher's string. Repeat with more tied beef middles until the meat mixture is used up.

Put the salami in a large roasting pan and cover with cold water. Put the pan over medium-high heat and bring the water to 145°F. Adjust the heat to maintain that temperature until the salami reaches an internal temperature of 145°F on a meat thermometer, 1 to 1^1/$_2$ hours. Remove from the water and immerse in a large bowl of ice water (or the emptied roasting pan) until the salami is cool.

Store in the refrigerator for up to 2 weeks. You can slice and serve this salami cold. But I like to sear pieces in a hot pan and serve them warm.

BEVERAGE—Paitin di Pasquera Elia-Langhe 2006 (Piedmont): This fresh Nebbiolo-Barbera blend has just the right acidity and earthy spiciness to keep pace with the rabbit.

Swordfish SAUSAGE

I got bored with making meat sausages, but all the seafood sausages I ever tried were weak and rubbery. Not these. Swordfish has enough fat and a firm enough texture to make a satisfying sausage. Of course, it is fish, so it's still somewhat delicate. Keep an eye on the temperature of your poaching water. If it's too hot, the sausage will lose all its juices. When poached carefully, it's amazing. As with the Rabbit Salami (page 144), I like to cut this sausage into medallions and quickly sear them in a hot pan in a little grapeseed oil. It gives the sausage a nice crispy crust.

Freeze the fish and fatback in a single layer on a baking sheet until firm but not solid, about 1 hour. At the same time, freeze all the parts to a meat grinder.

Fit the meat grinder with the large die, then put on plastic gloves and stick your hands in a large bowl of ice until very cold, almost painful. Place the bowl of a stand mixer in the large bowl of ice, then set the grinder on high speed. Grind the fish and fat into the mixer bowl.

Add the kosher salt, sugar, pepper, coriander, garlic, and water. Mix with the paddle attachment on medium speed until the mixture is sticky, like wet bread dough, 3 to 4 minutes.

Attach a large sausage stuffer tube to the food grinder and grease the tube with some of the fish mixture. The next step of stuffing the sausage is much easier with two people: if you can, have one person feed in the fish mixture and the other person handle the casing as it fills up. Feed some of the fish mixture into the feed tube on high speed until it just starts to poke out the end of the sausage stuffer. Turn off the machine. Slip the open end of a hog casing onto the stuffer all the way to the end, like putting a sock on your foot. Put pressure on the end of the casing so it's gently pressed against the stuffer. Turn the machine to high speed and feed in the fish mixture. Keep gentle pressure on the casing so the mixture packs into the middle of the casing as tightly as possible. You want no air in there. As the fish gets stuffed into the casing, it should surround at least 1 inch of the end of the stuffer tube to prevent air from getting into the sausage. Constantly check the sausage for air bubbles, working them out the open end of the casing as necessary. Continue stuffing the mixture into the casing, and when you reach the length of a link (I like 6-inch lengths for these sausages), twist the link a few times to seal one end. Continue stuffing until you reach another link length, then twist that link in the opposite direction. This will keep the links from unraveling. Continue stuffing until the casing is full and all the mixture is used, using additional hog casings as necessary.

MAKES ABOUT 3 POUNDS

2$1/2$ pounds (1125 g) swordfish, cubed

12 ounces (375 g) pork fatback, cubed

3 tablespoons (25 g) kosher salt

1$1/2$ teaspoons plus $1/8$ teaspoon (6.25 g) sugar

$1/2$ teaspoon (1.5 g) ground pepper

$1/2$ teaspoon (1.5 g) ground coriander

1 small clove garlic (2.5 g), minced

$1/4$ cup (55 g) water

Hog casings, soaked in cold water for 1 hour, then rinsed inside and out

Remove the stuffed casing from the stuffer, grab the open end, and squeeze it down tightly against the fish to pack it firmly. Twist the open end several times against the fish until the sausage is firm and sealed. Tie off the twisted end with butcher's string. Repeat with more tied beef middles until the fish mixture is used up.

Put the sausage in a large roasting pan and cover with cold water. Put the pan over medium-high heat and bring the water to 160°F. Adjust the heat to maintain that temperature until the sausage reaches an internal temperature of 150°F on a meat thermometer, 10 to 15 minutes. Remove from the water and immerse in a large bowl of ice water until the sausage is cool.

Cut between the links and store in the refrigerator for up to 2 weeks or freeze for up to 1 month. You can grill or pan-sear this sausage whole, but I like to slice it into coins and sear the coins in a little oil in a hot pan.

BEVERAGE—Anselmi, San Vincenzo 2008 (Veneto): From the Soave region of the Veneto, this Garganega/Chardonnay blend exhibits some weight on the palate, and the intensity of its citrus, pear, and hazelnut aromas picks up on the coriander and garlic in the sausage.

DRY-CURED SALAMI

Soppressata CALABRESE

This is one of my favorites. Years ago, when I started making dry-cured salami, Calabrese was the first. For me, it is the perfect combination of salt and spice. It's kind of like pepperoni, but sooo much better. If you like it really spicy, up the amount of red pepper flakes and black pepper.

MAKES ABOUT 3¹/₂ POUNDS (ABOUT TWO 12-INCH-LONG SALAMI)

4 pounds (2 kg) boneless pork butt (shoulder), cubed

1 pound (500 g) pork fatback, cubed

1 small clove garlic (2.5 g), smashed

¹/₄ cup plus 4 teaspoons (75 g) dry red wine

¹/₂ cup plus 1¹/₂ teaspoons (70 g) kosher salt

5¹/₄ teaspoons (12.5 g) dextrose powder, or 4 teaspoons (10.5 g) superfine sugar

2 teaspoons (4 g) red pepper flakes

1 teaspoon (6 g) curing salt No. 2

1 teaspoon (3.5 g) cracked black pepper

¹/₂ teaspoon (1.5 g) ground white pepper

Beef middles, soaked in cold water for 1 hour, then rinsed inside and out

Freeze the pork and fatback in a single layer on a baking sheet until firm but not solid, about 1 hour. At the same time, freeze all the parts to a meat grinder.

Soak the garlic in the wine for 30 minutes, then discard the garlic and keep the wine.

Fit the meat grinder with the large die, then scatter the kosher salt, dextrose, red pepper flakes, curing salt, black pepper, and white pepper over the cold meat and fat. Put on plastic gloves, then stick your hands in a large bowl of ice until very cold, almost painful. Place the bowl of a stand mixer in the large bowl of ice. Mix together the meat and seasonings with your hands, then set the grinder on high speed. Grind the meat, fat, and seasonings into the mixer bowl. Dump the mixture back onto the baking sheet and grind it a second time.

Pour the wine over the meat, then set the bowl in the stand mixer fitted with the paddle attachment. Mix on medium speed until the mixture is sticky, like wet bread dough, about 2 minutes.

Cut the beef middles to 1¹/₂-foot lengths and tie one end tightly with butcher's string. Attach a large sausage stuffer tube to the food grinder. Grease the stuffer tube with some of the meat mixture. The next step of stuffing the sausage is much easier with two people: if you can, have one person feed in the meat and the other person handle the casing as it fills up. Feed some of the meat mixture into the feed tube on high speed until it just starts to poke out the end of the sausage stuffer. Turn off the machine. Slip the open end of a beef middle (casing) onto the stuffer all the way to the end, like putting a sock on your foot. Put pressure on the end of the casing so it's gently pressed against the stuffer. Turn the machine to high speed and feed in the meat. Keep gentle pressure on the casing so the meat packs into the middle of the casing as tightly as possible. You want no air in there. As the meat gets stuffed into the casing, the meat should surround at least 1 inch of the end of the stuffer tube to prevent air from getting into the sausage. Constantly check the sausage for air bubbles, working them out the open end of the casing as necessary. Continue stuffing the meat into the casing until you have a firm sausage about 1 foot long.

Remove the stuffed casing from the stuffer, grab the open end, and squeeze it down tightly against the meat to pack it firmly. Twist the open end several times

continued, page 150

Soppressata Calabrese, continued

against the meat until the sausage is firm and sealed. Tie off the twisted end with butcher's string, leaving enough extra string for hanging. Repeat with more tied beef middles until the meat mixture is used up.

Ferment the sausage in a warm (80°F to 90°F), dark place with 100 percent humidity for 36 hours. See page 128 for options on setting up the fermentation environment.

After fermentation, hang the sausage in a cool (50°F to 55°F), dark place with some air circulation and 75 percent humidity until the salami feels firm yet slightly pliable, usually 6 to 8 weeks (see page 132). Check the salami every couple of days. It should feel a little tacky on the surface and lose 25 to 30 percent of its weight. Some white mold is okay. A thick covering of mold usually means the humidity is too high. If the casing becomes hard and brittle, the humidity is too low.

Remove and store in the refrigerator for several months.

BEVERAGE—Librandi, Ciro Rosato 2008 (Calabria): Soppressata is rich, salty, and supremely satisfying. The wild berry, date, and spice aromas of this fresh rosato—as well as its solid acidity—act as the perfect foil.

So Young and So Good

If you want to be inspired by salumi, go to Italy. You can get mortadella the size of tree trunks in one city and tender, young sausages no more than three days old in another. When I went back to visit friends in Bergamo in 2008, we ate at La Brughiera in Villa d'Almè. They served a soppressata made in the traditional way, but instead of aging it until it was firm, they served it after only three days. It was so soft, you could spread it with a butter knife. The bread on the side of the plate was there for just that purpose. It was the most flavorful sausage I have ever tasted. This soft, young dry-cured sausage opened my eyes to so many new things about sausage making. When I got home, I immediately cut into my dry-cured sausages to see how they would taste. They were a little more aged than three days, but one bite told me that I would be serving sausages in new ways from there on out.

Fennel SALAMI

I like my salami very young. I only age them for about six weeks. But you could age them even less. Do an experiment: when you make dry-cured salami, cut into one of them after a week and taste it. Wait another week, then cut into another one. The next week, another one. It can be very satisfying to watch and taste how the salami changes as it ages. Maybe you'll find out that you prefer your salami after eight weeks of curing, and that's fine.

Freeze the pork and fatback in a single layer on a baking sheet until firm but not solid, about 1 hour. At the same time, freeze all the parts to a meat grinder. Soak the garlic in the wine for 30 minutes, then discard the garlic and keep the wine.

Fit the meat grinder with the large die, then scatter the kosher salt, dextrose, black pepper, fennel seeds, and curing salt over the cold meat and fat. Put on plastic gloves, then stick your hands in a large bowl of ice until very cold, almost painful. Place the bowl of a stand mixer in the large bowl of ice. Mix together the meat and seasonings with your hands, then set the grinder on high speed. Grind the meat, fat, and seasonings into the mixer bowl. Dump the mixture back onto the baking sheet and grind it a second time.

Pour the wine over the meat, then set the bowl in the stand mixer fitted with the paddle attachment. Mix on medium speed until the mixture is sticky, like wet bread dough, about 2 minutes.

Cut the beef middles toto 1¹/₂-foot lengths and tie one end tightly with butcher's string. Attach a large sausage stuffer tube to the food grinder. Grease the stuffer tube with some of the meat mixture. The next step of stuffing the sausage is much easier with two people: if you can, have one person feed in the meat and the other person handle the casing as it fills up. Feed some of the meat mixture into the feed tube on high speed until it just starts to poke out the end of the sausage stuffer. Turn off the machine. Slip the open end of a casing onto the stuffer all the way to the end, like putting a sock on your foot. Put pressure on the end of the casing so it's gently pressed against the stuffer. Turn the machine to high speed and feed in the meat. Keep gentle pressure on the casing so the meat packs into the middle of the casing as tightly as possible. You want no air in there. As the meat gets stuffed into the casing, the meat should surround at least 1 inch of the end of the stuffer tube to prevent air from getting into the sausage. Constantly check the sausage for air bubbles, working them out the open end of the casing as necessary. Continue stuffing the meat into the casing until you have a firm sausage about 1 foot long.

MAKES ABOUT 3¹/₂ POUNDS (ABOUT EIGHT 12-INCH-LONG SALAMI)

4 pounds (1.8 kg) boneless pork butt (shoulder), cubed

1 pound (500 g) pork fatback, cubed

2 cloves garlic (7.5 g), smashed

¹/₄ cup plus 4 teaspoons (75 g) red wine

¹/₂ cup plus 1¹/₂ teaspoons (70 g) kosher salt

5¹/₄ teaspoons (12.5 g) dextrose powder, or 4 teaspoons (10.5 g) superfine sugar

¹/₂ teaspoon (1.5 g) cracked pepper

2 teaspoons (5.5 g) fennel seeds

1 teaspoon (6 g) curing salt No. 2

Beef middles, soaked in cold water for 1 hour, then rinsed inside and out

Remove the stuffed casing from the stuffer, grab the open end, and squeeze it down tightly against the meat to pack it firmly. Twist the open end several times against the meat until the sausage is firm and sealed. Tie off the twisted end with butcher's string, leaving enough extra string for hanging. Repeat with more tied casings until the meat mixture is used up.

Ferment the sausage in a warm (80°F to 90°F), dark place with 100 percent humidity for 36 hours. See page 128 for options on setting up the fermentation environment.

After fermentation, hang the sausage in a cool (50°F to 55°F), dark place with some air circulation and 75 percent humidity until the salami feels firm yet slightly pliable, usually 6 to 8 weeks (see page 132 for options on setting up the curing environment). Check the salami every couple of days. It should feel a little tacky on the surface and lose 25 to 30 percent of its weight. Some white mold is okay, but a thick covering of mold usually means the humidity is too high. If the casing becomes hard and brittle, the humidity is too low.

Remove and store in the refrigerator for several months.

BEVERAGE—Casa Girelli, Primitivo 2007 "Virtuoso" (Puglia): Herbal spice and rich, dried fruit and earth flavors characterize this Primitivo, which is the genetic equivalent of Zinfandel.

Chorizo

I have tasted chorizos for years, but I never really had one I liked until I went to Barcelona. There, in La Boqueria, the big main market, I found the perfect texture and flavor: firm yet pliable, not quite spicy, but redolent with the smoky aroma of pimentón, and perfectly salted. Everything was dead on. When I got home, I started experimenting to re-create that exact flavor and texture. I think this is pretty damn close. It's milder than the heavily spiced Spanish chorizo you might be used to. And don't confuse it with Mexican chorizo, which is an uncooked fresh sausage.

Freeze the pork and fatback in a single layer on a baking sheet until firm but not solid, about 1 hour. At the same time, freeze all the parts to a meat grinder. Soak the garlic in the wine for 30 minutes, then discard the garlic and keep the wine.

Fit the meat grinder with the large die, then scatter the kosher salt, dextrose, pimentón, black pepper, and curing salt over the cold meat and fat. Put on plastic gloves, then stick your hands in a large bowl of ice until very cold, almost painful. Place the bowl of a stand mixer in the large bowl of ice. Mix together the meat and seasonings with your hands, then set the grinder on high speed. Grind the meat, fat, and seasonings into the mixer bowl. Dump the mixture back onto the baking sheet and grind it a second time.

Pour the wine over the meat, then set the bowl in the stand mixer fitted with the paddle attachment. Mix on medium speed until the mixture is sticky, like wet bread dough, about 2 minutes.

Cut the beef middles into 1¹/₂-foot lengths and tie one end tightly with butcher's string. Attach a large sausage stuffer tube to the food grinder. Grease the stuffer tube with some of the meat mixture. The next step of stuffing the sausage is much easier with two people: if you can, have one person feed in the meat and the other person handle the casing as it fills up. Feed some of the meat mixture into the feed tube on high speed until it just starts to poke out the end of the sausage stuffer. Turn off the machine. Slip the open end of a casing onto the stuffer all the way to the end, like putting a sock on your foot. Put pressure on the end of the casing so it's gently pressed against the stuffer. Turn the machine to high speed and feed in the meat. Keep gentle pressure on the casing so the meat packs into the middle of the casing as tightly as possible. You want no air in there. As the meat gets stuffed into the casing, the meat should surround at least 1 inch of the end of the stuffer tube to prevent air from getting into the sausage. Constantly check the sausage for air bubbles, working them out the open end of the casing as necessary. Continue stuffing the meat into the casing until you have a firm sausage about 1 foot long.

**MAKES ABOUT 3¹/₂ POUNDS
(ABOUT EIGHT 12-INCH-LONG SALAMI)**

4 pounds (1.8 kg) boneless pork butt (shoulder), cubed

1 pound (500 g) pork fatback, cubed

2 cloves garlic (7.5 g), smashed

¹/₄ cup plus 4 teaspoons (75 g) red wine

¹/₂ cup plus 1¹/₂ teaspoons (70 g) kosher salt

10¹/₂ teaspoons (25 g) dextrose powder, or 8 teaspoons (21 g) superfine sugar

3 tablespoons (24 g) pimentón (smoked paprika)

1 tablespoon (10 g) cracked pepper

1 teaspoon (6 g) curing salt No. 2

Beef middles, soaked in cold water for 1 hour, then rinsed inside and out

Remove the stuffed casing from the stuffer, grab the open end, and squeeze it down tightly against the meat to pack it firmly. Twist the open end several times against the meat until the sausage is firm and sealed. Tie off the twisted end with butcher's string, leaving enough extra string for hanging. Repeat with more tied casings until the meat mixture is used up.

Ferment the sausage in a warm (80°F to 90°F), dark place with 100 percent humidity for 36 hours. See page 128 for options on setting up the fermentation environment.

After fermentation, hang the sausage in a cool (50°F to 55°F), dark place with some air circulation and 75 percent humidity until the salami feels firm yet slightly pliable, usually 6 to 8 weeks (see page 132 for options on setting up the curing environment). Check the salami every couple of days. It should feel a little tacky on the surface and lose 25 to 30 percent of its weight. Some white mold is okay, but a thick covering of mold usually means the humidity is too high. If the casing becomes hard and brittle, the humidity is too low.

Remove and store in the refrigerator for several months.

BEVERAGE—Bastianich, Rosato 2008 (Friuli)/Beba, Toro Doppio Malto NV (Piedmont): The Rosato is made from the Refosco grape, which produces a deep rosy color, a hefty mouthfeel, and pronounced spice and red fruit flavors that stand up well to the smoky, spicy chorizo. Or try a beer with this sausage. Toro Doppio Malto from Piedmont complements the chorizo by imparting a nutty caramel component that softens its spice.

WHOLE-MUSCLE SALUMI

Beef Speck

The region of Tyrol is part Italian, part Austrian, and famous for the lightly smoked, juniper-scented dry-cured ham called speck. Even though pork leg is traditional, I wanted to show you that beef makes great speck, too. I love it sliced paper-thin and draped on a plate like carpaccio, with some lumps of Gorgonzola cheese and pickled vegetables.

MAKES ABOUT 4 POUNDS

5 pounds (2.25 kg) beef top round

2/3 cup plus 1 1/4 teaspoons (100 g) kosher salt

5 1/4 teaspoons (12.5 g) dextrose or 4 teaspoons (10.5 g) superfine sugar

1/2 teaspoon (2 g) crushed garlic

1 teaspoon (1.5 g) ground black pepper

1 teaspoon (6 g) curing salt No. 2

1/2 teaspoon (2 g) ground juniper berries

1/4 teaspoon (0.5 g) red pepper flakes

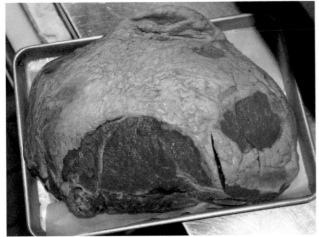

Rinse the beef and pat it dry. Combine all the remaining ingredients in a shallow plastic tub with an airtight lid.

Wearing plastic gloves, add the beef to the cure and rub the cure all over the meat. Cover and refrigerate for 10 days. Wearing gloves, turn over the beef every day or so and rub with the liquid from the bottom of the tub.

Rinse the beef, pat it dry, and set it on a wire rack. Cover and refrigerate for 1 day to dry the surface and form a sort of "skin" known as a pellicle. The surface should feel somewhat tacky, a texture that helps absorb smoke aromas.

Lightly smoke the beef using very low heat (100 to 125°F) and oak or hickory wood for 30 minutes. On a stove top, you can put wood chips or shavings on one side of a large roasting pan, then put a small wire rack on the other side of the pan. Set the chips side of the pan over a burner on medium-high heat until you see smoke (turn on your hood vent or open a window). Lower the heat to medium and set the beef on the rack on the opposite side of the pan, away from the heat. Cover tightly with aluminum foil and smoke for 30 minutes. Peek under the cover once or twice to make sure the chips are still smoking. If they burn up, replenish them.

After smoking, if there is any moisture on the surface of the beef, pat it dry. Tie butcher's string securely around the beef in several places or lengthwise through the top of it using a trussing needle. You could also put the beef in a mesh meat bag.

Hang the speck in a cool (50°F to 55°F), dark environment with some air circulation and 75 percent humidity until it feels firm yet slightly pliable, usually 4 to 5 months. It should feel a little tacky on the surface and lose 20 to 25 percent of its original weight. A little white mold is okay. See page 130 for options on setting up the curing environment.

BEVERAGE—Piccolo Birrificio "Chiostro": The herbal spice from the juniper in this salumi is what sets it apart on a charcuterie board. I can think of nothing better to drink with it than Chiostro, a witbier from Liguria that's scented with wormwood from a dash of absinthe in the beer.

Coppa

When I started making salumi, I messed around with coppa a lot. I made it with whole pork butt and with cut-up pieces. I tried hanging the coppa with nothing around it, and I tried stuffing it in cheesecloth. What I liked best was stuffing the whole muscle into beef bungs. Pork butt, or shoulder, is an uneven cut because of all the bone that is removed, and stuffing it into a big casing helps it hold its shape so it's easier to slice when fully cured. By the way, this is the "cold cut" that you often find on submarine sandwiches called "capicola" or, even worse, "gabagool." Let's just call this salumi what it is: coppa. Be sure to slice it paper-thin or it will be too chewy.

Rinse the pork and pat it dry. Combine all the remaining ingredients except the bung in a shallow plastic tub with an airtight lid.

Wearing plastic gloves, add the pork to the cure and rub the cure all over the meat. Cover and refrigerate for 15 days. Wearing gloves, turn over the pork every day or so and rub with the liquid from the bottom of the tub.

Rinse the pork and pat dry, then stuff it into the beef bung, packing it in tight and massaging the bung so the meat takes the oblong shape of the bung. Twist the open end of the bung tightly against the pork. Tie butcher's string tightly around the twisted end to seal it, leaving extra string for hanging.

Hang the coppa in a dark environment with some air circulation at 50°F to 55°F and 75 percent humidity until it feels firm yet slightly pliable, 2 to 3 months. It should feel a little tacky on the surface and lose 20 to 25 percent of its original weight. See page 130 for options on setting up the curing environment.

BEVERAGE—Monteflor, Friulano 2009 "Satis" (Friuli): Friulano is the classic wine to pair with salumi. The wine has bright acidity and light flavors of lemon oil with salty minerality. This is a great example of how a modest wine can be elevated by its food pairing.

MAKES ABOUT 4 POUNDS

5 pounds (2.25 kg) boneless pork butt (shoulder) in one piece

2/3 cup plus 1 1/4 teaspoons (100 g) kosher salt

5 1/4 teaspoons (12.5 g) dextrose powder, or 4 teaspoons (10.5 g) superfine sugar

1 teaspoon (3.5 g) cracked pepper

2 cloves garlic (7.5 g), minced

1 teaspoon (6 g) curing salt No. 2

Leaves from 3 to 4 sprigs rosemary (6 g), chopped (about 1 tablespoon)

1 beef bung, about 1 1/2 feet long, soaked in cold water for 1 hour, then rinsed inside and out

Pancetta

Americans tend to like pork bellies smoked and cured with lots of sugar. That's American bacon. Italians usually skip the smoke and let the pork belly speak for itself. Pure and simple. You often see pancetta rolled, but this flat method is much easier. When you roll pancetta, you need to make it airtight. If you don't, there will be air pockets that let bacteria grow, which can ruin the pancetta. Making flat pancetta gives you the same flavor and texture but without the added risk. You can use this pancetta anywhere you would normally use bacon.

MAKES ABOUT 4 POUNDS

5 pounds (2.25 kg) pork belly

2/3 cup plus 1¼ teaspoons (100 g) kosher salt

5¾ teaspoons (25 g) granulated sugar

1 teaspoon (6 g) curing salt No. 2

1 teaspoon (3 g) ground pepper

½ teaspoon (1.5 g) ground cinnamon

Rinse the pork belly and pat it dry. Combine all the remaining ingredients in a shallow plastic tub with an airtight lid.

Wearing plastic gloves, add the pork belly to the cure and rub the cure all over the belly. Cover and refrigerate for 10 to 12 days. Wearing gloves, turn over the belly every day or so and rub with the liquid from the bottom of the tub.

Rinse the belly and pat it dry. Tie butcher's string securely around the belly in several places or lengthwise through the top of it using a trussing needle, leaving extra string for hanging. You could also put the belly in a mesh meat bag.

Hang the pancetta in a dark environment with some air circulation at 50°F to 55°F and 75 percent humidity until it feels firm yet slightly pliable, 2 to 3 months. It should feel a little tacky on the surface and lose 20 to 25 percent of its original weight. See page 130 for options on setting up the curing environment.

BEVERAGE—Cantina di Montecchia, Lessini Durello NV Brut (Veneto): Here's a compelling Venetian sparkling wine: floral with stone fruit aromas and lots of minerality on the palate to complement the saltiness of the pancetta but cut through the fat.

Lardo

If you've never tasted cured pork fatback—lardo—pull up a chair. It's one of the most luxuriously rich things you will ever put in your mouth. Three important points here: first, you need extra-thick fatback. It will be hard to find, but look for it at your local butcher shop or farmers' market. Better yet, if you know a pig farmer in the area, ask the farmer for extra-thick fatback. Whatever you do, don't bother trying this recipe with fatback that's less than 1 inch thick. It just won't work. Two inches thick is even better. Second, I like a lot of spice in my lardo. It gives the fat such great flavor. I cure the lardo with spices, then rub the same spices on it again before storing it. Third, it's important to add water to the lardo after a few months and let it soak. It really enhances the soft, melting texture. Italians usually soak the lardo in a marble tub. But any container will do. After it's done, just thinly slice the lardo and enjoy it naked. Maybe put a thin slice or two on toasted Rustic Loaf (page 24) or on Pesca Pizza (page 51).

Rinse the fatback and pat it dry. Combine all the remaining ingredients except for the separate herb mixture in the bottom of a large, dark plastic trash bag.

Wearing plastic gloves, add the fatback to the cure and rub the cure all over the fatback. Press the air out of the bag, seal with a twist tie, and put the sealed bag in a shallow plastic tub with an airtight lid.

Put the tub in a cool (50°F to 55°F), dark place with some air circulation for 4 months. After 4 months, add enough water to the plastic bag to completely cover the fatback. Reseal the bag, put the lid on the container, and return to the same cool, dark place for at least 2 months or up to 6 months.

Remove the fatback from the water and pat dry. In a small bowl, combine all the ingredients for the herb mixture. Rub the herbs over the fatback and wrap tightly in plastic. Store in the refrigerator for up to 6 months. You can also vacuum seal the seasoned fatback and refrigerate it for up to 1 year.

MAKES ABOUT 5 POUNDS

5 pounds (2.25 kg) pork fatback at least 1 inch thick

1 teaspoon (3.5 g) cracked pepper

1 teaspoon (6 g) curing salt No. 2

1 teaspoon (2.5 g) ground coriander

1/2 teaspoon (1.5 g) ground cinnamon

1/2 teaspoon (1.5 g) ground cloves

1/2 teaspoon (1.5 g) grated nutmeg

2 cloves garlic (12.5 g), minced

Leaves from 2 sprigs rosemary (3 g), chopped (about 1 1/2 teaspoons)

5 fresh sage leaves (2 g), chopped (about 1 1/4 teaspoons)

3 cups plus 3 tablespoons (450 g) kosher salt

HERB MIXTURE

1 teaspoon (3.5 g) cracked pepper

1 teaspoon (2.5 g) ground coriander

1/2 teaspoon (1.5 g) ground cinnamon

1/2 teaspoon (1.5 g) ground cloves

1/2 teaspoon (1.5 g) grated nutmeg

Leaves from 2 sprigs rosemary (3 g), chopped (about 1 1/2 teaspoons)

5 fresh sage leaves (2 g), chopped (about 1 1/4 teaspoons)

BEVERAGE—Elisabet, Prosecco di Valdobbiadene NV (Veneto): Prosecco's soft effervescence, green-apple aroma, and tart citrus flavor makes it an enchanting counterpoint to the creamy luxury of lardo.

To Each His Own

It is scientifically proven that certain flavors will affect other flavors in very well-documented ways. Salt suppresses bitterness, as does sugar. But I firmly believe that those flavor alterations don't mean the same thing to everyone. If that were true, we would all add cream to our coffee or squeeze citrus into our Diet Coke. The real truth is that tasting is very personal. A platter of salumi is a great opportunity to discover your own preferences. An assortment of spicy Chorizo (page 154), creamy Lardo (page 160), tender cooked salami, and all the other foods on the plate, like pungent Mostarda (page 172) and acidic pickles, gives you plenty of beverage options. You could play off the salt with a tannic wine, or choose a beer to tame the spicy chorizo, maybe try a Franciacorta or other frizzante with the lardo. But how will it taste with the Fennel Salami (page 152)? Try different flavor combinations to find out what you enjoy most!

SHORTCUT Guanciale

Italians cure both pork bellies and pork jowls. But the jowls are where it's at. With more fat and more collagen, cured jowl (guanciale) has a phenomenally rich mouthfeel. It's so good that I can't always wait for a full cure as in Pancetta (page 159). So I came up with a quick-curing method that takes less time and still gives you an awesome flavor. After curing the seasoned jowls for a few days in the refrigerator, you slow-roast them with very low heat for a few hours to dry them out a bit. Cubed and browned in a pan with some tomatoes, red pepper flakes, and pecorino, guanciale is perfect in Bucatini alla Matriciana (page 72). Or use it anywhere you would use bacon. Just keep in mind that the quick-cure method means that it won't keep as long. Try to use it up within a week, which shouldn't be a problem once you have your first taste.

Rinse the pork jowl and pat it dry. Combine all the remaining ingredients in a shallow plastic tub with an airtight lid.

Wearing plastic gloves, add the jowl to the cure and rub the cure all over the jowl. Cover and refrigerate for 3 days.

Preheat the oven to 275°F. Rinse the jowl, pat it dry, and place on a roasting rack in a roasting pan. Roast until tender, 2 1/2 to 3 hours.

Store in the refrigerator for up to 1 week.

BEVERAGE— Brouwerij Bosteels, Deus Brut de Flanders (Belgium): You will likely be using your guanciale as an addition to another dish that will dictate what you drink. However, if you want to nibble on the guanciale by itself, I would go for something effervescent and light in body to lift the salty, fatty meat. Sour ale could work, but so would sparkling wine. That leads me to this great Belgian ale, which is technically a "Biere de Champagne." A beer that acts like champagne—perfect!

MAKES ABOUT 14 OUNCES

1 pound (500 g) pork jowl

2 tablespoons plus 1 teaspoon (20 g) kosher salt

2 teaspoons (5 g) dextrose powder, or 1 1/2 teaspoons (4 g) superfine sugar

1/2 teaspoon (1.5 g) ground coriander

1 teaspoon (3.5 g) ground pepper

1 teaspoon (6 g) curing salt No. 1 (pink salt)

1 teaspoon (4 g) crushed garlic

Leaves from 4 sprigs rosemary (6 g), coarsely chopped (about 1 tablespoon)

WARM Pork Belly

I like pig. It's just a fact. I like it cold, sliced, roasted, seared—any way you serve it, I like it. In 2008, we were getting ready for the Great Chefs Event that I host in Philadelphia to benefit Alex's Lemonade Stand. That year, Bobby Flay, Michael Symon, Paul Kahan, John Besh, Suzanne Goin, and several other chefs were coming out to support the cause. We had about forty chefs from around the globe, including my friend Marco Rossi from Italy, all helping to raise money for pediatric cancer research. The night before the event, I always host all the chefs at a big dinner at Osteria. Jeff Michaud and I usually come up with a fun menu. That year, we decided to switch up our usual charcuterie platter of house-cured soppressatta, coppa, and lardo. This pig ended up being the best thing on the platter.

MAKES 4 SERVINGS

1/4 cup (35 g) kosher salt

1 tablespoon (15 g) sugar

1/2 teaspoon (3 g) curing salt No. 1 (pink salt)

2 teaspoons (6 g) freshly ground pepper

1/2 teaspoon (1.5 g) ground coriander seeds

1 clove garlic (3 g), minced

2 1/2 pounds (1.25 kg) pork belly

Mix together the kosher salt, sugar, curing salt, pepper, coriander, and garlic, then rub all over the pork belly. Wrap the belly in plastic wrap and refrigerate for 4 days.

Preheat the oven to 350°F. Unwrap the pork and put it on a rimmed baking sheet or in a shallow roasting pan. Cover the pan with aluminum foil and cook in the oven until tender, about 1 1/2 hours.

Remove the pork from the oven and let cool in the pan. Slice it like you would a thick slab of bacon—into strips about 6 inches long and 1/4 inch thick. Cook the slices in a skillet over medium-high heat or on a grill over medium heat until the pieces are crisp and browned, about 2 minutes per side. Serve warm.

PREP AHEAD

The curing takes 4 days, but you can cool the roasted pork belly and refrigerate it in an airtight container for up to 4 days. Slice off strips and crisp them as you need them.

BEVERAGE—Abbazia di Novacella, Lagrein 2008 (Alto Adige): From one of the most interesting wineries in the region, which belongs to a twelfth-century monastery, comes this earthy, full-flavored red. With hints of violet, Lagrein always pairs well with fattier meats.

YOU MIGHT THINK homemade pickles have gone the way of the dodo bird, but they're making a comeback as part of the hand-crafted foods movement. And they make total sense. Just ask any Italian woman who grew up during the Depression (or anyone, anywhere who has lived through lean times) and she'll tell you how important it was to

PICKLES AND PRESERVES

pickle the harvest. When I first opened Vetri restaurant in 1998, I pickled everything. We opened in September and so much was coming up—peppers, tomatoes, cucumbers, cauliflower, beets, parsnips, radishes—you name it. I pickled it all. And I still do, every season. Great food is fleeting. It's here one day and gone the next. You don't find ramps in the fall. And you don't get sweet tomatoes in the winter. Certain foods ripen in certain seasons, and that's the time to enjoy them. Don't bother eating fresh corn on the cob in January. If you really want to eat with the seasons, the way to make the season last longer is to capture ripe fruits and vegetables in a jar. Preserve them. I love surprising people in November with pickled ramps from April. It's like giving them a gift.

CANNING

Pickling and preserving are very simple processes. Don't be scared off by them. The two main types of pickles and jams are those that are shelf-stable and those that must be refrigerated.

To make a vegetable or fruit shelf-stable in a jar, you need to set up a boiling-water canner. Bring a big pot of water to a boil, like a pasta pot. Drop a small wire rack into the pot; it will give you good water circulation and keep the jars off the bottom of the pot, where they could overheat. The pot should be deep enough to keep your canning jars submerged. I usually use 1-pint canning jars, the standard ones with two-part metal lids you can buy in most supermarkets. Or look for different shapes and sizes of canning jars online.

To eliminate bacteria in the jars, I wash them in hot soapy water, then sterilize them with their lids and rings in the boiling-water canner for about 5 minutes, usually while I'm mixing up the pickling liquid or jam on the stove. Pickling liquid is basically brine, a simple mixture of salt, sugar, and water. I typically pickle with a fair amount of vinegar, too. The salt and vinegar (acid) discourage bad bacteria from growing, and the sugar and spices

flavor the pickles. For extra-crisp pickles, I use unrefined sea salt or pickling salt. Why does the salt matter? Because table salt and kosher salt are refined to remove trace minerals, but unrefined sea salt and pickling salt retain calcium and magnesium. Those minerals help keep pickled vegetables crisp by interacting with pectins in the cell walls of the vegetables. Nerdy, I know, but the science works. If you want softer pickles, on the other hand, use kosher salt. Or just cook the vegetable in the pickling liquid.

For jams, you simply peel, core, or pit the fruit, then chop it and cook it down with some sugar and whatever spices you like. Adding lemon juice (or another acid) and a little powdered pectin helps the mixture form a gel. Depending on the natural pectin in the fruit, you add more or less powdered pectin to form the gel. (Check out the recipes for a few examples.) Then ladle the hot jam into pint jars. The only thing to keep in mind when cooking jams and pickles is that you need to use nonreactive pans such as stainless steel. The acid in the jam or pickling liquid will corrode other metals.

After packing the pickles or jam into jars, I like to make sure everything is clean by wiping around the rims before screwing on the lids. Then into the boiling water they go. Here's where the "magic" happens. When you boil a sealed jar, air is driven out of the jar. As it cools, a vacuum forms that prevents air from getting back into the jar. The thin metal lid of the jar will actually get sucked down by the vacuum. If the lid has a "button," you'll probably hear an audible ping or thwunk. That's how you know the jar is airtight. If the lid flexes up and down when you press on it, put the jar back in the boiling-water canner until the lid does eventually get sucked down as it cools. You can use a special jar lifter, good sturdy tongs, or heatproof silicone gloves to move the jars in and out of the boiling water.

That simple combination of salt, acid, and a lack of air—and in some cases, a little cooking—keeps microorganisms from growing inside the jar. Voilà, preserves! Let them cool on a wire rack, then label and date everything. For gifts, I like to use a decorative label and tie a colorful ribbon around the lid. How long will they last? Up to one year is a good rule of thumb. But by then, whatever you preserved should be at the peak of ripeness again, and you can enjoy it fresh.

HOMEMADE Spicy Pickles

Here's a universal pickling recipe. Use it with almost any vegetable you like. Just match the cooking time to the size and density of the vegetable. If it's a bigger or denser vegetable like carrots, cook it a little longer. Change the spices to suit the vegetable. And if you want crisper pickles, use unrefined sea salt instead of kosher (use a little less—about 2 teaspoons here). In early spring, I love dialing back the red pepper flakes and using this recipe with freshly dug ramps. Then in the summer or fall or winter, I can open the jar and still enjoy them.

Set up a canner by bringing a large stockpot of water to a boil. Drop a wire rack into the bottom of the pot. Using tongs, a jar lifter, or silicone gloves, immerse 4 pint jars and their metal lids and rims in the boiling water for 5 minutes. Remove and keep warm.

Meanwhile, combine all of the ingredients except the cucumbers in a medium saucepan and bring to a boil. Cut the cucumbers if needed to fit them in the jar (4-inch lengths work well for pint standard jars). Add the cucumbers to the hot pickling liquid and cook until tender yet crunchy, 1 minute.

Use tongs to transfer the pickles upright into the warm jars, packing them in. Ladle the liquid to within $1/8$ inch of the top of the jars, including some spices, garlic, and bay leaf in each jar. Wipe the rims clean, put on the lids, and tightly screw on the caps. Using tongs, a jar lifter, or heatproof silicone gloves, immerse the sealed jars in the boiling water for 10 minutes.

Remove and let cool on a wire rack. As the jars cool, the centers of the lids should get sucked down. To test, press on the centers of the lids, which should feel firm, not flexy. If they feel flexy, immerse the jars in the boiling water for another 5 minutes.

PREP AHEAD

Store in a cool, dark place for up to 1 year. Refrigerate after opening and use within 3 weeks.

MAKES ABOUT 4 PINTS

3 cups distilled white vinegar

2 cups water

$1/4$ cup sugar

$1^1/_2$ tablespoons kosher salt

$1^1/_2$ tablespoons dill seeds or coriander seeds

$1/2$ to 1 teaspoon red pepper flakes

$1/4$ teaspoon whole black peppercorns

2 cloves garlic, halved

2 small bay leaves, each broken in half

$2^1/_2$ pounds small pickling cucumbers, preferably no longer than 4 inches

PICKLED Eggs

I remember saying to myself about the Potted Trout Terrine (page 135), "What are you going to serve with it?" and I replied to myself, "I don't know, chef." "Well, how about a hard-boiled egg? Like you would serve with caviar." "That works! But how about we pickle the eggs?" "That works!" Yes, I talk to myself. That's what happens when you work in a kitchen all day and night. You get a little crazy, but you get some great ideas!

MAKES ABOUT 2 PINTS

8 eggs

1 1/2 cups red wine vinegar

1 1/2 cups water

1/2 cup kosher salt

1/2 cup sugar

2 bay leaves, broken in half

1/2 teaspoon black peppercorns

Put the eggs in a large saucepan in a single layer and cover with cold water by 1 inch. Bring to a boil over high heat. As soon as the water boils, remove the pan from the heat, cover, and let stand for 15 minutes. Drain and run under cold water to cool the eggs. When cool, peel the eggs.

Meanwhile, sterilize 2 pint jars and their metal lids and rings by bringing a large stockpot of water to a boil. Drop a wire rack into the bottom of the pot. Using tongs, a jar lifter, or heatproof silicone gloves, immerse the jars and lids in the boiling water and boil for 5 minutes. Remove and keep warm.

Bring the red wine vinegar, water, salt, sugar, bay leaves, and peppercorns to a boil in a medium nonreactive saucepan. Boil until the sugar and salt dissolve, then let cool until warm.

Loosely pack the hard-boiled eggs into the warm jars (about 4 per jar) and ladle the pickling liquid to within 1/8 inch of the top of the jars, including some peppercorns and bay leaf in each jar. Wipe the rims clean, put on the lids, and tightly screw on the rings. Refrigerate for at least 2 days before using.

PREP AHEAD

The eggs can be refrigerated in the sealed jars for up to 3 weeks. The eggs pick up a nice pink color from the red wine vinegar in the brine. Use the eggs within a week after opening the jars.

PICKLED Mustard Seeds

Back in 2007, I was in the kitchen with my chef, Brad, and he was working on something to pair with the leg of lamb we were roasting. It needed some kind of sauce, but I generally don't like making classic sauces (except béchamel). We wanted something more like a condiment. Brad came up with these mustard seeds simmered in pickling liquid. They are so good that the simplicity of them is disarming. We started serving them with fish, meat, vegetables—just about everything. I love them with salumi like Soppressata Calabrese (page 149) and Rabbit Salami (page 144).

Combine all the ingredients in a medium nonreactive saucepan and bring to a simmer over medium heat. Simmer until most of the liquid evaporates and the seeds start to clump together, about 2 minutes.

Remove from the heat and let steep in the liquid for 1 hour. Cover and refrigerate for up to 2 days, but serve at room temperature.

MAKES ABOUT 1/2 CUP

1/4 cup white wine vinegar

1/4 cup water

1 tablespoon sugar

1 1/2 teaspoons kosher salt

1/4 cup yellow mustard seeds

1/4 cup brown mustard seeds

PRESERVED Cherry Tomatoes

You want simple? You got it. This pickle has only two ingredients: tomatoes and basil (and a little salt and pepper). Save this recipe for when you get those crazy sweet cherry tomatoes in the middle of the summer. Then later in the year, crack open the pickles and you've got summer in a jar.

Set up a canner by bringing a large stockpot of water to a boil. Drop a wire rack into the bottom of the pot. Using tongs, a jar lifter, or heatproof silicone gloves, immerse 2 pint jars and their metal lids and rings in the boiling water and boil for 5 minutes. Remove and keep warm.

Bring a large pot of salted water to a boil. Salt the water a little less than you would pasta water, about 1 tablespoon salt per quart of water. Immerse the tomatoes in the water until blanched, 10 to 15 seconds. Remove and immerse in a bowl of ice water. Let the hot blanching water cool down (it will become the canning liquid). Peel the tomatoes, which is a little time-consuming, but necessary. The easiest way

MAKES ABOUT 2 PINTS

Unrefined sea salt

1 pound small cherry, grape, or pear tomatoes

Freshly ground pepper

4 large fresh basil leaves

is to hold the ends of a tomato in each hand and use a fingernail to tear a hole in the blossom end (the smoother end). Then use the other hand to gently squeeze and pop the tomato through the hole to remove the skin. Get someone to help (hey, kids!) and it will go much faster.

Divide the tomatoes between the pint jars, adding some black pepper and a couple of basil leaves tucked down inside each jar so you can see the leaves through the glass. Ladle in the cooled blanching liquid to within $1/8$ inch of the top of the jars. Wipe the rims clean, put on the lids, and tightly screw on the rings. Using tongs, a jar lifter, or heatproof silicone gloves, immerse the sealed jars in the boiling water for 10 minutes.

Remove and let cool on a wire rack. As the jars cool, the centers of the lids should get sucked down. To test, press on the centers of the lids, which should feel firm not flexy. If they feel flexy, immerse the jars in the boiling water for another 5 minutes.

PREP AHEAD

The tomatoes look beautiful on a sunny windowsill, but should be kept in a cool, dark place for longer storage, up to 8 months. Refrigerate after opening and use within 3 weeks.

Shallot MARMALADE

If you like caramelized onions, you'll love this spread. It's made with caramelized shallots and rosemary briefly buzzed in a food processor to the texture of marmalade. Spoon a little bit onto a plate along with any of the salumi from pages 135–163.

MAKES ABOUT 1 CUP

1 pound shallots (about 1$1/2$ cups)

$1/2$ cup (1 stick) unsalted butter

$1/4$ cup olive oil

2 sprigs rosemary

Salt and freshly ground pepper

$1/2$ to 1 teaspoon sherry vinegar

Pinch of sugar (optional)

Peel the shallots and cut them in half. Melt the butter with the olive oil in a medium saucepan over low heat, then add the shallots and rosemary and season lightly with salt and pepper. Cook very slowly until the shallots caramelize, about 1 hour. Toss the shallots now and then to break them up and separate the layers.

Remove the rosemary sprigs and season the shallots lightly with sherry vinegar and a pinch of sugar if necessary. Blend briefly with an immersion or upright blender until chunky, like a marmalade. Taste and add vinegar, salt, pepper, and sugar as needed.

PREP AHEAD

You can keep the marmalade in an airtight container in the refrigerator for up to 2 weeks. The mixture will solidify, so return it to room temperature or warm it briefly before serving.

Mostarda

For years, whenever I went to Italy, I would stop in a pharmacy and pick up a few bottles of mustard essence and bring it back home on the plane. But it's basically liquid mustard gas. If one of those bottles ever fell and broke on the floor of the plane, everyone would need a gas mask. Just one drop of this stuff is plenty to put the pungent edge on a whole batch of mostarda, which is Italian fruit preserves in mustard syrup. This recipe offers a safer alternative: mustard powder, or even better, pure mustard oil. In India, mustard oil is used for cooking and for massages. Look for the oil at Indian grocery stores or some gourmet stores (see Sources, page 279). Federal Drug Administration regulations require that imported mustard oil be labeled "for external use only." But Indians have been cooking with mustard oil for centuries with no ill effects, and I have made and eaten mostarda with it many times with no harm whatsoever.

What you do need to watch out for here is the timing and temperatures. Follow the recipe to the letter. It's important to strain the fruit or vegetable without touching it. Don't pluck out the fruit or vegetable by hand, which can cause the sugar mixture to crystallize. You can use any fruit or vegetable you like, but when using soft fruit like mangoes or even apples, instead of returning the fruit to the mixture and heating it as directed here, just pour the hot liquid over the fruit on Day 2 and again on Day 3. Then proceed as directed. Serve the mostarda, including any of the variations below, like a relish. It goes well with roasted or braised meats, a salumi or cheese plate, or anywhere you want a sweet and spicy counterpoint.

DAY 1: Toss the prepared fruits or vegetables with the sugar in a bowl. Let stand overnight, uncovered, at room temperature.

DAY 2: Empty the sugary fruits or vegetables into a colander or strainer set over a larger saucepan. With the colander over the saucepan, rinse the fruit or vegetables with some of the 4 cups water and rinse the bowl with the rest (you want all the sugar to remain in the water). Set the rinsed fruit or vegetables aside. Add the glucose or corn syrup to the sugar water and attach a candy thermometer to the pan. Boil over high heat until the mixture reaches 220°F. Return the fruits or vegetables along with any additional flavorings (as in the variations below) and reheat to 220°F. Immediately remove from the heat and let stand, uncovered, overnight at room temperature.

DAY 3: Drain the fruits or vegetables over a saucepan and boil the liquid in the pan over high heat until it reaches 222°F, 10 to 15 minutes. Return the fruits or vegetables and boil the mixture to 222°F. Immediately remove from the heat and let stand, uncovered, overnight at room temperature.

continued, page 174

MAKES 1½ TO 2 CUPS

1 pound fruits or vegetables, such as quince or squash, peeled, seeded and/or cored as necessary, and chopped

1²/₃ cups sugar

4 cups water

¼ cup liquid glucose or light corn syrup

2 drops essential oil of mustard, or 1 to 2 teaspoons pure mustard oil or mustard powder

Mostarda, continued

DAY 4: Drain the fruits or vegetables over the saucepan again and boil the liquid to 224°F. Return the fruits or vegetables and boil to 224°F. Immediately remove from the heat and let stand, uncovered, overnight.

DAY 5: Leave the fruits or vegetables in the liquid and heat to 226°F. Remove from the heat and let cool to room temperature. The fruits or vegetables should be softened, broken down, and covered in a medium-thick syrup. Stir in the essential oil of mustard, or add the oil or powder to taste. If using mustard powder, first carefully transfer 1/4 cup of the syrup to a small saucepan. Heat over medium heat and stir in the mustard powder until dissolved, then stir the mixture back in with the rest of the syrup.

PREP AHEAD

Use the mostarda immediately or spoon it into an airtight container, seal, and refrigerate for up to 3 weeks.

ARTICHOKE MOSTARDA

Use 1 pound small to medium artichokes. Trim off the stems. Snap off and discard the dark green leaves down to the tender green-yellow leaves. Trim all the dark green stem bases down to the white inner part of the stem. Cut each artichoke in half crosswise, and discard the top half of the leaves. When adding the artichokes to the saucepan, add the juice of 1 lemon, the leaves of 1 sprig rosemary, and 8 cracked black peppercorns to the pan.

WALNUT MOSTARDA

Use 1 pound walnut halves, the best ones you can find. Skip the macerating process for Day 1. Instead, just mix the sugar and liquid glucose or corn syrup in the saucepan with enough water to make the mixture look a little wetter than sand. Bring it to 220°F, then proceed as directed.

QUICK BELL PEPPER MOSTARDA

Seed and devein 2 large red and 2 large green bell peppers. Cut the peppers into 1 1/2-inch squares (you should have about 4 cups). Then put them in a saucepan along with 2/3 cup sugar to the pan. Cook over low heat until syrupy, 1 1/2 to 2 hours. Stir in 1 drop essential oil of mustard or 1 to 2 teaspoons mustard powder or pure mustard oil along with a pinch each of red pepper flakes and ground black pepper. Great with veal or pork.

QUICK SPRING ONION MOSTARDA

Combine 4 cups water, 4 cups sugar, $^1/_4$ cup liquid glucose or light corn syrup, 5 black peppercorns, 2 sprigs rosemary, 3 whole cloves, and the zest (in short, narrow strips) of $^1/_2$ lemon in a saucepan. Add 1 pound spring onions, trimmed and coarsely chopped, and cook over medium heat until the mixture reaches 217°F on a candy thermometer, occasionally brushing down the sides with a wet pastry brush to prevent the sugar from crystallizing on the sides of the pan. Remove from the heat and let cool to room temperature. Stir in 1 to 2 drops essential oil of mustard or 1 to 2 teaspoons mustard powder or pure mustard oil.

Quince BUTTER

I liked to spread quince paste (membrillo) on toast. But I always thought it was a little too firm, almost rubbery. I wanted to make something softer that would spread more like butter. Here's the result. It needs no added pectin because quince has plenty of natural pectin. Caramelizing the sugar gives the spread a deep, dark flavor that lingers nice and long in your mouth.

Set up a canner by bringing a large stockpot of water to a boil. Drop a wire rack into the bottom of the pot. Using tongs, a jar lifter, or heatproof silicone gloves, immerse 3 pint jars and their metal lids and rings in the boiling water and boil for 5 minutes. Remove and keep warm.

Meanwhile, peel, core, and chop the quince (you should have about 10 cups). Scatter on the cinnamon and toss to mix.

Put the sugar and water in a small saucepan. Using a small knife, split the vanilla bean lengthwise and scrape the seeds into the saucepan. Bring to a simmer over medium heat and cook without stirring until the mixture turns a deep amber, 4 to 5 minutes. Add the quince and apple cider and cook until the quince is tender, about 20 minutes (it will take a few minutes for the caramel to dissolve).

Puree the mixture in a blender, then ladle the quince butter into the warm jars to within 1/8 inch of the top. Wipe the rims clean, put on the lids, and tightly screw on the rings. Using tongs, a jar lifter, or heatproof silicone gloves, immerse the sealed jars in the boiling water for 10 minutes.

Remove and let cool on a wire rack. As the jars cool, the center of the lids should get sucked down. If they don't, immerse them in the boiling water for another 5 minutes.

Refrigerate after opening and use opened jars within 3 weeks.

MAKES ABOUT 3 PINTS

4 pounds quince (about 6)

1 tablespoon ground cinnamon

1 1/2 cups sugar

1/2 cup water

1/2 vanilla bean

2 cups apple cider

APPLE BUTTER

If you don't have quince or prefer apples, use 4 pounds of apples, such as Pippin, Bramley, Cortland, or McIntosh, and omit the apple cider.

PREP AHEAD

You can keep the sealed jars of quince butter in a cool, dark place for up to 8 months. It will keep for 3 months in the refrigerator after opening.

Hazelnut HONEY

For such a simple recipe, this little condiment packs a lot of flavor. I love it drizzled on sliced cooked sausage and meat terrines. When I'm making sandwiches with Lamb Mortadella (page 142), I even use it as a spread. Any honey variety will work, but single-flower honeys like orange blossom, sage, and tupelo are some of my favorites.

MAKES ABOUT 2³/₄ CUPS

1 cup hazelnuts

³/₄ cup plus 1 tablespoon honey, preferably single flower rather than wildflower

1 cup extra-virgin olive oil

2 teaspoons fresh thyme leaves

Pinch of red pepper flakes

Salt and freshly ground black pepper

Toast the hazelnuts in a dry pan over medium heat or in a preheated 350°F oven, shaking the pan often, until fragrant and lightly browned, 5 to 7 minutes. If the hazelnuts have skins, wrap them in a cloth and rub off the skins while still warm. Then coarsely chop the nuts.

Meanwhile, whisk together the honey and olive oil in a bowl until blended. Stir in the thyme, pepper flakes, and hazelnuts. Taste and season with salt and pepper.

PREP AHEAD

The honey keeps in an airtight container at room temperature for up to 3 weeks. A cool, dark place is best. You can also refrigerate this, but the honey may crystallize. If it does, just reheat the jar under hot tap water until the honey can be stirred smooth.

Strawberry PÂTÉ DI FRUTTA

When they're done, these soft, sweet little cubes will charm the pants off your guests. But when you're making them, the recipe is all about pectin and temperature. Different fruits have different amounts of natural pectin, which is what causes them to clump together after they cook and cool as in, say, a jam. Apples and pears have a lot of pectin. Watermelon has very little. So you have to adjust the amount of added pectin according to the fruit. Experiment with different fruits (see the variations on page 180 for a few examples). When cooled, the pate should be soft and squishy rather than firm and jiggly. Two to 3 teaspoons of powdered pectin is a good base amount to add. But you may need to go up to 1$^{1}/_{2}$ tablespoons or down to 1$^{1}/_{2}$ teaspoons depending on the fruit. Try mixing low-pectin fruit like cherries with high-pectin fruit like apples for different flavors and colors. Adjust the sugar according to how sweet and ripe the fruit is. Either way, these make delicious nibbles after a meal or between courses. Or anytime.

Line a 9 by 7-inch baking dish with microwaveable plastic wrap. Puree the strawberries in a food processor, then strain through a fine-mesh sieve. Measure out 3$^{1}/_{3}$ cups of the puree and pour into a medium saucepan. Warm over low heat.

Mix the pectin and $^{1}/_{4}$ cup of the sugar together, then stir into the warmed puree. Bring to a boil and add the remaining 2$^{1}/_{2}$ cups sugar in three stages, stirring each addition until dissolved before adding the next.

Stir in the glucose or corn syrup and bring to a boil over high heat, stirring to prevent clumping. Attach a candy thermometer to the side of the pan. When the mixture reaches 230°F, stir in the lemon juice and remove from the heat. When the mixture stops bubbling, immediately pour it into the prepared baking dish, where it will begin to set. Let stand on a rack at room temperature until fully set and cooled, about 1$^{1}/_{2}$ hours. The pate should be like soft, squishable Jell-O, set, but not so hard that it's jiggly and would bounce if it fell on the floor.

Store at room temperature covered in plastic wrap. Do not refrigerate, or the sugar may separate out.

When ready to serve, cut the pâté into 1-inch squares. Put the sugar for coating in a bowl and add about 5 cubes to the bowl at a time, tossing to coat.

continued, page 180

MAKES ABOUT FORTY 1-INCH SQUARES

2 pints fresh strawberries

1 tablespoon powdered pectin

2$^{3}/_{4}$ cups sugar, plus more for coating

$^{1}/_{2}$ cup liquid glucose or light corn syrup

$^{1}/_{4}$ teaspoon fresh lemon juice

PINEAPPLE

Use $1^3/_4$ cups pineapple puree and a scant 1 tablespoon pectin. Make the puree by peeling and coring the fruit, pureeing it in a food processor, then straining the puree. One medium pineapple will yield about 3 cups puree.

APPLE OR PEAR

Use $1^1/_2$ cups apple or pear puree and $1^3/_4$ teaspoons pectin. Make the puree by peeling and coring the fruit, pureeing it in a food processor, then straining the puree. Three medium apples or pears will yield about $1^1/_2$ cups puree.

BLACKBERRY OR RASPBERRY

Use 4 cups fresh berries, pureed and strained to remove the seeds, and $2^3/_4$ teaspoons pectin.

BLUEBERRY

Use 4 cups fresh blueberries, pureed and strained, and 2 teaspoons pectin.

PREP AHEAD

The pate will keep, covered, at room temperature for up to 5 days. Cut out and remove squares from the pan as needed.

Honeycrisp Apple JAM

Let it be known: there is one apple that is the best. They come early in the season and are as sweet as candy. The Honeycrisp is, hands-down, my favorite eating apple ever. It makes an amazing jam, too. When you make this, the jam will look loose, but don't worry. As the liquid cools, it will gel and get firmer.

MAKES ABOUT 2 PINTS

3 or 4 Honeycrisp apples, peeled, cored, and chopped (3 1/2 cups)

1/4 cup fresh lemon juice

1/2 cup water

3 cups sugar

1 tablespoon powdered pectin

Toss the apples in a bowl with the lemon juice.

Set up a canner by bringing a large stockpot of water to a boil. Drop a wire rack into the bottom of the pot. Using tongs, a jar lifter, or heatproof silicone gloves, immerse the pint jars and their metal lids and rings in the boiling water for 5 minutes. Remove and keep warm.

Bring the water and 2 1/2 cups of the sugar to a boil in a large saucepan. Mix together the remaining 1/2 cup sugar and the pectin, then whisk the mixture into the boiling sugar water. Add the apples and cook until they are tender and just starting to fall apart, 10 to 15 minutes. Mash with a potato masher.

Let cool slightly, then ladle into the warm jars to within 1/8 inch of the top. Wipe the rims clean, put on the lids, and tightly screw on the rings. Using tongs, a jar lifter, or silicone gloves, immerse the sealed jars in the boiling water for 10 minutes.

Remove and let cool on a wire rack. As the jars cool, the center of the lids should get sucked down. To test, press on the centers of the lids, which should feel firm, not flexy. If they feel flexy, immerse the jars in the boiling water for another 5 minutes.

APPLE-CHESTNUT MARMALADE

Add 2 cups cooked and chopped chestnuts along with the apples. After cooking, stir in the zest (in short, narrow strips) of 2 oranges. You can use prepared cooked chestnuts or roast them yourself: Cut a slit in the flat part of each chestnut, then roast at 400°F for 20 minutes. Using a kitchen towel or oven mitts, remove the shells and skins while the nuts are still hot.

PREP AHEAD

The sealed jars of apple jam keep well in a cool, dark spot at room temperature for up to 8 months. They look stunning in the sunlight, shimmering a translucent gold color. Tie some ribbon on the jars and give them away as gifts. Refrigerate after opening and use within 3 weeks.

Apricot JAM

The whole purpose of making marmalades and jams is to capture the flavor of perfectly ripe fruit. Then six months later, when you're craving that taste, you can pull out a jar and enjoy the fruit all over again. Sometimes, I like to mix a little butter into the fruit as it's boiling to give the jam a richer mouthfeel. Try it.

Mix the apricots, 1¹/₂ cups of the sugar, and the lemon juice in a stainless-steel or other nonreactive saucepan, stirring vigorously to mash up the fruit a little. Let stand for 1 hour at room temperature.

Set up a canner by bringing a large stockpot of water to a boil. Drop a wire rack into the bottom of the pot. Using tongs, a jar lifter, or heatproof silicone gloves, immerse the pint jars and their lids and rings in the boiling water and boil for 5 minutes. Remove and keep warm.

Put the pan of apricots over medium heat until the mixture is warm, 3 to 4 minutes, mashing the fruit with a potato masher or large spoon as it heats. Mix the remaining 1¹/₂ cups sugar with the pectin and stir into the warm fruit. Attach a

candy thermometer to the pan and increase the heat to medium-high. Bring to a boil, stirring gently and skimming any foam from the surface, and heat to 217°F. Stir in the butter and let it cool slightly. Ladle the mixture into the warm jars to within ¹/₈ inch of the top. Wipe the rims clean, put on the lids, and tightly screw on the rings.

Using tongs, a jar lifter, or silicone gloves, immerse the sealed jars in the boiling water for 10 minutes.

Remove and let cool on a wire rack. As the jars cool, the center of the lids should get sucked down. To test, press on the centers of the lids, which should feel firm, not flexy. If they feel flexy, immerse the jars in the boiling water for another 5 minutes.

2 pounds apricots, pitted and finely chopped

3 cups sugar

6 tablespoons fresh lemon juice

1 tablespoon powdered pectin

¹/₂ teaspoon unsalted butter

KIWI JAM

Mix 5 cups peeled and chopped kiwi (about a dozen kiwi or 2³/₄ pounds), 2 tablespoons fresh lemon juice, and 1³/₄ cups sugar in the pan. Let stand for 2 hours, then heat as directed. Mix another 1³/₄ cups sugar with 1¹/₂ teaspoons pectin and stir it into the pan. Proceed with the recipe.

PEACH JAM

Mix 10 cups pitted, peeled, and sliced peaches (about 18 peaches or 4¹/₄ pounds), ³/₄ cup sugar, and ¹/₄ cup fresh lemon juice in the pan. Let stand for 1 hour, then heat as directed. Mix ¹/₄ cup sugar with 2 tablespoons pectin and stir it into the pan. Proceed with the recipe.

CHERRY JAM

Mix 4 pounds pitted cherries, 1¹/₄ cups sugar, and ¹/₂ cup fresh lemon juice in the pan. Let stand for 1 hour, then heat as directed, mixing another 1¹/₄ cups sugar with 2 tablespoons pectin and stirring it into the pan. Proceed with the recipe.

BLACKBERRY JAM

Mix 5¹/₂ pounds blackberries, ³/₄ cup sugar, and ¹/₄ cup fresh lemon juice in the pan. Let stand for 1 hour, then heat as directed, mixing another ¹/₂ cup sugar with 2¹/₂ tablespoons pectin and stirring it into the pan. Proceed with the recipe.

PREP AHEAD

You can keep the sealed jars of jam in a cool, dark place for up to 8 months. Refrigerate after opening and use within 3 weeks.

MEATS AND FISH

M**Y GRANDMOTHER JENNY LIVED IN SOUTH PHILLY** on 725 League Street, right behind the Italian market. When I was growing up, we went to her house every Sunday for a family meal. My brother, Adam, and I, and our cousins would run around the alleys until dinner was ready. We used to play stickball right in the middle of the street. At one o'clock, my mother would yell out the door, "Dinner's ready!"

That was my favorite part of Sunday. We would walk in the house all sweaty and there would be a bowl of fruit on the table. I would grab an apple right away for something juicy. And there was always a bowl of nuts with nutcrackers and shells strewn all over the table. My grandfather Mario would be sitting in his lounge chair smoking a cigar. Jenny sat in a chair next to the oven in the kitchen. She'd get up, finish prepping some food, put it on the big family table, and sit back down again. Mario would help out and put a few dishes on the table here and there.

There were thirty of us on Sundays, and everyone pitched in. My father, Sal, usually made the meatballs. He would mix together ground veal, pork, and beef; soak some bread in milk; toss in some Parmesan and parsley; and mix the whole thing up by hand. He rolled and rolled and rolled dozens of perfect little meatballs. Sal learned to make them from his Sicilian grandmother Angelina in 1946 or '47. Back then, all people did was cook on Sundays because they didn't have refrigerators. You went to the market, bought food fresh, and cooked it that day. You were always in the kitchen.

It hadn't changed much when I was growing up in the 1970s. Sure, we played outside as kids, but we also spent time in the kitchen helping with family meals. We did have refrigerators, of course, but Jenny still bought food fresh every Sunday and started cooking it in the morning. She made all kinds of things: mussels, stuffed calamari, macaroni and gravy, lasagna, sausage and eggs, sausage and peppers, stuffed artichokes—Italian dishes that were always simple yet completely delicious. Jenny's artichokes had a wet stuffing of Parmesan, garlic, and bread crumbs. It was salty, moist, and crunchy, all at the same time. I couldn't get enough of it as a kid. She always had some kind of cutlet, too—a breaded fish or chicken or eggplant or pork Milanese. And always a braised meat. Some kind of braciole (meat rolls). If it was a special occasion, we had a straightforward roast of veal, lamb, pork, or beef.

When everything was ready, we all sat down together. Nobody answered the phone. Nobody got up from the table. If you got up and left before you were excused, you usually got a whack on the back of the head. This was family meal. It was a special time. We ate slowly, and the meal lasted from one to four in the afternoon. I loved it then, and I still love it today with my family.

It's not surprising, then, that whenever I go to Italy, the best meal I have is always a family meal in someone's home. It's not at the Michelin-starred restaurants—although I have had some amazing meals in those, too. It's usually a spur-of-the-moment invitation, when a friend says, "Why don't you just come over, and I'll invite a few people."

Two things happen at these dinners: there is always a wood fire going, and there is always a piece of meat with a story behind it. Someone's uncle shot this wild boar the other day and made it into ragù. Or those beef cheeks come from the finest cattle raised in the mountains. Or my friend raises pigs and he feeds them acorns or hazelnuts or almonds to make the ham richer and more tender. It doesn't matter. There is always meat. There is always a story. And there is always a wood fire.

The Sunday dinner—or any leisurely meal with family or friends—brings out so many stories in people that it gives you a deeper connection to everyone at the table. Somehow, it also gives you a deeper connection to the food itself.

BRINING MEAT

I realize that my favorite way to cook meat is to keep it simple. Just brine it and roast it over wood. I've cooked meat every way you can imagine, from sautéed to sous-vide, and to this day I have not found any cooking method more satisfying.

Soaking meat in saltwater is nothing new. It's one of those techniques with years of proven success behind it. It just makes the meat taste better. Salt is the reason. The salt in a brine makes meat juicier, more tender, and more flavorful. The most important effect is juiciness. What happens is that the salt starts to break down the protein in the meat, and exposes more surface area for water in the brine to bond with that protein. So when the meat cooks, it has more water in it than before and stays about 10 percent juicier throughout the cooking. Brining gives you a flavor boost, too, because the extra water that enters the meat also carries the flavors of your brine's herbs, spices, and other seasonings deep into the meat. Plus, you get some tenderness because the salt loosens up the muscle fibers that cause muscles in meat to contract, making the meat softer and less chewy when cooked.

Just be sure not to overbrine your meat, or the salt will have the opposite effect. It will actually dry out the meat by causing the proteins to tighten and force out all that the moisture you wanted to get in there. As a rule of thumb, dense and thick meats like whole suckling pig can brine for a few days, but tender and thin meats like boneless chicken breasts need only a few hours. Check out the brining times in the recipes in this chapter to get a sense of how long to brine various meats.

ROASTING AND GRILLING

I put a wood grill in my restaurant, Osteria, because it creates a welcoming atmosphere, like a fireplace in someone's home. That restaurant is like my second home. And I love roasting meat in it. Some people swear by charcoal for grilling and roasting, while others can't be bothered with anything but gas. Personally, I love wood and wouldn't trade it for anything else. Wood burns the hottest and gives off the most incredible smoky flavor. I usually use a mixture of red and white oak in my wood grill. If you have a charcoal grill, add some chunks of oak to the coals for a similar smoky aroma. You could even use a gas grill or grill pan (minus the woodsmoke aromas).

No matter what kind of grill you have or even if you decide to roast in a gas oven instead, the most important factor to bear in mind is the heat itself. What creates delicious flavor on the surface of roasted and grilled meat is high heat. As the outside of the meat gets hotter and hotter, sugars and proteins on the surface react with each other and change color, becoming a darker and darker brown. These browning reactions (called Maillard reactions) form hundreds of new flavor compounds that make roasted and grilled meats taste delicious. It's where those deep, savory, toasted, malty, earthy flavors in roasted meats come from. Simply put, the higher the heat, the deeper the browning, and the better the flavor. Of course, you don't want to take things too far and burn the meat. Then all you get is bitterness. Sometimes, as with thick steaks and small roasts, that means searing the meat over a high fire, then moving it to a lower-heat area of the grill—or just farther away from the heat—to finish cooking. Other times, usually for larger roasts and whole animals, it means roasting at a short distance from a more moderate fire throughout the cooking so the meat can gradually brown on the surface while cooking all the way through.

Two other notes about browning: it doesn't happen when foods are wet. If the food is wet when it hits the grill or oven, it won't brown as easily and will take longer to develop that great roasted flavor. Moisture can only reach 212°F before it evaporates, but browning doesn't start to happen until about 250°F. Pat your meats dry before roasting or grilling to get rid of the surface moisture so the meat can brown better.

Second, you don't want to take cold meat right from the fridge to a hot grill or oven. The fact is, warm meat sears and browns better than cold meat does. Put your finger over a candle and you'll see what I mean. When your finger is warm, it will feel the heat right away. But if you stick your hand in ice and then put it over the candle, you'll be able to hold your finger there longer before you feel the heat. When cooking meat, you want it to feel the heat right away. Before you grill or roast, let the meat warm up at room temperature for 15 minutes or so to take the chill off. Large roasts may take 30 minutes. Feel the meat to see if it is cool but not cold. You'll get better flavor—and better grill marks when you take the chill out of the meat.

While we're on the subject, be sure to keep your grill grates clean and well oiled. I can't tell you how many times I've started to grill something and the last person who used the grill didn't scrape it clean. It's like putting a dirty dish in the sink and just leaving it there! Think of your grill like a grill pan. You want it clean and hot with a little oil on there before you add the meat. A clean grill is important because it helps prevent sticking (especially when grilling fish), and it gives you better grill marks. I usually scrape the grill when it's hot, then I rub some fat on the grate to lubricate it. Sometimes, I'll use a chunk of fat trimmed off a piece of meat; sometimes it's a paper towel dunked in grapeseed oil. Rubbing some fat on the grill pulls any fine soot off the metal grate, and the oil helps prevent sticking. The fat also helps the heat of the grill transfer more quickly and evenly to the meat.

FISH FRESHNESS

The same principles apply when roasting or grilling fish. But the flesh of fish is less dense and more delicate, so you want to turn down the heat to keep from drying it out. Fish is also much wetter, so don't expect them to brown quite as well. If anything, undercook the fish a little bit. Even after you take it off the grill or out of the oven, the heat in it will continue to cook it as it rests.

In 1994, at a restaurant outside Venice called Dall'Amelia, I got the best seafood education a chef could ever hope for. I had been working there for a few months, and they had the best seafood I had ever seen. The most impressive dish on the menu was always the fish of the day. Whatever fish was running that day ended up on your plate. Sometimes it was plump scampi or lean sole; other times it was seppie (cuttlefish), squid, briny clams, or meaty swordfish. We just grilled the seafood for two, four, six, eight, or more people and put it on giant silver trays. People would smile and even cheer when they saw those platters coming to them.

We would lightly grill the fish, because the whole dish was all about capturing the freshness of the food itself. Taking fish from water to grill to plate is a simple way to illustrate that food is a fleeting pleasure in life; you have to enjoy it while you can. And freshness is still the best guide for buying fish today. I encourage you to forget about your favorite variety of fish. Everybody loves salmon. But it isn't always fresh. And there's so much more to taste and enjoy! Just walk into the market and ask them, "What is the freshest fish you have today?" No matter what it is, buy it. Whatever they have, you can use it to make Fish Poached in Olive Oil (page 213) or Mixed Seafood Grill (page 211). I put these two recipes in this book for that very reason. There are lots of ways to prepare fish and various factors to consider—bone-in, boneless, whole, fillets, steaks, fat content, firmness, roasted, grilled, broiled, sautéed, pan-seared, poached—it's endless. But none of it matters if the quality isn't there. No matter what variety you like, fish is one of the most perishable foods we eat. Freshness trumps variety here. If the fish is very fresh, you have a better chance of it tasting good no matter how it is prepared.

SLOW-ROASTED Lamb Shoulder

I first tried brined and roasted lamb in Rome years ago, and I've never had more flavorful lamb in my life. I now follow the same basic process for most of my roasted meats: brine it, roast it, and slice it into portions, then crisp up the slices in a hot pan. I like to serve the lamb slices on a plate with Rosemary Roasted Potatoes (page 228). You might think 8 pounds of lamb will cost you an arm and a leg. But while lamb chops are expensive, lamb shoulder is cheaper. This recipe turns an economical cut of meat into an incredible meal.

Put a large, heavy-duty trash bag in a large bowl or tub (something large enough to hold the lamb) and carefully pour in the brine. Add the lamb and push it down until it is completely submerged. Press the air out of the bag, tie it closed, and put the container and bag in the refrigerator for 3 days.

Preheat the oven to 300°F. Make a layer of the vegetable chunks on the bottom of a roasting pan that is large enough to fit the lamb. Pull the lamb from the brine and discard the brine. Place the lamb on the vegetables and roast until fork-tender, 4 to 5 hours. Let cool to room temperature.

Remove the cooled lamb to a cutting board and remove the bones. The lamb should be tender enough to pull the bones right out of the meat. Try to keep the sections of meat as whole as possible.

Slice the lamb sections into 1-inch-thick pieces. Heat the oil in a large skillet over high heat. Brown the lamb pieces in the hot oil until crispy, 3 to 4 minutes per side, turning occasionally. Serve the seared lamb pieces on a platter sprinkled with salt, pepper, and fresh rosemary leaves.

PREP AHEAD

The brine can be prepared up to 2 days in advance. You'll need another 3 days for brining the lamb. After you roast the lamb, you can cool the sections and refrigerate them for a day or two before searing them in a hot pan. Plenty of options here for working ahead.

BEVERAGE—Cantina Santadi, Carignano 2007 "Grotta Rossa" (Sardinia): The deep flavor of lamb pairs well with the richness of this warm-climate Carignano. The wine feels soft in the mouth, with a nice, full body.

MAKES 6 SERVINGS

Rosemary-Garlic Brine (page 274)

1 bone-in lamb shoulder, about 8 pounds

1 large onion, cut into large chunks

2 large carrots, peeled and cut into large chunks

3 ribs celery, cut into large chunks

3 tablespoons grapeseed oil

Coarse salt and freshly ground pepper

Fresh rosemary leaves, for garnish

SPIT-ROASTED Suckling Pig

We make one of these every day at Osteria. If you've never spit-roasted and are at all intrigued, give it a try. You can make this recipe with a backyard spit-roaster (see Sources, page 279), which is exactly how we tested it for the book. But I will say up front: this recipe is not for the faint of heart. Trussing a whole animal onto a spit is fairly graphic. Invite some friends over to help hoist the animal to and from the spit-roaster. And enjoy the feast.

Put the brine in a clean cooler or tub just large enough to hold the pig (at least an 8-gallon cooler or tub). Submerge the pig in the brine. If you're using a cooler, put a sealed bag of ice on top of the brined pig to keep it down and cold. If you have a refrigerator big enough to hold an 8-gallon tub, stick the tub in the fridge. Brine the pig for 4 days, replenishing the ice as necessary if using a cooler.

Start a high-burning wood fire. I like to use a mixture of red and white oak, but apple and cherry woods—even a little hickory—all work well. If you can't get wood, use charcoal briquettes (they last longer than lump charcoal) and toss on some soaked wood chunks now and then for smoke. Let the fire burn down until medium-hot, at least 30 minutes. To test the temperature, hold your hand 6 inches over the fire and start counting, "1 one thousand, 2 one thousand . . ." You should only make it to 4 or 5.

Meanwhile, put the pig on a large, clean work surface, like a picnic table covered with aluminum foil, and pat it dry. Insert a spit through the mouth or chest of the pig and out under the tail. Tie, wire, or pin the backbone of the pig to the spit (see "Trussing a Pig to a Spit," opposite). Once the backbone is secured to the spit, slide a pronged skewer (if your spit has one) onto the rear of the pig, pushing it firmly into the hams of the pig and tightening it to the spit. Position the hind legs under the belly and the forelegs under the chin, then tie butcher's twine or wire very tightly around the pig in several places from head to tail to ensure that all parts are firmly secured to the spit. You don't want anything to slip or rotate unevenly.

Rake the coals of the fire to a length just a few inches longer than the pig. Put your spit set-up near the fire, positioning the pig along the length of the fire, just behind the fire instead of directly over it (to prevent flare-ups). The pig should be fairly close to the fire, no more than 2 feet away. Put drip pans beneath the pig to catch any drippings. Spit-roast the animal, turning constantly, until an instant-read thermometer registers 140°F in the hams and shoulders. Maintain a relatively hot fire, about 375°F ambient temperature, to crisp the skin, replenishing the wood and/ or coals as necessary. A 20-pound pig will take anywhere from 2^{1}/$_{2}$ to 3^{1}/$_{2}$ hours to

continued, page 194

MAKES 14 TO 16 SERVINGS

Fennel Brine (page 274)

1 suckling pig, dressed for spit-roasting, about 20 pounds

1 cup grapeseed oil

^{1}/$_{3}$ cup olive oil

1^{1}/$_{2}$ tablespoons chopped mixed fresh herbs (rosemary, parsley, thyme, chives)

1^{1}/$_{4}$ teaspoons fennel seeds, toasted and ground (see Prep Ahead, page 194)

^{1}/$_{4}$ teaspoon freshly ground pepper

2 recipes Rosemary Roasted Potatoes (page 228)

Procuring a Spit and a Suckling Pig

If you can borrow a friend's spit, that's the easiest way to go. You can also rent one from a local all-purpose renter. If you plan to spit-roast often, it pays to buy one. We tested this recipe on a SpitJack with internal spit forks and spit pins for pinning the backbone to the spit (see Sources, page 279). It worked great. Don't forget the fuel: you'll need about a fourth of a cord of wood or 60 pounds of charcoal and 4 quarts of wood chunks like oak, apple, or cherry. As for the pig, I order my sucklers from D'Artagnan (see Sources, page 279). You could do the same, or find a good country butcher or farmer who sells pork at farmers' markets. He or she should be able to get you a suckling pig. Order one in the A weight range (12 to 24 pounds), dressed for spit-roasting. Be sure to order the pig at least 2 weeks ahead of time to make sure you can get it in time for brining and cooking. Remember: it brines for 4 days.

Trussing a Pig to a Spit

Most spit rods are round, so it's not enough to just wrap butcher's string around the outside of the pig once it's on the spit. The round spit will just spin inside the animal, and the pig won't turn. The best way to prevent spinning is to secure the animal's backbone to the spit. Secure trussing can take an hour or more, but it goes much faster if you have someone to help you.

Option 1: Tie or wire the backbone. Use this method if your spit rod is not drilled with holes to accommodate spit pins. Push the spit rod through the pig, along the backbone. Lay the pig on its side, with the cavity facing you so that you can wire the backbone to the spit. Using a trussing needle and a double thickness of butcher's string or 18-gauge wire and pliers, insert the string or wire through the inside of the pig near the backbone and spit. When the string or wire pokes through the back of the pig, bend the string or wire around the outside of the backbone and push it back through the pig. The entire length of string or wire should be wrapped around the backbone and spit. Tie the string tightly, or use pliers to twist the two ends of the wire together, securing the string or wire very tightly around the spit. Repeat this process at roughly 4-inch intervals toward the rear and front of the pig until the backbone is securely fastened to the spit.

Option 2: Pin the backbone. Some spits are drilled with holes so you can insert pins through both animal and the spit to easily secure the backbone to the spit. In that case, insert the pins or internal forks as directed by your spit manufacturer, tightening them as much as possible to fasten the backbone to the spit.

Spit-Roasted Suckling Pig, continued

reach 140°F. It could take up to 4 hours, but start checking it after 2¹/₂ in case your fire is hot, the wind is making it hotter, or the air is cool.

Transfer the spitted pig to a large clean work surface and let rest for 20 minutes. Remove the skewers, spit pins, and/or string and pull out the spit.

Just before you're ready to carve, preheat the oven to 375°F. If you have convection, turn it on. If not, preheat the oven to 400°F.

Starting at the belly of the beast, use a boning knife to remove the skin, leaving as much meat on the animal as possible. The skin should be crisped enough to come off in large sheets. Place the skin on a baking sheet and bake at 375°F with convection (400°F without convection) until very crisp, 15 to 20 minutes (5 to 10 minutes longer without convection). Remove the crisp cracklings and break into 2-inch pieces.

Butcher the pig by removing the head first with a heavy cleaver. A few strong blows across the neck should sever the head. Then remove the hind legs/hams and forelegs/shoulders by driving the cleaver straight through the primary joints. It's easiest to put the pig on its back, lift the leg away from the body, then drive the cleaver through the hip joint or shoulder joint to remove the hind legs and forelegs. Carve the meat from the leg and shoulder bones, keeping the sections of meat in fist-size portions as much as possible. Remove the ribs from the backbone by cutting through the rib bones on either side of the backbone. Carve the tenderloins (the lean meat along the length of the backbone on either side), keeping them as whole as possible. Separate each rib by cutting between them (they will be small).

Heat a grill or griddle to medium-high heat. Combine the grapeseed oil, olive oil, mixed herbs, fennel seeds, and black pepper in a shallow dish. Dip the pieces of meat in the seasoned oil and sear all sides on the grill or griddle until lightly browned, 3 to 4 minutes per side. Depending on the size of your grill or griddle, you'll probably have to work in batches to avoid crowding. Divide the meat among plates, including at least one rib and a piece of loin, shoulder, or leg in each serving. Each serving should weigh 6 to 7 ounces, the size of an average half chicken breast. Serve with a crackling or two, a drizzle of the seasoned oil, and the crispy potatoes.

PREP AHEAD

Toast the fennel seeds up to a few hours serving the pork. Put them in a dry skillet over medium heat and toast until fragrant, 3 to 5 minutes, shaking the pan.

BEVERAGE—Tenuta San Nicola, Primitivo 2008 (Puglia): Purportedly the granddaddy of what we have come to know as Zinfandel, this Primitivo adds a hint of spice to the pig. But unlike many Zins, its assertive flavor complements the dish instead of overpowering it.

Shaved Pork WITH SUMMER FRUIT

In 2005, my wife, Megan, and I tied the knot in sunny Boulder, Colorado, at the Flagstaff House. Instead of a big reception, we had a casual after-party at Frasca with our good friends Lachlan Mackinnon-Patterson (the chef) and Bobby Stuckey (the wine director). These guys are serious about food. They even have a winery in Fruili called Scarpetta. We drink their wines all the time. Anyway, they surprised Megan and me on our wedding day with a dish of shaved pork and ripe plums. I was blown away by its simple beauty. Megan and I both fell in love with the dish, and when I got home, of course I had to re-create it. This is a little different from Lachlan's version, but it carries all the tender memories of that day.

MAKES 8 SERVINGS

Peppercorn Brine (page 274)

2 pounds boneless pork butt (shoulder)

1 tablespoon red wine vinegar

1 tablespoon whole-grain mustard

1/2 cup extra-virgin olive oil, plus more for drizzling

1/2 cup chopped fresh flat-leaf parsley

Salt and freshly ground pepper

4 ounces arugula

2 red plums, pitted and thinly sliced

1 cantaloupe, peeled, seeded, and cut into 1/2-inch cubes

Maldon sea salt, for garnish

Put a gallon-size ziplock plastic bag in a large bowl and carefully pour in the brine. Add the pork, squeeze out any excess air, and seal the bag. Refrigerate for 2 days.

Preheat the oven to 300°F. Remove the pork from the brine and discard the brine. Put the pork in a shallow roasting pan and roast to an internal temperature of 145°F, about 55 minutes. It won't brown much and will still be red in the center when sliced. Remove the pork from the oven and let rest for 20 minutes.

Whisk together the vinegar and mustard in a small bowl until blended. Whisk in the 1/2 cup olive oil in a slow, steady stream until incorporated. Stir in the parsley, then taste and season with salt and pepper.

Cut the pork into thin shavings or slices, using a meat slicer if you have one, or a sharp knife. Toss the pork shavings in the dressing, then put them in a skillet and cook over medium heat until heated through, about 5 minutes.

Arrange the pork on a platter or plates and top with the arugula, plums, and cantaloupe. Drizzle with olive oil and garnish with Maldon salt and pepper to taste.

PREP AHEAD

You can make the brine up to 2 days ahead. You need another 2 days to brine the pork. And you can refrigerate the roasted pork for up to 2 days after shaving it. Bring the shavings almost to room temperature, then toss them in the dressing and heat them in a pan as directed.

BEVERAGE—Ferrando, Erbaluce di Caluso 2008 "La Torrazza" (Piemonte): Lush flavors of baked stone fruits characterize this lesser-known varietal from the north. It makes a well-balanced match for the summer fruits with the pork.

Chicken Halves ON THE GRILL

The only dish that Jeff Michaud and I argued about when we opened Osteria was the chicken. I wanted to put chicken on the menu and he didn't. I had in mind a beautifully brined chicken cooked over a wood fire—a simple crowd-pleaser. I would butcher it in a way that kept it intact but took out all of the bones (see the photos opposite). Jeff kicked and frowned and scratched his head until the day we opened. I'm happy to say that this chicken was, is, and will always be the best seller on the menu. Serve with almost any of the vegetables or sides beginning on page 216.

Put the cooled brine in a 2-gallon ziplock plastic bag or a clean plastic container big enough to hold the chicken (and fit in your fridge). Add the chicken, submerging it completely, squeeze out the air (if using a bag), seal, and refrigerate for 12 to 18 hours. Remove the chicken and discard the brine.

Using kitchen shears, cut the bird in half lengthwise, starting at the bottom of the breast (between the legs) and cutting right through the center of the breastbone. Open up the bird like a book and remove the backbone and ribs by cutting straight through the ribs along the backbone. This will give you 2 bone-in chicken halves. If you want them completely boneless, which is a bit more work, see the box opposite for how to do it.

When you're done cutting the bird, combine the oil, rosemary, thyme, and garlic in a 1-gallon ziplock plastic bag. Add the chicken halves, massage to coat, and squeeze out any excess air. Seal the bag and refrigerate for 2 to 3 hours.

Meanwhile, light a grill for medium heat. Let the chicken sit at room temperature to take the chill off while the grill heats up. When the grill is hot, scrape the grill rack clean and oil it with an oily paper towel. Grill the chicken, skin side down, until nicely grill-marked on both sides and the thigh meat registers 165°F on an instant-read thermometer, 10 to 12 minutes per side. If you're grilling boneless chicken halves, they will cook faster, about 5 to 6 minutes per side. Cut into pieces and serve.

PREP AHEAD

The chicken can be brined overnight, then prepped, seasoned, and refrigerated for up to 24 hours before grilling.

BEVERAGE—Falesco, Roscetto 2007 "Ferentano," or Paitin, Dolcetto d'Alba 2008 "Serra" (Piedmont): The chicken brine calls out for the weight and slightly oaked finish of the Roscetto; however, I cannot pass up the Dolcetto. Its tobacco and chocolate nose makes it my go-to wine for meats with a hint of smoke.

MAKES 4 SERVINGS

Thyme Brine (page 274)

1 chicken, about 3½ pounds

½ cup olive oil

1 teaspoon chopped fresh rosemary

1 teaspoon chopped fresh thyme

1 clove garlic, chopped

Preparing a Chicken for Grilling

There are lots of ways to grill a whole chicken. You can spatchcock it by removing the backbone and keeping the rest of the bird intact, kind of like an opened book. You can cut it in half and remove the backbone. Or you can cut it in half and remove all the bones. Boning a bird is a little more work, but that's how I like to grill my chicken.

a-b. Put the bird on its back on a work surface with the legs facing away from you. Using a boning knife, slice down through the center of the bird to the breast bone, always keeping the knife against bone. Put the knife just to one side of the breast bone and slice down around the bone to remove the breast meat from the bone.

c-d. Cut down through the soft bone near the neck (the end nearest you). Pull the released half of the bird from the carcass and continue cutting around the rib cage to the back of the bird.

e-f. Hold the thigh in one hand and push up from the bottom to pop the hip bone. Cut through the center of the hip bone to remove that side. Repeat on the other side to remove the other half of the bird from the carcass. You will be left with two chicken halves with the wing and leg bones still attached.

g-h. For each half, remove the wing by cutting through the second joint (the remaining "drummette" bone is the only bone that will be left in the bird). Put the bird-half skin side down with the breast meat facing up. Put the tip of the knife in the center of the leg and cut down to the bone.

i-j. Holding the knife against bone at all times, cut along the leg bone up toward and along the thigh bone to remove the leg and thigh meat from the bone on one side. Cut through the knee joint to separate the thigh bone from the leg bone, then release the meat from the thigh bone by cutting around the bone and pulling the bone from the meat. Repeat with the other leg bone to remove the leg bone from the meat. Save the chicken carcass and bones to make stock.

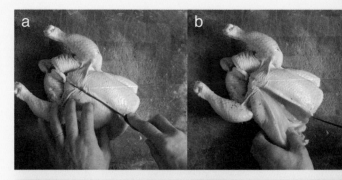
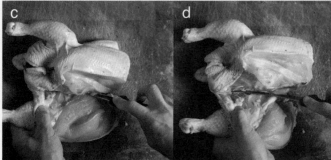
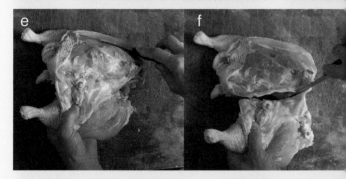
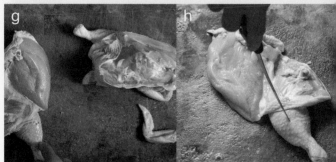

SAL'S OLD-SCHOOL Meatballs

My father instilled three things in me: (1) Always work for yourself—no matter what, be the boss; (2) Always have integrity—you are only as good as your word; (3) Always use veal, pork, and beef in meatballs. Life really is that simple!

Combine the veal, pork, beef, bread, milk, eggs, 2 cups Parmesan, pecorino, 6 tablespoons parsley, salt, pepper, and garlic in a stand mixer fitted with the flat blade. Mix on medium-low speed for 1 minute.

Scoop out $^1/8$-cup pieces of meat and gently roll them between your hands into balls about the size of a golf ball. The meat will be soft, so don't compress it too much. Put the flour in a bowl and toss the meatballs in the flour as you work.

Heat the grapeseed oil over medium heat in a large skillet and, working in batches, add the floured balls, cooking them until golden brown all over, 8 to 10 minutes total. The internal temperature should be about 155°F.

Divide the meatballs among plates; sprinkle with Parmesan and parsley.

BRAISED MEATBALLS

If you like, braise the browned meatballs in Pizza Sauce (page 267). Add the sauce directly to the pan you're browning the meatballs in, cover, and simmer for 5 minutes. You can also serve the braised meatballs over cooked pasta.

SWORDFISH MEATBALLS

Freeze $4^1/2$ pounds cubed swordfish and $1^1/2$ pounds cubed fatback until firm but not solid, about 45 minutes. Freeze all parts to a meat grinder too. Grind the fish and fatback through the small die of a meat grinder along with $^1/2$ cup golden raisins and $^1/2$ cup toasted pine nuts. Soak 9 slices of white bread in 2 cups milk for 5 minutes, then squeeze out the excess milk and add the soaked bread to the meatball mixture. Put the meatball mixture in the bowl of a stand mixer and add 2 cups grated Parmesan cheese, 2 cups grated pecorino cheese, $^1/4$ cup kosher salt, 4 eggs, 5 tablespoons chopped fresh parsley, 2 minced cloves garlic, and pepper to taste. Mix with the paddle attachment for 1 minute, then scoop out $^1/8$-cup pieces of meat and roll into meatballs the size of a golf ball. Dust the meatballs in flour and sear in oil as directed, cooking to an internal temperature of 125°F. I like to braise the swordfish meatballs in Pizza Sauce (page 267) for a few minutes, then serve them over Polenta Squares (page 230) and garnish with Parmesan, parsley, and olive oil.

MAKES ABOUT SIXTY 1-OUNCE MEATBALLS (THIRTY 2-OUNCE BALLS OR TWENTY 3-OUNCE BALLS)

1 pound ground veal

1 pound ground pork

1 pound ground beef

4 slices white sandwich bread, torn

$1^1/2$ cups milk

3 eggs

2 cups freshly grated Parmesan cheese, plus more for garnish

1 cup grated pecorino cheese

6 tablespoons chopped fresh flat-leaf parsley, plus more for garnish

2 tablespoons kosher salt

$^1/2$ teaspoon freshly ground pepper

1 clove garlic, minced

$1^1/2$ cups tipo 00 flour or all-purpose flour

$^1/4$ cup grapeseed oil

PREP AHEAD

The meatballs can be rolled in flour and frozen in a single layer on a baking sheet. Put the frozen balls in a freezer bag and freeze for up to 2 months. Thaw and sear as directed.

BEVERAGE—Torre Quarto, Don Marcello Rosso 2007 (Puglia): This Southern Italian blend is ideal with these meatballs. Primarily Sangiovese with Cab and Merlot, this slightly tannic blend is aged in stainless steel and brings a surprising flavor of fresh fruit that makes it as rustic as the dish it complements.

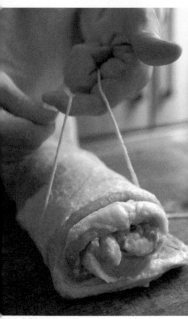
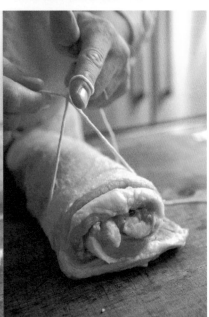

Veal Breast "al Latte" WITH FRIED SAGE

In 1994, when I was in working in Tuscany at La Chiusa, we used to braise goat in milk all the time. It made it so tender. The milk did something to the meat. Then we would blend the juices with the cooked milk and make an incredibly creamy sauce. It's a very traditional Tuscan way to cook. After it's braised and sliced, I like to serve the veal with cipollini onions roasted in a hot oven until soft and browned. Or try the Shallot Marmalade on page 171.

MAKES 8 SERVINGS

1¹/2 pounds pork fatback, cubed

2 cloves garlic

Leaves of 3 sprigs rosemary, plus 2 sprigs more for braising

Coarse salt and freshly ground pepper

1 boneless veal breast, about 5 pounds

3 to 4 tablespoons grapeseed oil

1 bay leaf

Juice of 1 lemon, plus 2 lemons, sliced

3 quarts to 1 gallon whole milk

20 fresh sage leaves, plus more for garnish

Put the fatback in a single layer on a baking sheet that will fit in your freezer and freeze until firm but not solid, 30 to 40 minutes. Puree the fat, garlic, and rosemary leaves in a food processor in small batches until it is the texture of softened butter. Season with salt and pepper to taste.

Place the veal breast, rough side up, on a work surface and lay it flat. Trim the excess fat to make the meat relatively flat and even, then season with salt and pepper. Spread three-fourths of the fat mixture evenly over the surface of the veal. Starting at a long side, roll the veal into a compact roll. Tie the roll with butcher's string at even intervals spaced 1 to 2 inches apart. Rub the outside of the roll with the remaining fat mixture.

Preheat the oven to 350°F. Heat 1 tablespoon of the oil over medium heat in an oval Dutch oven or a heavy ovenproof casserole big enough to hold the veal roll (roughly 16 to 18 inches at the widest spot). Add the veal and cook until it is dark brown on all sides, about 10 minutes, turning now and then.

Tie the bay leaf and 2 rosemary sprigs together with kitchen twine, then toss it in the pan. Add the lemon juice and slices to the pan. Pour in enough milk to come about two-thirds of the way up the side of the veal. Reduce the heat to medium-low and bring to a simmer. Cover the pan and cook in the oven until the veal is fork-tender, about 2 hours.

Remove the pan from the oven and transfer the veal to a cutting board. Remove the lemon slices and the herb sachet from the cooking liquid, which will be curdled. Let the liquid cool for a few minutes, then skim some of the fat from the surface.

Boil the liquid over medium-high heat until it reduces in volume by about one-third, 15 to 20 minutes. Puree the liquid using an immersion blender or regular blender until the mixture is smooth. Taste and season with salt and pepper.

continued, page 206

Cut the veal roll crosswise into 3/4-inch-thick slices. Heat 1 tablespoon of the remaining oil in a large skillet over medium-high heat and sear the slices in batches until crisp, about 4 minutes per batch, adding oil as necessary. Sauté the 20 sage leaves until they are crisp as well. Arrange the meat and sage leaves on a warm serving platter or individual plates.

Discard any remaining oil in the pan and pour in the pureed braising liquid. Simmer it gently over medium-low heat until warm. Drizzle the sauce over the veal and garnish with sage leaves.

PREP AHEAD

It's best to start the veal several hours before you plan to serve it, preferably the day before. You can also braise the veal roll, remove the roll from the braising liquid, and cover and refrigerate it for 1 day before slicing it. Allow the slices to sit at room temperature for about 1 hour before searing them.

BEVERAGE—Tenuta di Capezzana, "Barco Reale di Carmignano" 2007 (Tuscany): For this succulent yet delicate dish, you might think Chianti, but I prefer this velvety Sangiovese/Cabernet/Canaiolo blend. It strikes a tremendous balance with just a hint of oak.

GRILLED Beef Cheeks

These days, you can find veal cheeks on many restaurant menus. It has become the "in" thing, probably because veal cheeks have a seductive, tender texture from all the collagen in the veal. But that tenderness comes at the expense of flavor. Veal is such a young animal that the muscles haven't developed. And the more developed a muscle is, the better the meat tastes. Beef cheeks taste much more robust, and plenty of Italian cooks use them instead of veal. The trick is to soften them without losing their beefy character. After cooking them every which way, I found that braising the cheeks in wine, then quickly grilling them, gives you the perfect combination of fork-tender, beefy-tasting meat and a crusty surface. I like to serve these with Celery Root Puree (page 270), but Roasted Mushrooms in Foil (page 227) work well too. A few small heirloom carrots on the side are nice, too. Blanch them with some of the stem on, then sauté them quickly and season with coarse salt and pepper.

MAKES 6 SERVINGS

3 pounds beef cheeks (4 cheeks, each about 12 ounces), trimmed of fat and sinew

Salt and freshly ground pepper

All-purpose flour for dredging

2 tablespoons grapeseed oil, plus a little more for coating

4 cups dry red wine

2/3 cup finely chopped carrot

2/3 cup finely chopped celery

2/3 cup finely chopped onion

2 tablespoons unsalted butter

Celery Root Puree (page 270)

Gremolata (page 270)

Maldon sea salt, for garnish

Preheat the oven to 350°F. Lightly season the beef cheeks with salt and pepper, then dredge in flour.

Heat the 2 tablespoons oil in a large sauté pan over medium-high heat. When hot, add the cheeks (in batches if necessary to avoid overcrowding) and sear until golden brown all over, about 5 minutes.

Discard the oil from the pan, then stir in the red wine so it bubbles, and scrape up the browned bits from the bottom of the pan (if the pan is too burned, exchange it for a clean pan). Add the carrot, celery, and onion and return the cheeks to the pan. Add just enough water to come about three-fourths of the way up the sides of the cheeks.

Cover the pan and cook in the oven until the cheeks are fork-tender but not falling apart, 3 to 4 hours. Pull the cheeks out of the liquid and let cool. Strain the cooking liquid into a medium saucepan and bring the liquid to a boil. Cook until reduced to about 2 cups, then swirl in the butter. Taste and season with salt and pepper. Set aside.

Light a grill for high heat. Cut the cooled beef cheeks into 3 or 4 slices each. Coat the slices in grapeseed oil and season with salt and pepper. When the grill is hot, scrape the grill rack clean and oil it with an oily paper towel. Put the beef slices on the hottest part of the grill. Grill just until the cheeks develop a nice crust, 2 to 3 minutes per side.

Heat the celery root puree in a small saucepan until hot. Reheat the beef sauce. Put 3 or 4 beef slices on each plate and ladle some sauce over the slices. Pour about 1/2 cup hot celery root puree alongside each serving and scatter some gremolata over each plate. Garnish with Maldon sea salt.

PREP AHEAD

Both the celery root puree and the gremolata can be made up to 8 hours in advance, covered, and refrigerated. After braising and cooling the cheeks, you can cover and refrigerate them for up to 8 hours before grilling. Let them sit at room temperature to take the chill off while the grill heats up.

BEVERAGE—Pio Cesare, Barolo 2005 (Piedmont): People often think of Cabernet Sauvignon when they think of beef, but this smoky, structured Barolo is perfect with the cheeks.

Turkey Cutlets MILANESE STYLE

You'll find this dish in home kitchens all over Northern Italy. When I was opening my restaurant Amis, I knew something milanese was definitely going on the menu. To do a little research, I took my wife, Megan, and my son Maurice to Cene, just outside of Bergamo in Northern Italy to visit Pina, the mother-in-law of my chef Jeff Michaud. We all loved her turkey milanese. She made it in the classic way with turkey cutlets pounded thin, breaded, and panfried. Served on a bed of arugula dressed with lemon and olive oil, it became something even more spectacular. The bite of arugula and the spark of lemon perk up the turkey, and a few shavings of Parmesan give it the perfect saltiness. It's still one of the most popular dishes on the Amis menu.

Place a slice of turkey between two sheets of plastic wrap. Using a flat meat mallet or small iron skillet, pound the turkey breast slice to an even thickness of about $1/4$ inch. Repeat with the remaining slices.

Put the flour in a shallow bowl, the eggs in a second one, and the bread crumbs in a third. Season the flour with salt and pepper to taste. Coat the flattened turkey slices in the flour, patting off any excess. Coat with egg using one hand, and immediately dredge in the bread crumbs using your other hand. Put each breaded slice on a wire rack to rest for 10 minutes.

Heat the oil in a large skillet over medium-high heat. When hot, add the butter and melt. In two batches, panfry the breaded turkey slices in the hot fat until browned and crisp, 2 to 3 minutes per side. Drain on paper towels and sprinkle with Maldon sea salt.

Dress the arugula with the lemon vinaigrette and a little salt. Mound a small pile of dressed arugula on each turkey slice. Top with a couple of Parmesan shavings and garnish with a wedge of lemon.

PREP AHEAD

The vinaigrette can be made a day or two ahead and refrigerated. You can also bread the pounded turkey and let it rest at room temperature for up to 30 minutes before panfrying it.

BEVERAGE—Elio Perrone, Barbera d'Asti 2009 "Tasmorcan" (Piedmont): White meat and red wine? Yes, it does work, and the Barberas from Asti prove that, especially with a lightly breaded dish like milanese. Fresh fruit, good acid, and a nice tart finish work magic with the turkey.

MAKES 4 TO 6 SERVINGS

$1^1/2$ pounds boneless, skinless turkey breast, cut into 8 slices on the diagonal

1 cup tipo 00 or all-purpose flour

2 eggs, lightly beaten

2 cups plain dried bread crumbs

Salt and freshly ground black pepper

$1/4$ cup grapeseed oil

2 tablespoons unsalted butter

Maldon sea salt, for sprinkling

4 ounces arugula

2 tablespoons Lemon Vinaigrette (page 273)

$1/2$ cup shaved Parmesan cheese

$1/2$ lemon, cut into 4 wedges

BRAISED Monkfish

I was never a big monkfish fan. I couldn't get over the chewiness and lack of flavor. Everyone told me, "Monkfish is the poor man's lobster," but I didn't see the likeness. Why not just eat lobster? One day at Vetri, years ago, I decided to give it a second chance. I braised the monkfish like ossobuco. And then I saw the light. I was starstruck! Monkfish is tough, like a beef cheek, but when you braise it, the meat tenderizes itself and becomes moist and juicy. White wine and tomatoes in the braising liquid give it great flavor, too. Even better than lobster! I used to break up the fish and toss it with papardelle. But more recently at Osteria, Jeff Michaud decided to serve it like ossobuco with some Saffron Puree (page 271) on the side.

MAKES 4 SERVINGS

1¹/2 pounds monkfish, cut into 4 equal pieces

Salt and freshly ground pepper

Tipo 00 or all-purpose flour for dredging

4 tablespoons unsalted butter

¹/4 cup grapeseed oil

4 leeks (white and light green parts only), trimmed, rinsed between leaf layers, and cut into half-moons

1 bottle (750 ml) dry white wine

1 cup canned peeled tomatoes, preferably San Marzano

4 sprigs thyme

2 bay leaves

Fresh lemon juice

Preheat the oven to 350°F. Season the monkfish with salt and pepper on all sides, then dredge in the flour.

Melt the butter with the grapeseed oil in a large ovenproof sauté pan over medium-high heat. Add the monkfish to the pan and brown all over, 4 to 6 minutes. Remove the monkfish from the pan and drain off all but ¹/4 cup fat.

Add the leeks to the pan and cook gently over medium-low heat until they start to look translucent, about 5 minutes. Increase the heat to high and pour in the wine, stirring to scrape the browned bits from the pan bottom. Simmer until the liquid reduces in volume slightly, 3 to 4 minutes.

Crush the tomatoes by hand, adding them to the pan. Return the monkfish to the pan and, if necessary, add enough water to barely cover the fish. Bring to a simmer over medium-high heat and add the thyme, bay leaves, and a few squeezes of lemon juice. Cover the pan and put it in the oven until the fish is tender, about 30 minutes.

Remove the pan from the oven and transfer the monkfish to a platter or plates. Remove the thyme and bay leaves from the braising liquid and ladle some of it over each serving.

BEVERAGE—Mastroberardino, Greco di Tufo 2006 (Campania): This Greco typifies the grape. Flavors of apricot and peach with just the right amount of acid create a lush mouthfeel that plays well with the full flavor of the monkfish.

Thanks for the Complement

When people taste wine they often say something like, "Oh, that imparts hints of citrus and honey," or "I'm getting some chocolate and strawberry on the finish." Reflect on those kinds of insights when trying to pair wine with food. If citrus, honey, chocolate, or strawberries are foods that could actually be used in the dish you're making, get those flavors on the table in the form of wine instead. That way, the wine will complement the food. Let's say you're making a seafood dish and considering a generous squeeze of lemon or a few grindings of fresh black pepper. Hold back a little on the seasonings and let the wine bring those flavors. The Mixed Seafood Grill (page 211) makes an excellent example. Pairing the Vermentino with this dish brings both the acid and the citrus you might achieve with a squeeze of lemon. This concept also explains why Zinfandel is such a food-friendly wine. Its peppery bite stands in for the fresh black pepper we often grind over our savory dishes.

MIXED Seafood Grill

For this dish, use whatever fish is freshest at your market. No scallops? Skip 'em. The swordfish came in yesterday, but the halibut this morning? Use halibut—no question. Freshness is everything. It all just gets grilled anyway. If you have a cast-iron griddle (plancha) on your grill, grill the polenta on that. If not, you can put the polenta squares right on the grill grate alongside the fish. Put the grilled fish on a big platter, spritz it with lemon and olive oil, toss on some herbs, and decorate with some sliced lemon. Perfection!

MAKES 4 SERVINGS

8 extra-large (16 to 20 per pound) shrimp in the shell, heads removed, shells split down the back, and deveined (leave shells on)

4 large diver sea scallops

4 small squid, cleaned, tentacles reserved

4 ounces swordfish, cut into four 1/2-inch-thick pieces

4 ounces skate wing, cut into four 1/2-inch-thick pieces

2 tablespoons grapeseed oil, plus more for brushing

Salt and freshly cracked pepper

Eight 2-inch chilled Polenta Squares (page 230)

1/2 cup Lemon Vinaigrette for Grilling (page 273)

4 tablespoons chopped fresh flat-leaf parsley

1/2 lemon, cut into 4 wedges

Light a grill for high heat. If you have a cast-iron griddle and enough grill space, heat the griddle on one side of the grill.

Gently toss the seafood with the 2 tablespoons grapeseed oil and season with salt and pepper to taste. Brush the polenta squares with oil.

When the grill is hot, scrape the grill grate clean and oil it with an oily paper towel. Grill the seafood until grill-marked and firm but not dry, about 2 minutes for the swordfish, skate wing, and squid bodies and tentacles; 3 minutes for the shrimp; and 3 to 4 minutes for the squid sacs and scallops, turning the pieces halfway through the cooking. Grill the polenta squares until nicely grill-marked, about 2 minutes per side, using the griddle if you have one.

Serve 2 polenta squares, 2 shrimp, 1 scallop, 1 squid, 1 swordfish piece, and 1 piece of skate wing per person, topped with 2 tablespoons lemon vinaigrette, 1 tablespoon parsley, and a lemon wedge.

PREP AHEAD

The polenta can be cooked, chilled, cut, and kept refrigerated for up to 2 days before grilling. The vinaigrette can also be made a couple of days in advance.

BEVERAGE—Argiolas, Vermentino di Sardegna 2008 "Costamolino" (Sardinia): The honeyed tropical fruit nose here is unmistakably Sardinian. With refreshing acidity and lemon-lime flavors right up front, it immediately calls to mind summer at the beach.

Halibut WITH PEAS

This is my Sunday go-to dinner. I learned it in 1995 from a woman nicknamed Titi. She was from Genoa and married to Giorgio Gallizio, the man who hired me to open Giorgio's at the Pier in Juneau, Alaska. Giorgio wanted his wife to put some of her dishes on the menu. I was skeptical at first, but then she started cooking for me. Skepticism be gone! She made me some incredible dishes, like ravioli genovese (sweetbread and brain ravioli), fried porcini mushrooms, and halibut with peas. The halibut was my favorite, and it went on the menu at Giorgio's. It was on my menu at Vetri for a while, too, but nowadays it shows up more often on my own kitchen table. My wife just loves it. Sometimes, I'll toss in a little chopped Pancetta (page 159) to make it richer. But don't even bother using anything but freshly shelled peas. The smaller, the better. Once they get too big, they go from sweet to starchy.

Heat the oil in a large skillet over medium heat and sauté the peas, shallot, and garlic until soft but not browned, 3 to 4 minutes. Add the wine, pepper flakes, and $^1/_2$ cup of the water and simmer rapidly over medium-high heat until only a few tablespoons of liquid are left in the pan, 5 to 6 minutes.

Cut the halibut into 6 pieces and season all over with salt and pepper. Add the halibut to the pan and drizzle in the sherry vinegar. Reduce the heat to medium and cook, turning a few times, until you can almost break the halibut apart with your fingers, 6 to 8 minutes, adding the parsley halfway through and spooning the liquid from the pan over the fish now and then. Transfer the fish to a platter or plates and keep warm.

Increase the heat to medium-high and add the remaining $^1/_2$ cup water in 2-tablespoon increments, stirring during each addition. Cook until the liquid in the pan reduces in

MAKES 6 SERVINGS

$^1/_4$ cup extra-virgin olive oil

2 cups freshly shelled green peas (about 2 pounds peas in the pod)

1 small shallot, minced

1 clove garlic, smashed

$^1/_2$ cup dry white wine

Pinch of red pepper flakes

1 cup water

1$^1/_2$ pounds halibut, skinned

Salt and freshly ground pepper

2 teaspoons sherry vinegar

1 tablespoon chopped fresh flat-leaf parsley

volume and thickens slightly and the peas are tender, 6 to 8 minutes total. Taste and season with salt and pepper.

Remove the garlic and pour the peas and sauce over and around the fish on the platter or plates.

BEVERAGE—Foradori, Teroldego 2007 (Trentino): Here is another pairing that successfully breaks the outdated "white with fish" rule. A fuller-bodied fish like halibut makes a great match for this red grape, which is indigenous to the Alto Adige. Herbaceous with a whisper of fennel, the wine brings deep flavor yet finishes softly and delicately.

Fish Poached IN OLIVE OIL

This is a surefire way to cook a great piece of fresh fish. It's much more flavorful than just poaching the fish in water. If you have a meaty fish like halibut or salmon, the texture gets unbelievably silky. Top with some coarse sea salt, and keep the side dishes simple. Fennel Gratin (page 232) works nicely, as does a green salad.

MAKES 4 SERVINGS

1¼ pounds halibut, salmon, cod, or bass fillet, cut into four 5-ounce pieces

1½ to 2 cups grapeseed oil

1½ to 2 cups olive oil

Salt and freshly ground pepper

Maldon sea salt, for garnish

Let the fish rest at room temperature for about 15 minutes to take the chill off.

Pour about 3 inches of the oils into a large sauté pan and heat over medium heat to 160°F. The oil will start to shimmer on top.

Season the fish with salt and pepper (go easy on the salt, because the fish will be finished with sea salt). Drop the fish into the oil, skin side down (if the skin is still on). Adjust the heat to maintain the 160°F oil temperature and cook until the fish is medium-rare or about 125°F on an instant-read thermometer, 5 to 8 minutes. Remove from the oil using a slotted metal spatula and drain on paper towels, then transfer to plates. Garnish with Maldon salt and enjoy.

PREP AHEAD

You can't really make anything ahead of time here, but you can save the poaching oil for a few days and use it for any other fish dish, like Tuna-Ricotta Fritters (page 240).

BEVERAGE—Tramin, Gewürztraminer 2009 (Alto Adige): The soft, rich texture of this dry Gewürztraminer is a beautiful complement to the succulent fish.

Tuna Tagliata WITH FENNEL AND ORANGE

Tagliata (tahl-ee-atta) means "sliced" in Italian, and trattorias often serve tagliata di manzo for lunch, a thinly sliced rib-eye steak served on a bed of arugula. Here, I have some fun with the whole idea of "sliced." Instead of beef, I use fish. Instead of slicing the fish like a steak, I pound it thin into one big slice. Instead of arugula, I serve it with fennel that has been cut into thin strips. Even the oranges are segmented to give you only the sweetness of orange and none of the bitterness of the membrane.

Put the tuna between sheets of plastic and pound to a $1/2$-inch thickness with a heavy pan or the flat side of a meat pounder. Put the fish in a ziplock plastic bag with the $2/3$ cup olive oil and the rosemary and marinate in the refrigerator for 4 to 6 hours.

Trim the stems and about 1 inch of the top of the fennel bulb. Thinly shave the fennel into $1/8$-inch-thick half-moons. The easiest way is to use a mandoline, even an inexpensive hand-held model, and pass the trimmed stem end of the fennel bulb gently and repeatedly over the blade. Discard the core, dark green parts, and tough root end or outer layers of the bulb. You should end up with about 2 cups of fennel strips.

Segment the oranges into supremes, working over a bowl to catch the juice (see Prep Ahead, opposite). Measure out 1 tablespoon of the juice, pour it into the bowl, and drink or reserve the rest. (It tastes awesome; you might as well drink it.) Gradually whisk the remaining 3 tablespoons olive oil into the juice in a slow, steady stream until blended. Taste and season lightly with salt and pepper. Add the fennel and oranges, taste, and season again with salt and pepper, tossing to coat.

Light a grill for medium-high heat. Lightly season the tuna with salt and pepper and let stand at room temperature until the grill heats up.

MAKES 4 SERVINGS

4 ahi tuna steaks, about 5 ounces each

$2/3$ cup plus 3 tablespoons extra-virgin olive oil

2 tablespoons fresh rosemary leaves, coarsely torn

1 fennel bulb

2 seedless oranges

Salt and freshly ground pepper

1 tablespoon chopped fresh flat-leaf parsley

When the grill is hot, scrape the grill rack clean and oil it with an oily paper towel. Grill the tuna on one side only, creating cross-hatch marks on that side. The easiest way is to look at your grill as if it were a clock and start the tuna pointing toward 10 o'clock. Grill until marked, 1 to 2 minutes, then point the steaks to 2 o'clock and grill until cross-marked. Use a wide metal spatula to flip the tuna onto plates so the grilled side is up.

Arrange the salad over the tuna, drizzling on some of the vinaigrette. Garnish with parsley.

PREP AHEAD

I love the taste of sliced oranges, but I don't always like the bitter, chewy membranes. To get rid of them, make orange supremes. Do it ahead of time because it's a little fussy. You can refrigerate the supremes in an airtight container for about 8 hours. Slice off about $1/2$ inch from the top and bottom of the oranges. Stand an orange on end and cut downward all around, cutting just beneath the white pith down to the flesh to remove the entire rind in strips. Steady the orange and remove one orange segment at a time by running the knife in a V shape as close to each side of each membrane as possible, releasing each segment into a bowl. Squeeze the remaining accordion-like "skeleton" of membrane to extract the juice.

BEVERAGE—DiGiovanna, Grillo 2008 (Sardinia): I love the fresh citrus in this indigenous varietal. Its diverse minerality and the fresh-cut grass on the nose make a perfect match for the orange and fennel.

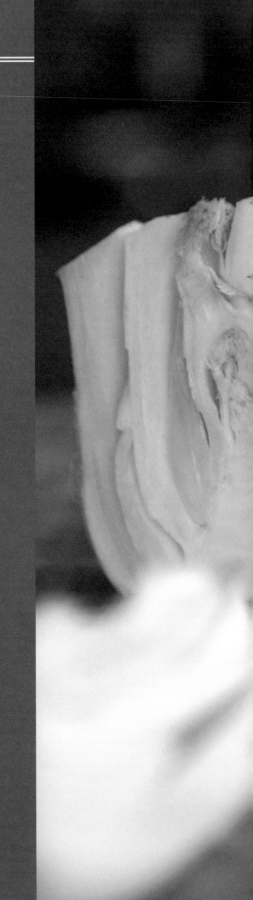

F ARMERS' MARKETS ARE BIG IN PHILADELPHIA. Every neighborhood has its own, and each claims theirs is the best. The reality is, they are all great. Some are smaller than others, but they all have great products. We have honey vendors, meat vendors, jam and marmalade purveyors, and, of course, sellers of incredible fruits and vegetables. Think about it. Pennsylvania was the country's first agricultural state. Dairy farms and fruit orchards are everywhere. Now that people like buying directly from farmers, there's even more variety and better-quality produce available.

SIMPLE VEGETABLES AND SIDES

It's a field day for chefs. I walk through my local farmers' market in a daze for the first few minutes. The colors, the smells, the bushels and baskets and tubs and tables filled with vegetables and fruit are just overwhelming. Then I start picking things up, feeling them, smelling them, and talking to the farmers. "When did you pull these carrots?" "What variety are they?" "Did you spray these peaches?" "Do you have Honeycrisp apples?" "How long ago was this corn picked?" "How many more weeks until you get fennel?" I start filling up my bags. I never have enough bags.

For my kids, the best thing is the flowers. They love to choose the bouquets and carry them home and help put them in water. It's a great family activity that we all look forward to. But more than anything I love watching their faces. When we get to the flower vendors, their faces just light up at the sight of all the colors and shapes and smells. A circle of yellow here, a cone of red there, a burst of pink, some shaggy purple—all of the flowers exuding a sweet perfume that sends you into a daydream. Watching their faces makes me feel like I'm five years old again. The way they take in all the sensations at the market, it reminds me to be thankful I'm alive. As a chef, it reminds me to use all my senses when I walk through the market—to let the colors wash over me, to breathe in the aromas at each stall, and to let my own instincts guide me toward what is good to eat.

CHOOSING PRODUCE

With our five senses, we have all the tools we need to choose good foods. Forget what you've been told and go with your instincts. By nature, fruits and vegetables are designed to be attractive. If you're attracted to them, there's a good chance you'll enjoy eating them. The colors should be vibrant, the skins should be taut, and the flesh should be plump and juicy. Who said vegetables can't be sexy? Pick one up and feel it. If it feels heavy for its size, it's voluptuous and full of juice. Choose that one.

PREPARING VEGETABLES AND FRUITS

If you start with great ingredients, then your job as a cook is merely to enhance the natural qualities of the food itself. When I look at a vegetable or fruit, I think about how I can respect the integrity of the food. What kind of preparation will enhance its best qualities without destroying its essential character? Let's say it's celery root. It's a root vegetable. Firm and crunchy. You may want to just leave it raw to show off those natural qualities, as in Cold Farro Salad with Crunchy Vegetables (page 224). If that's the case, then you'll want to finely chop the vegetable so it's easier to chew.

But root vegetables also become nice and creamy when pureed. Think mashed potatoes or pureed carrots or whipped sweet potatoes. You could decide to highlight that characteristic of celery root by making Celery Root Puree (page 270).

Think about the nature of the specific fruit or vegetable. Is it juicy like an apple? Or starchy like a potato? Try to pick a preparation that will amplify those essential qualities. For instance, I would never puree fresh fennel. It's just too fibrous. And that's what's so great about it. It's crunchy and juicy. For Fennel Gratin (page 232), I just cut the bulb into wedges and roast the wedges in the oven with some oil. The oil softens the fennel and makes it taste even more juicy—still with a little bit of crunch.

Potatoes are starchy. So I slice them as thinly as possible for Potato Torta (page 229) so they will release lots of starch and meld together into a torta when layered and cooked. But the Roasted Mushrooms in Foil (page 227) are left whole so you can still see their beautiful folds after cooking them.

Whenever you're working with a piece of produce, keep in mind its defining characteristics and try to enhance those characteristics as best you can. In choosing a cooking technique, I usually try to make fennel taste more fennel-y, potatoes more potato-y, and mushrooms more mushroom-y. But sometimes, it's better to just get out of the way and let the produce speak for itself by simply cutting it up and making a salad like Apple and Endive Salad with Lemon and Thyme (page 221) or Lima Bean Salad with Shaved Red Onion (page 220).

SEASONING

It's important to taste as you go. This principle applies to all cooking, but especially to produce. Fruits and vegetables taste different at different times of year and in different regions and from variety to variety. Taste them raw by taking a bite. What you're tasting for is sweetness, bitterness, acidity, and pungency. Fruits and vegetables are very much alive, and each one will have a different balance of these essential flavors. You need to taste the produce so you can adjust the balance when you're preparing the dish. If the apples taste super sweet, add a little salt to balance them out. If the endive tastes really bitter, add a pinch of sugar. Spritz the red onion with a little sherry vinegar to offset the pungency. You get the idea. You're looking for balance.

Lima Bean Salad WITH SHAVED RED ONION

Every fall, I look forward to the lima beans at the farmers' market. They're like the most tender little fava beans, bright green and soft and sweet. You just have to get them when they're small and use them fresh—not frozen. I use fresh limas all over my menus. This is a beautiful preparation that I like to serve as an amuse-bouche or even on coarsely torn Rustic Loaf (page 24) as it comes out of the oven. My son Maurice loves to peel the limas and nibble on them while we're making dinner in the kitchen.

Bring a large pot of water to a boil. Add the lima beans and blanch for 1 minute, then transfer to a bowl of ice water. When cool, pinch open the pale green skin and pop out the deep green inner lima beans. You should have about 2 cups.

Put the vinegar in a medium serving bowl and gradually whisk in the olive oil in a steady stream until incorporated. Add the limas, onion, mint, parsley, and pepper flakes and let stand at room temperature for 10 minutes. Taste and season with salt and pepper.

Just before serving, top with shaved pecorino.

MAKES 4 SERVINGS

2 1/2 cups shelled lima beans (about 2 1/2 pounds in the pod)

1 tablespoon red wine vinegar

4 tablespoons olive oil

1/2 small red onion, sliced as thinly as possible

2 teaspoons chopped fresh mint

2 teaspoons chopped fresh flat-leaf parsley

Pinch of red pepper flakes

Salt and freshly ground black pepper

3/4 cup shaved or grated pecorino cheese

PREP AHEAD

You can blanch and peel the limas 1 day in advance and keep them covered in the refrigerator. You can also assemble the whole salad 1 day ahead and refrigerate it.

BEVERAGE—PAUSA Café, Tipopils NV (Piedmont): Bright with citrusy hops and subtle caramel flavors, PAUSA's Tipopils beer makes a refreshing match for the hearty flavor of lima beans.

Apple and Endive Salad WITH LEMON AND THYME

Whenever new chefs comes to work with me, I have them rummage through the fridge and use up stuff. I help them out. "Look, you have four endives here and a couple of apples there. Let's make a salad." You can make a salad out of almost anything, but pairing bitter flavors with sweet is one of my favorite ways to do it. The combination always works. With endives and apples, the salad comes out so crisp and delicious, it only needs some fresh herbs and squeeze of lemon to bring it all together. Perfect with Chicken Halves on the Grill (page 198).

MAKES ABOUT 4 SERVINGS

1 tablespoon fresh lemon juice

2 tablespoons extra-virgin olive oil

1 tablespoon fresh thyme leaves

3 apples (Honeycrisps are my favorite), peeled and cored

2 Belgian endives

Salt and freshly ground pepper

Pinch of sugar (optional)

Put the lemon juice in a medium bowl and gradually whisk in the olive oil in a steady stream until blended. Then whisk in the thyme leaves.

Cut the apples and endives into thin strips about 2 inches long. Add the apples and endives to the dressing, then taste and season with salt, pepper, and a little sugar if necessary.

PREP AHEAD

The salad can be assembled, covered, and refrigerated for up to 2 hours before serving.

BEVERAGE—Germano Ettore, Riesling 2008 "Herzu" (Piedmont): Riesling is incredibly food-friendly, and Herzu, with its classic profile of apple, citrus, and tingling acidity, is just perfect here.

Celery Puntarelle Salad WITH ANCHOVY DRESSING

Puntarelle is a bitter green found in the winter in Italy. It tastes a little like dandelion greens, and has serrated leaves attached to a pale green and bright white base. It's hard to find in the States, but if you have a source or can grow it yourself, by all means use puntarelle. Otherwise, endive makes a fair substitute. On Sundays, I make this salad for my wife, and she can't get enough of it.

Refrigerate the celery in ice water until slightly curled, 30 to 40 minutes. Drain, pat dry, and toss with the puntarelle and parsley in a bowl.

For the dressing: Put 2 tablespoons of the olive oil, the garlic, and anchovies in a small saucepan over medium heat. Simmer until the anchovies break up, about 1 minute.

Add the tomato, pinching off and removing the core. Tear the tomato into pieces and drop into the pan. Reduce the heat to low and simmer until the tomato breaks down a little, 3 to 4 minutes.

Remove from the heat and let cool for 2 to 3 minutes (or it will splatter when the vinegar is added). Stir in the vinegar and the remaining 6 tablespoons olive oil. Remove and discard the garlic clove and vigorously whisk the dressing or puree it with an immersion blender or in a small blender. Taste and season lightly with salt and pepper.

Add 6 to 8 tablespoons of the dressing to the salad bowl and toss until mixed. Season lightly with salt and pepper.

Divide equally among chilled plates, piling the ingredients into small mounds. Garnish with the Parmesan shavings.

PREP AHEAD

The dressing can be made up to 1 day in advance, covered, and refrigerated. Mix it with the salad just before serving.

BEVERAGE—Araldica, Gavi di Gavi 2008 "La Luciana" (Piedmont): Made from the Cortese grape, Araldica's Gavi di Gavi is the perfect summer wine—light and fresh with soft acidity and briny minerality.

MAKES 6 TO 8 SERVINGS

2 ribs celery, cut lengthwise into very thin strips 3 to 4 inches long

1/2 small head puntarelle, or 2 heads endive, trimmed, cut in thirds on a diagonal, and separated

1/2 cup fresh flat-leaf parsley leaves

DRESSING

8 tablespoons extra-virgin olive oil

1 clove garlic, smashed

2 salted whole anchovies, rinsed and boned (4 fillets)

1 canned peeled San Marzano tomato

2 tablespoons red wine vinegar

Salt and freshly ground pepper

Salt and freshly ground pepper

1/3 cup Parmesan shavings

Cold Farro Salad WITH CRUNCHY VEGETABLES

I love cold bean and grain salads. With some crunchy baby vegetables, they're just so simple and beautiful. Now that farro is easy to get in the States, you should try it in this salad. It's like barley but with an earthier, wheatier flavor, because farro is one of the oldest forms of wheat. I usually use pearled or semipearled farro, but if you have whole farro, just allow a little more cooking time.

Combine the water, 2 tablespoons of the oil, and the salt in a medium saucepan and bring to a boil. Stir in the farro and reduce the heat to medium-low. Cover and cook until the farro is just tender, about 20 minutes. Pour off any excess water, then spread the farro on a baking sheet.

Scrape the cooled farro into a bowl and mix with the carrot, celery, onion, celery root, mint, vinegar, and remaining 4 tablespoons oil. Taste and season with salt and pepper. Serve cold or at room temperature.

PREP AHEAD

You can cook the farro up to 1 day ahead, then cover and refrigerate it. Mix it with the rest of the salad ingredients a few minutes before serving. Or prepare the entire salad, cover, and refrigerate for up to 3 days before serving.

BEVERAGE—Bastianich, Refosco Rosato 2009 (Friuli): Refosco, a grape varietal indigenous to Fruili, yields a vibrant rosato with exciting plum, spice, and vegetal notes that highlight the taste of the farro and vegetables.

MAKES 4 TO 6 SERVINGS

1½ cups water

6 tablespoons olive oil

1 teaspoon salt

1 cup pearled or semipearled farro

1 carrot, peeled and diced

2 ribs celery, diced

¼ red onion, diced

½ small celery root, peeled and diced

2 tablespoons chopped fresh mint

2 tablespoons sherry vinegar

Salt and freshly ground pepper

Vegetarians Welcome

I love it when people call or e-mail the restaurant and say, "We are coming in tonight and wanted to let you know that we are vegetarians. Will you have something for us to eat?" Will I have something for you to eat?!? I mean—seriously? This is Italian food. We do vegetables, and we do them well. In the late spring, summer, and early fall, more than 50 percent of my menus are vegetarian. The right vegetable, picked at just the right time, served in a way that enhances its natural qualities, can be a breathtaking experience.

Once a year, I take my Vetri chefs out for a great culinary experience. Sometimes, we fly to Italy or take a weekend field trip. One year, I decided to take them to Blue Hill at Stone Barns just upstate from New York City. I have known Dan Barber for ten or fifteen years, since the days when I worked in New York. But I had never eaten his food. Dan gave us a tour of the farm and talked about growing food with such passion and commitment that my chefs were already impressed. Afterward, we sat down for a truly memorable evening. But how can I tell you what we ate so you will understand how great it all was? We had baby cherry tomatoes on a toothpick. Big deal, right? Anybody can do that! Beautiful young carrots dipped in brine and served as is. Purple potato chips. Zucchini just cooked past al dente and wrapped in pancetta. Squash, lettuces, celtuce (which I had never heard of until then),

all just brought from the earth to our plate. Nothing composed. Nothing over manipulated. Some people may ask, "When do you get to the cooking part?" I mean, putting baby cherry tomatoes on a plate is not cooking—or is it? Well, I think it is. Appreciating what comes from the earth is one of the most important first steps in cooking. We didn't see a piece of fish or meat until two hours into our meal. And then it was simply a piece of exceptional fish. A beautiful roasted suckling pig. Ninety percent of our meal was from the vegetable garden, and it was masterful. Vegetables are not just a side dish. They should be respected as if they were rare jewels and cooked or prepared with care to highlight their best qualities. You need to truly understand the differences among vegetables and fruits to serve them with only the barest of preparations.

For me, that meal underscored just how important vegetables are in Italian cooking. It inspired me to change the way I present my tasting menus at Vetri. Instead of a complicated amuse-bouche, I like to start everyone with a sampling of the season's finest little bites, most of which are vegetables or fruits.

So, yes, I will have something for vegetarians to eat. And not just something, but something truly delicious. To make it clear that vegetables aren't just for the side of the plate, wine pairings are included with all of the dishes in this chapter.

Corn Crema WITH CORN SAUTÉ AND SCALLIONS

When I make risotto, I like to make a vegetable crema, or puree, then dice up some more of the vegetable for a different texture. That's the concept here. You get the whole kernels of corn, deliciously browned on a grill, surrounded by a smoother, simpler puree of corn. It allows you to taste the vegetable in two different ways and enjoy it even more. Try the same method with other vegetables, too.

Light a grill for medium heat. Grill the ears of corn, turning them every 3 or 4 minutes, until the kernels are tender and tipped with brown, about 12 minutes. You can also use the broiler, keeping the corn 4 inches from the heat, turning as directed. Let cool enough to handle, then cut the kernels from the cobs. You should have about 3 cups.

Heat the corn crema in a large sauté pan until simmering. Add the grilled corn and scallions and heat through. Taste and season with salt, pepper, and vinegar as needed.

PREP AHEAD

You can make the crema a day or two in advance, then reheat it in a saucepan.

BEVERAGE—Movia, Ribolla Gialla 2006 (Brda, Slovenia): Tropical, smoke, caramel, and earth flavors make this wine a great match for both crunchy corn kernels and creamy puree.

MAKES 6 SERVINGS

6 ears fresh sweet corn, shucked

Corn Crema (page 272)

5 scallions, trimmed and thinly sliced on the diagonal

Salt and freshly ground pepper

$1/2$ to 1 teaspoon sherry vinegar

Roasted Mushrooms IN FOIL

Turn to this side dish when you run out of burners on your stove top, or when you're cooking outside. You can put the packet of mushrooms on a grill, over a wood fire, or in an oven. The oven method is easiest, but if you put them right over a fire, just keep moving the packet around so the mushrooms don't scorch on the bottom.

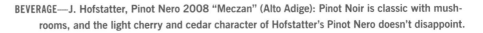

MAKES 4 TO 6 SERVINGS

1¹⁄₄ pounds chanterelle mushrooms, cleaned and halved if small or quartered if large

3 cloves garlic, smashed

4 sprigs rosemary, or 6 sprigs thyme

3 tablespoons extra-virgin olive oil

1 tablespoon sherry vinegar

Salt and freshly ground pepper

Preheat the oven to 450°F. Pile the mushrooms on 2 large sheets of aluminum foil, then scatter on the garlic, rosemary, oil, and vinegar. Season with salt and pepper to taste.

Fold over the foil and crimp it down tightly over the mushrooms. Pop the packet in the oven and roast until you can hear the mushrooms simmering when you put your ear near the packet, 12 to 15 minutes. Remove the packet from the oven and let stand for 5 to 6 minutes before opening.

Open the packet, remove the herbs, and transfer the mixture to a platter or plates, drizzling the juices over the top.

BEVERAGE—J. Hofstatter, Pinot Nero 2008 "Meczan" (Alto Adige): Pinot Noir is classic with mushrooms, and the light cherry and cedar character of Hofstatter's Pinot Nero doesn't disappoint.

ROSEMARY Roasted Potatoes

These potatoes are the epitome of simplicity: you just toss them with oil and seasonings and roast them. I like to serve them with roasted meats like Slow-Roasted Lamb Shoulder (page 190) and Spit-Roasted Suckling Pig (page 192). Double the recipe to serve these with the pig.

Preheat the oven to 500°F. Toss the potatoes with the rosemary, butter, and oil, then season with salt and pepper to taste. Spread the potatoes on a baking sheet in a single layer, then bake for 15 minutes, until the bottoms are browned. Add the garlic and dislodge the potatoes from the pan with a flat metal spatula, then toss and bake another 15 minutes, or until golden brown and crisp.

PREP AHEAD

I like to bake these potatoes and then refrigerate them for several hours before serving. Then I toss them in a hot pan with a little grapeseed oil and crisp them up minutes before they go on the plates.

BEVERAGE—Alois Lageder, Pinot Bianco (Alto Adige): Rosemary is the deciding factor here. With Pinot Bianco's clean mouthfeel, fresh fruit, and hint of herbaceousness, it's as if you've added more seasoning to the potatoes.

MAKES 6 TO 8 SERVINGS

4 pounds Yukon Gold potatoes, peeled and cut into 2-inch pieces

Leaves from 8 sprigs rosemary, chopped

3 tablespoons unsalted butter, melted

1 tablespoon extra-virgin olive oil

Coarse salt and freshly ground pepper

2 cloves garlic, minced

Potato TORTA

I make frittatas all the time, and this dish is a play on the Italian frittata and the Spanish torta: thin slices of potato are roasted, then mixed with eggs, onions, garlic, and parley and packed in a big sauté pan until it's almost overflowing. After the bottom cooks, the Spanish usually flip it to cook the other side. It's easier to just put the pan in the oven, so that's the method here. Just be careful not to cook the torta too fast or you'll have scrambled eggs. To gild the lily, top this with mozzarella or Parmesan and broil it until browned. I like to serve it with roasted tomatoes and a hunk of Rustic Loaf (page 24) for a light meal.

MAKES 8 TO 10 SERVINGS

7 russet potatoes, about 12 ounces each

1/4 cup plus 5 tablespoons olive oil

Salt and freshly ground pepper

1 onion, finely chopped

12 eggs

1/4 cup chopped fresh flat-leaf parsley

1 clove garlic, minced

Peel and slice the potatoes about 1/8 inch thick. A mandoline, even an inexpensive handheld model, makes the slicing go much faster.

Put the potato slices on a large rimmed baking sheet (or 2 small ones) and drizzle with the 1/4 cup olive oil. Using your hands, toss and rub the potatoes with the oil and season generously with salt and pepper. Spread into a thin, nearly single layer. Roast for 22 minutes, then let the potatoes cool down a little.

Meanwhile, heat 2 tablespoons of the oil in a 12-inch ovenproof nonstick sauté pan over medium heat. Add the onion and sauté until soft but not browned, 5 to 7 minutes.

Whisk the eggs in a large bowl until blended, then season with salt and pepper. Stir in the cooked potatoes, sautéed onion, parsley, and garlic.

Preheat the oven to 350°F. Heat the remaining 3 tablespoons oil in the sauté pan over medium heat until just smoking. Add the potato mixture and pack it into the pan to form a cake. Cook until the bottom and sides are set, about 5 minutes.

Put the torta in the oven and bake until firm and cooked through, 25 to 30 minutes. Remove and let cool for 5 minutes, then cut into wedges.

PREP AHEAD

You can bake the torta up to 1 day in advance, then reheat it in the same pan in the oven for about 20 minutes.

BEVERAGE—DeForville, Chardonnay 2008 (Piedmont): This Chardonnay is lean and focused, with medium body and green apple, pineapple, and lime flavors along with a vegetal earthiness. It's a great accompaniment to the earthy potato torta.

Polenta SQUARES

Italians make these with whatever is left in the pot after pouring out enough hot porridge for the meal. You spread it flat, then leave the polenta in the fridge overnight. The next morning, you slice it and grill it or sear it in a pan. Nothing wasted. Everything gained.

Bring the water to a boil in a medium saucepan over high heat, then add the salt. Very gradually add the polenta while constantly stirring with a whisk.

Reduce the heat to low and cook, stirring frequently with a wooden spoon, until the polenta is thick enough to pull away from the sides of the pan, about 1 hour. It should have a consistency similar to mashed potatoes. In the last half hour of cooking, you'll need to stir more often to keep the polenta from scorching on the bottom.

Stir in the $1/4$ cup oil and taste it. Add more salt as needed.

Pour the polenta onto a rimmed baking sheet and spread into an even layer about $1/2$ inch thick and 8 inches square. Let cool, then cut into 2-inch squares.

To grill the squares, coat them with a little olive oil, then grill them over a medium fire until nicely grill-marked, about 2 minutes per side. You could also sear them in a hot cast-iron pan the same way.

MAKES 3 CUPS, ENOUGH FOR SIXTEEN 2-INCH SQUARES

6 cups water

2 teaspoons kosher salt

1 cup polenta

$1/4$ cup extra-virgin olive oil, plus more for coating

BUCKWHEAT POLENTA

Increase the water to $6 2/3$ cups. Replace $2/3$ cup of the polenta with $2/3$ cup freshly milled buckwheat flour, adding it gradually along with the polenta.

PREP AHEAD

The polenta can be cooked, cooled, cut, and refrigerated for up to 3 days in advance. For the best taste, look for polenta that is freshly milled and made from "polenta integrale," which is whole cornmeal rather than degermed cornmeal. I get mine from Cayuga Pure Organics in upstate New York (see Sources on page 281).

BEVERAGE—Castello della Sala, Chardonnay 2008 "Bramito del Cervo" (Tuscany): Think Chardonnay with polenta—or corn in general—particularly a buttery Chardonnay!

Tuna and White Bean BRUSCHETTA

Don't bother buying expensive tuna loin for this dish. You'll just be wasting your money. Ask your fishmonger for the scraps. The ends and the stuff with all the white veins are perfect here.

MAKES 8 TO 10 SERVINGS

TOPPING

1/2 cup dried white beans, rinsed and picked over

1/2 ounce Pancetta (page 159) or purchased pancetta, preferably in a chunk

1/4 onion in one big chunk

1 pound tuna scraps, cut into chunks

1 teaspoon kosher salt

Juice of 1 lemon

Leaves from 2 sprigs rosemary

1 rib celery, finely chopped

1/4 cup finely chopped red onion

1/2 teaspoon dried oregano

Pinch of red pepper flakes

2 tablespoons red wine vinegar

1/4 to 1/3 cup extra-virgin olive oil

Salt and freshly ground black pepper

1 Rustic Loaf (page 24) or baguette, sliced 1/2 inch thick

Extra-virgin olive oil for brushing

1/2 cup Lemon Vinaigrette (page 273)

2 tablespoons chopped fresh flat-leaf parsley

For the topping: Soak the beans overnight in water to cover by 2 inches. Drain the beans, then put them in a saucepan with water to cover by 2 inches; add the pancetta and the onion. Bring to a boil, then reduce the heat to medium-low and simmer until the beans are tender, about 1 hour. Drain and remove the pancetta and onion. Let the beans cool.

Rub the tuna with the salt until evenly coated, then cover and refrigerate for 1 hour. Rinse the tuna and put it in a wide pan deep enough to submerge the fish in water. Cover with cold water and add the lemon juice and rosemary. Bring to a bare simmer over medium-high heat; the water should register 165°F. Adjust the heat to maintain the 165°F water temperature and gently poach the fish until it is just firm and registers about 120°F internal temperature. Remove from the heat and let cool in the poaching liquid.

Remove the tuna from the liquid and break it into small pieces, dropping them into a bowl. Add the celery, red onion, oregano, pepper flakes, vinegar, and just enough olive oil to moisten everything. Fold in the beans, taste, and season with salt and pepper. Makes about 3 cups.

To serve, brush both sides of the sliced bread with oil and toast the slices until golden brown on both sides, preferably on a grill (but you could broil them in a pinch). Arrange the toasts around the bowl of topping and put the vinaigrette and parsley on the table. Allow guests to make their own bruschetta by spooning some of the topping onto a toast and drizzling on some vinaigrette with a pinch of parsley.

PREP AHEAD

To skip the overnight soaking, cover the beans with water by 2 inches and bring to a boil; cook for 2 minutes, then remove from the heat and set aside for 1 hour. Drain and proceed with the cooking as directed.

BEVERAGE—Nicodemi, Cerasuolo Rosé di Montepulciano 2008 (Abruzzi): Flavor intensity is so important in food and beverage pairings. Here, the earthy meatiness of tuna and beans is counterbalanced by an intensely fruity, spicy rosé from Nicodemi.

Fennel GRATIN

Once you start, you won't be able to stop eating these salty little jewels of fennel. You cut the bulb into wedges, scatter on some red pepper flakes and Parmesan, and slowly roast the fennel wedges in oil. After this cools a little, it's almost like fennel confit. The Parmesan gets nice and crispy, so you have soft, crunchy, sweet, salty, and spicy all in one bite. I love serving this alongside roasted meats and fish.

Preheat the oven to 350°F. Trim the base of the fennel and remove all dark and light green parts down to the white bulb. Slice each bulb in half lengthwise. Cut each half lengthwise into 4 wedges and remove the cores. Lay the wedges on a rimmed baking sheet and add olive oil to a depth of $1/4$ inch. Sprinkle each wedge with a pinch each of salt, black pepper, and red pepper flakes. Top each with about 1 teaspoon of Parmesan.

Bake until fork-tender, about 30 minutes. Remove from the oven and let cool in the oil until just warm.

Using a slotted metal spatula, transfer the fennel to plates and garnish with the reserved fennel fronds.

MAKES 4 TO 6 SERVINGS

2 fennel bulbs (about 2 pounds), fronds trimmed and reserved

About $2^1/_2$ cups olive oil

Salt and freshly ground black pepper

$1^1/_4$ teaspoons red pepper flakes

$1/_3$ cup freshly grated Parmesan cheese

PREP AHEAD

You can make this 1 hour ahead because it needs to cool until just warm. It tastes great cold, too.

BEVERAGE—Pieropan, Soave 2008 (Veneto): Soave is enjoying a surge in quality, and Pieropan is at the forefront of this movement, making exciting, delicious, and affordable wines. Pieropan Soave, with its palate of apple, pear, almond, and citric notes, provides a welcome counterpoint to the herbal intensity of the fennel gratin.

Escarole Gratin WITH RAISINS AND PARMESAN

I'll say it again: you can't go wrong combining something bitter with something sweet. Raisins provide the sweet here, and anchovies give you some salt to balance out the escarole's bitterness. It's just the perfect combination. Always has been, always will be.

Preheat the broiler. Cut the escarole in half lengthwise. Finely chop the anchovies and discard the tails.

Put the olive oil, garlic, and anchovies in a large ovenproof sauté pan and heat over medium heat until the anchovies start to break down, about 1 minute. Add the escarole to the pan, cut sides down, and sprinkle in the raisins. Season with salt and pepper to taste, then cover and cook until a knife easily pierces the stem ends of the escarole, 5 to 8 minutes.

Top the escarole with the Parmesan and broil until lightly browned, about 1 minute. Cut into wedges to serve.

BEVERAGE—Planeta, La Segreta Bianco 2008 (Sicily): Often the best beverage pairing for food is a local wine. The bitter and sweet qualities of escarole and raisins brings Sicily to mind, and Planeta is one of the wineries that put Sicily on the wine map.

MAKES 4 TO 6 SERVINGS

2 heads escarole (about 1½ pounds total)

2 salted whole anchovies, rinsed, boned, and tails discarded

¼ cup olive oil

2 cloves garlic, minced

½ cup golden raisins

Salt and freshly ground pepper

1 cup freshly grated Parmesan cheese

Birds of a Feather

When you are considering what to drink with your meal, keep in mind that this is not a chemistry exam. You do not need a science degree to analyze all the flavor compounds in wine and food and then match them up. Successful pairings can be much simpler. One of the principles that works consistently well is that of geographical complements. Before intercontinental commerce, you drank what you had. The Piemontese drank Barbera, and the Tuscans drank Sangioviese. Those were the grapes that grew in the region, and those were the wines drunk with the meals. That could easily explain why so many of the dishes from these regions have the "ideal" pairing right out the back door. On my travels to Rome, I drank much of the wine from the Roman province of Lazio. The best known of the wineries north of the city is Falesco, owned by the renowned wine makers Renzo and Ricardo Cottarella. Their entry-level whites and reds called Vitiano exhibit many of the key flavors that play well with those of the local fare. Drinking a Falesco Vitiano with Snails alla Romana (above) serves to illustrate this concept.

Eggplant Fries AND ZUCCHINI WAFFLE CHIPS

Back in 1994, this recipe was one of the coolest things I learned working at Dall'Amelia outside Venice. We cut these zucchini chips on a mandoline and crisscrossed them into a waffle shape, then soaked them in milk, dredged them in flour, and fried them. I started doing the same thing with other vegetables that had a similar consistency, like eggplant, but it's more fun to serve different shapes on the same plate. So I cut the eggplant into thick sticks here. I like to serve the eggplant fries by themselves with Rigatoni with Swordfish (page 65).

MAKES ABOUT 6 SERVINGS

1 Italian globe eggplant, about 1 pound

1 zucchini, about 6 ounces

Canola oil for deep-frying

2 cups whole milk

1 cup all-purpose flour

Salt and freshly ground pepper

Peel and cut the eggplant into sticks about $1/2$ inch thick and $2^1/2$ inches long. Cut the zucchini $1/8$ inch thick on a mandoline (a handheld one works fine), preferably with the waffle cutter, though a flat blade is fine, too.

Pour 2 inches of oil into a Dutch oven or deep fryer and heat to 350°F on a deep-fat thermometer. Meanwhile, dip the eggplant pieces and zucchini chips in the milk, then dredge in the flour. Working in batches to maintain the 350°F temperature, drop the vegetables into the hot oil and fry until golden brown, 2 to 3 minutes for the zucchini, 3 to 4 minutes for the eggplant.

Using a wire skimmer, transfer the vegetables to paper towels to drain, then season with salt and pepper to taste. Serve hot.

BEVERAGE—Castaldi, Franciacorta Brut Rosé (Lombardy): Fried foods and sparkling wine are a match made in heaven. Try Franciacorta or Champagne with French fries! Here, Castaldi's sparkling rosé, with its notes of herbs, red berries, and cedar, lends just the right spark.

Snails ALLA ROMANA

My Italian friends hike up the Dolomites and come back with huge bushels of snails. They soak them in water with polenta for a day so the snails eat and get fatter. When the snails eat, it helps clean out their insides so they can be safely eaten by us! To cook them, they scrub the shells, then boil the snails for 5 minutes in water with a little salt and vinegar. Then they follow the simple preparation below. Fresh snails can be hard to come by, so I wrote the recipe using canned snails, which are ready to use. Look for high-quality canned snails from Potironne (see Sources, page 279). If you're lucky enough to have fresh snails, soak and boil them before following the recipe below.

Drain the snails and cut each one into halves or thirds, depending on the size. You want them in nice little bites.

Heat the oil in a medium skillet over medium-low heat. Add the garlic and cook until fragrant, about 1 minute, shaking the pan a few times. Add the anchovy, cover, and cook until fragrant, about 30 seconds. Stir in the snails and cook until heated through, about 1 minute.

Add the tomatoes, white wine, and water and bring to a simmer. Simmer gently, stirring frequently, until the liquid thickens a little and becomes creamy, about 5 minutes. Stir in the parsley, taste, and season with salt and pepper.

BEVERAGE—Falesco, Rosso 2009 "Vitiano" (Lazio): From the hills north of Rome, Falesco's Cabernet, Merlot, and Sangiovese blend offers the right amount of freshness and concentration with a distinct herbal hit to enliven th

MAKES 4 TO 6 SERVINGS

3 dozen canned extra-large wild Burgundy snails (about one 14-ounce can)

1 tablespoon grapeseed oil

1 clove garlic, smashed

1 salted whole anchovy, rinsed, boned, tail discarded, and finely chopped

2 canned peeled tomatoes, preferably San Marzano, torn into pieces

1 cup dry white wine

1 cup water

3 tablespoons chopped fresh flat-leaf parsley

Salt and freshly ground pepper

Eggplant CAPONATA

People swear by salting eggplant first to leach out the bitterness. The truth is, bitterness has already been bred out of most eggplant varieties, so there's no need to salt them. If you use small eggplants, you don't have to peel them either. This recipe uses whole eggplant as is and makes a beautiful caponata that you can serve with almost anything. I usually make a big batch because it goes so quickly. People have asked me to jar it and sell it at supermarkets. Not a bad idea!

MAKES 8 TO 10 SERVINGS

5 tablespoons grapeseed oil

3 or 4 small Italian eggplants (2 pounds total), stemmed and cut into 1-inch cubes

1 fennel bulb, trimmed, cored, and cut into bite-size pieces

1/2 red onion, finely chopped

1 clove garlic, minced

3 canned peeled tomatoes, preferably San Marzano, coarsely chopped

3 tablespoons pine nuts, toasted (see Prep Ahead)

1/3 cup golden raisins

2 to 3 teaspoons red wine vinegar

Salt and freshly ground pepper

Heat 4 tablespoons of the grapeseed oil in a large, heavy skillet over medium-high heat. Add the eggplant cubes and sauté until nicely browned, about 10 minutes. Remove with a slotted spoon and drain on a wire rack set over a drip pan or paper towels.

Add the remaining 1 tablespoon oil to the pan and sauté the fennel and onion until lightly browned, about 5 minutes. Add the garlic and cook for 1 minute. Stir in the tomatoes, scraping up any brown bits from the bottom of the pan.

Add the sautéed eggplant, pine nuts, and raisins and mix gently so that you don't break up the eggplant. Add 2 teaspoons of the vinegar, then taste and season with salt, pepper, and vinegar as needed.

Let cool to room temperature before serving.

PREP AHEAD

Make the caponata up to 5 days ahead and keep it covered in the refrigerator. Before serving, bring it back to room temperature for the best flavor.

To toast the pine nuts, heat them in a dry skillet over medium heat until fragrant, 3 to 5 minutes, shaking the pan now and then.

BEVERAGE—Proprieta Sperino, Rosa del Rosa 2008 (Piedmont): Eggplant and tannin make good bedfellows. The soft tannins of this Nebbiolo-based rosé coupled with its rose petal aroma and spicy berry palate create a complex wine and a remarkable pairing of a Northern wine with a Southern dish.

Artichokes ALLA GUIDIA

This is a classic Roman ghetto dish: Jewish-style fried artichokes. They were the bane of my existence for six months when I opened my restaurant Amis. I had such perfect ones in Rome, but when I started making them, they were inconsistent. I found out that the size of the artichoke is important. About 3^1/$_2$ inches in diameter is perfect. If they're much bigger or much smaller, this preparation won't work. The other thing I discovered during my six months of hell is that it's best to leave the choke in. Just trim the outer leaves well and trim the stem. That way they develop amazing texture inside and out. It's like biting into an ice cream cone—you get the crunch outside, then the tender heart inside. It's a welcome change of pace from plain old steamed artichokes.

Fill a large nonreative container with water and add the lemon juice. Snap off and remove 2 or 3 layers of the outer green leaves from each artichoke until you are left with only light green-yellow leaves in a bullet shape. Leave the stem on but trim the outer layer with a paring knife down to the light green inner flesh. Pare off any dark green leaf bases around the outside of the artichoke so you reveal the inner white part. Cut the artichoke in half crosswise and remove and discard the top half. Drop each artichoke into the lemon water to prevent it from browning as you work.

Pour 3 inches of oil into a Dutch oven or deep fryer and heat to 300°F on a deep-fat thermometer.

Line a baking sheet with paper towels and top with a large wire rack. Remove the artichokes from the lemon water, shake off the excess water, and place them upside down on the rack.

Gently stretch the remaining leaves of each artichoke to separate the leaves. Mix together the salt and pepper and season the artichokes inside and out with the mixture.

Working in batches to maintain the 300°F temperature, fry the artichokes in the hot oil for 5 minutes. Using a slotted spoon, transfer the cooked artichokes to the

MAKES 6 SERVINGS

1 cup fresh lemon juice

12 artichokes, each about 6 inches long and 3^1/$_2$ inches in diameter

Grapeseed oil for deep-frying

1^3/$_4$ teaspoons coarse salt

^{1}/$_4$ teaspoon freshly ground pepper

1 tablespoon chopped fresh flat-leaf parsley

1 tablespoon chopped fresh mint, plus a few fresh sprigs for garnish

wire rack and drain upside down for 5 minutes. When all the artichokes are fried and have drained, refrigerate them on the wire rack for at least 10 minutes.

Just before serving, heat the oil in the fryer to 350°F. Working in batches to maintain the 350°F temperature, fry the artichokes until very crisp and browned on the edges, about 2 minutes. Drain upside down on a paper towel–lined baking sheet and season with a pinch of salt and pepper.

Mix the parsley and 1 tablespoon mint together. Serve 2 artichokes on each plate and sprinkle on all sides with the herb mixture. Garnish with mint sprigs.

PREP AHEAD

After the first frying, let the artichokes drain and cool, then loosely cover and refrigerate them for up to 8 hours. Fry the second time just before serving.

BEVERAGE—Tenuta Pietra Porzia, Frascati 2008 "Regillo" (Lazio): Perfumed with fresh flowers, pears, and almonds, this Frascati has enough natural acidity and dry character to pair well with artichokes.

Tuna-Ricotta FRITTERS

Last year, I went to Italy and had lunch in Cene, just outside Bergamo, at Pina Cagnoni's house. She's my chef Jeff Michaud's mother-in-law. When I walked in the door, I opened my mouth to say hello and Pina shoved some food in there instead. It was hot and crunchy on the outside, soft and creamy on the inside. What was that flavor? I couldn't quite get it, and she never did give me the recipe. But I figured it out on my own. If you like, add about $^1/_2$ cup finely chopped onion and $^1/_2$ cup chopped fresh flat-leaf parsley to the mix. And if you can't find robiola, substitute mascarpone or cream cheese.

Rub the tuna with salt until it is evenly coated, then cover and refrigerate for 1 hour.

Rinse the tuna and put it in a large sauté pan with water to cover. Bring to a low simmer (165°F) over medium-high heat. Adjust the heat to maintain the 165°F temperature and gently poach the fish until it is just firm and registers about 120°F internal temperature. Remove from the heat and let cool in the poaching liquid.

Remove the fish from the water and buzz it briefly in a food processor until it's still a little chunky. Transfer to a medium bowl and stir in the robiola, ricotta, egg, and bread crumbs. Season lightly with salt and pepper.

Add 2 inches of oil to a Dutch oven or heavy ovenproof casserole and bring to 350°F on a deep-fat thermometer.

For the breading: Put the flour in one shallow bowl, the eggs in a second bowl, and the bread crumbs in a third. Form the tuna mixture into $1^1/_2$-inch diameter balls (about the size of a golf ball) and roll in the flour, then the egg, then the bread crumbs. Transfer the balls to a wire rack set on a rimmed baking sheet as you work.

Working in batches, fry the balls until golden brown, 1 to 2 minutes, maintaining the oil temperature at 350°F. Cool on a rack set over a baking sheet lined with paper towels.

PREP AHEAD

If you can't find ricotta impastata, drain whole-mik ricotta instead. Line a sieve with cheesecloth or paper towels and place over a bowl. Put the ricotta in the sieve, cover, and let drain in the refrigerator for at least 8 hours or up to 24 hours.

You can mix, cover, and refrigerate the tuna mixture up to 3 days ahead. Let the mixture stand at room temperature for 15 to 20 minutes to take off the chill, then roll it into balls and bread it just before frying.

BEVERAGE—Planeta, Rosé 2009 (Sicily): Planeta's Syrah rosé, with its light and fresh strawberry and spice flavors, will take you straight to the Southern Italian seaside.

MAKES 32 SMALL FRITTERS

TUNA MIXTURE

1 (9-ounce) tuna steak

2 teaspoons kosher salt

9 ounces robiola cheese

9 ounces ricotta impastata or drained whole-milk ricotta cheese

1 egg, lightly beaten

$^1/_2$ cup dried bread crumbs

Salt and freshly ground pepper

Grapeseed or olive oil for deep-frying

BREADING

1 cup tipo 00 or all-purpose flour

3 eggs, lightly beaten

2 cups dried bread crumbs

Montasio CHEESE FRICO

Certain foods come from certain places. Montasio is a semifirm cow's milk cheese from Friuli. Frico was invented there with this cheese. It's just the local cheese, so that's what they used. But you could use another semifirm cow's milk cheese, like Bitto or Crucolo. The cheese shouldn't be as hard as Parmesan or as soft as Taleggio—somewhere in the middle. Fruilians grate it, layer it with potato and onion in a pan, and make a little pancake out of it. I mean, fried cheese with potato—is that ever going to be bad? It's like sex. Even when it's bad, it's good!

MAKES 4 TO 6 SERVINGS

1 Yukon Gold potato, peeled

1/2 onion

Salt and freshly ground pepper

3 cups shredded Montasio cheese

Preheat the oven to 300°F.

Slice the potato on a mandoline, even an inexpensive handheld model, so the slices are about 1/8 inch thick. Slice the onion to the same thickness, then lay both the onion and the potato on a baking sheet. Bake until the potatoes are tender, about 15 minutes. Remove from the oven and let cool slightly on the pan.

Leaving some gaps so you can see the bottom of the pan, make a thin layer of the potatoes and onions in a 12-inch nonstick sauté pan and season lightly with salt and pepper. Scatter an even layer of cheese over the potatoes and onions. The cheese should be about 1/2 inch thick, with no gaps.

Set the pan over a medium heat. As the cheese melts through to the pan bottom, it will crisp up and create a lightly browned crust. Push the sides of the "pancake" in toward the center to help shape it into a firm cake. Cook until golden brown on the bottom, 10 to 15 minutes. Then flip it with a wide metal spatula and cook until brown on the other side and gooey in the center, about 10 minutes.

Transfer to a cutting board and let cool slightly. Cut into 4 wedges.

PREP AHEAD

You can shred the cheese and keep it covered and refrigerated for up to 4 hours in advance, but the rest of the preparation is so simple, it should be done on the spot.

BEVERAGE—Anselmi, Friulano 2009 (Friuli): Local to Friuli, Anselmi's wine is perfect here. Its mineral and citrus flavors clean the palate for the next bite of frico.

I N 1994, I WAS WORKING THE PASTRY STATION at Taverna Colleoni dell'Angelo in Bergamo. I had been at the meat, fish, and pasta stations for months and needed a change. Plus, no one else seemed to want to work the pastry station. A Canadian chef named Peter Zambri was staging at the Taverna at the time, and sometimes we worked together on pastries. The boss, Pierangelo Cornaro, wanted us to make a layer-cake version of tiramisù. We tried it umpteen different ways, but the cream kept sliding off the cake. Finally, we just made a flat ladyfinger cake in a sheet pan, cut it up, and layered it with the mascarpone cream. It worked great and tasted delicious.

RUSTIC DESSERTS

About a week later, on our day off, one of the waiters invited us to his mother's house for dinner. This was on a Monday, and they had the wood grill going, with a big copper pot of polenta over the fire, and a plate of Taleggio cheese, and they were getting ready to grill horse-meat steaks. It was incredible! After the meal, they brought out an old-school tiramisù with store-bought ladyfingers, mascarpone cream, and espresso. Peter and I looked at each other and started laughing. When we tasted it, we looked at each other again and I said to Peter, "We suck!" He agreed. This tiramisù was way better than anything we had made over the past several weeks of hell. We laughed the rest of the night—and changed the recipe the next morning. We went back to a traditional tiramisù, and it was perfect. The boss agreed, too.

SIMPLICITY AND SEASONALITY

I'm a simple-dessert kind of guy. Some chefs like fancy dessert carts and crazy designed plates. Others prefer tarts and cakes. On the whole, I'm more inter-ested in perfecting the classics than spinning sugar cages. I like the simple things. In the late summer, I will serve a peach tart or a whole roasted peach. In the early spring, Rhubarb Strudel (page 256). In the early summer, Blueberry Custard Tarts (page 254). I let the seasons dictate the menu. When great strawberries come in around May, I just serve them with lightly sweetened whipped cream—maybe with some essential oil of orange in the cream for a whisper of citrus. Anything more than that would do a disservice to a perfect strawberry.

You can change many of the recipes in this chapter to match the season. If you want a strudel in the fall, make the Rhubarb Strudel (page 256) with apples instead. Or pears. Or figs. Use whatever is fresh and ripe. Just remember to taste the raw fruit first. Always go a little lighter on the sugar rather than a little heavy. I can't tell you how many times I've heard guests say, "Oh, this is great, but it's a little too sweet." I don't like too sweet. It masks the real flavor of the fruit.

CHOCOLATE

I have to admit, while I love fruit all year long, I'm also a total chocoholic. I don't need quantity. Just quality. I need to end a meal with at least one little piece of chocolate, or else I feel sad and incomplete. I prefer bittersweet chocolate but not too bitter. Most of the time, I use chocolate with 58 percent cocoa solids, which has a good balance of deep chocolate flavor, sweetness, and a bitter edge. Vahlrona and Cocoa Barry are my favorite brands. Sometimes I'll jump up to Vahlrona's 64 percent (Manjari) or 72 percent (Aranguani) chocolate for different desserts. But in that case, I like to add flavors that complement the bitterness and depth of the chocolate. For instance, Aranguani has notes of licorice, brown sugar, and raisins. So I will add something aromatic like Candied Citrus Peel (page 278) to balance out the flavors.

Don't sweat the percentages, though. In the end, some chocolate is better than no chocolate. Just buy the best you can find, taste it, and balance the flavors until it tastes good to you. But don't even bother with white chocolate. I think it should be banned from civilization completely. If you're lucky, you might find a brand with some real cocoa butter in it, but most have vegetable oil instead and none of them have chocolate liquor, the stuff that tastes so awesomely bitter and delicious in chocolate. White chocolate isn't really chocolate. You would be better off eating a stick of butter with some sugar on it.

TRADITIONAL Tiramisù

I walked into Amis one day and Brad Spence brought me some ladyfingers he had made—three different kinds. We had a classic back-and-forth. "What are those for?" I asked. "For the tiramisù," he said. "Just use the ones from the store," I told him. "But I made these!" he shot back. "Why?" I asked. "I was trying to make the tiramisù something nice," he pleaded. "Na, na, na," I soothed him, "just use the ones from the store. They hold up better. The ones you made will just get mushy in the tiramisù." He stood there with his mouth open like I'd just killed his dog. So I threw him a bone, "Use the ones you made for decoration." He sulked a little, but if there's one thing I learned in Italy, it's that store-bought ladyfingers work best for tiramisù. When Brad tasted it with the store-bought cookies, he understood.

MAKES 12 SERVINGS

8 eggs, separated

1 1/2 cups sugar

2 pounds mascarpone cheese, at room temperature

24 store-bought ladyfingers, plus a few for garnish

4 cups brewed espresso or strong brewed coffee, cooled

1/4 cup unsweetened cocoa powder, plus more for garnish

Put the yolks in the bowl of a stand mixer along with 1 cup of the sugar. Beat with the paddle attachment on medium-high speed until nice and thick, 1 to 2 minutes. Transfer to another bowl.

Put the mascarpone in the mixer bowl and beat with the paddle attachment briefly to soften it. Beat in the yolk mixture on medium speed until smooth, about 1 minute.

In a clean mixer bowl, beat the egg whites and remaining 1/2 cup sugar with the whisk attachment until glossy and thick. Using a rubber spatula, fold the whites into the mascarpone mixture in 3 increments.

Soak the ladyfingers in the espresso just until softened and saturated, about 1 minute. Make a layer of ladyfingers in a 3-quart serving dish or bowl, or in 12 individual serving dishes or bowls. Top with the mascarpone mixture, another layer of ladyfingers, and a final layer of mascarpone. Let stand at room temperature for 30 minutes before serving.

Sprinkle the top with the 1/4 cup cocoa. Garnish each portion with another ladyfinger dusted on one side with a little cocoa.

PREP AHEAD

I use Forno Bonomi ladyfingers, which you can pick up at Italian grocery stores or at Amazon and other online retailers (see Sources, page 279). The tiramisù keeps for about 3 days in the refrigerator. Let the tiramisù stand at room temperature for at least 10 minutes before serving to take the chill off.

BEVERAGE—Miscela d'Oro Espresso/Caffe Corretto: The espresso in a classic tiramisù calls for not much more than espresso to drink. However, if you're like me and enjoy the digestive powers of grappa, pour 1 ounce in your coffee and make a caffè corretto.

Baked Peaches WITH ALMOND FRANGIPANE

Peaches and almonds are one of those slam-dunk flavor combinations. When peaches are in season, I love nothing more than roasting them with some frangipane, or sweetened almond paste, in the hollows of the pitted peaches. The frangipane oozes over the sides and browns up crisp on the edges, yet stays creamy soft in the center.

MAKES 8 SERVINGS

8 ounces almond paste, broken into small pieces

1/2 cup (1 stick) unsalted butter, softened

3 tablespoons sugar

2 eggs

1/2 cup white pastry flour

4 large, ripe peaches

Put the almond paste, butter, and sugar in the bowl of a stand mixer and beat on high speed, using the paddle attachment, until well incorporated, 1 to 2 minutes. Add the eggs, 1 at a time, beating until each egg is incorporated before adding the next. Scrape down the bowl with a rubber spatula as needed. Reduce the speed to low and mix in the pastry flour until it becomes incorporated and the frangipane becomes a thick, wet paste. Makes about 1 cup.

Preheat the oven to 400°F. Cut the peaches in half and flick out the pits. If the pits don't come out easily, ease them out with a spoon. Put the pitted peaches, cut side up, in a shallow baking dish that holds them snugly. Bake just until heated through, about 10 minutes.

Spoon 2 tablespoons of frangipane into the hollow of each peach half and bake until the frangipane develops a golden crust, 10 to 15 minutes. As it bakes, the frangipane will spread over the cut surface of each peach. Serve warm.

PREP AHEAD

Make the frangipane up to 2 days ahead and keep it refrigerated in an airtight container.

BEVERAGE—Vietti, Moscato d'Asti 2007 (Piedmont): The sweet peachy, floral character of Moscato is ideal here or as an aperitivo.

Olive Oil CAKE

It's so funny when people see a slice of this next to the other desserts we serve. You would think it's not much of anything. Then they take a bite and smile. This is a very special cake. The olive oil makes it taste light and rich at the same time. And the orange brightens the whole thing with an awesome perfume. Serve this with gently whipped cream and chopped Candied Hazelnuts (page 275).

Preheat the oven to 350°F. Line a lower oven rack with aluminum foil in case the cake leaks out a little batter. Coat a 10-inch springform pan with cooking spray and cut a piece of parchment to fit in the pan and come up the sides about $1/2$ inch. Fit the parchment into the pan and spray the parchment.

Whisk together the flour, baking powder, baking soda, and salt in a medium bowl. In a large bowl, whisk the eggs and granulated sugar until blended. Whisk in the oil, milk, and orange zest. Add the dry ingredients and stir until blended.

Pour the batter into the prepared pan and bake on the middle oven rack until a toothpick inserted into the center comes out clean, 45 to 55 minutes. The cake will be very moist. Cool it in the pan on a wire rack for 10 minutes. Run a knife around the edge to loosen the pan and remove the springform sides.

Let cool completely, then dust with confectioners' sugar.

PREP AHEAD

The cake can sit at room temperature, loosely covered, for up to 3 days. Cut slices as needed.

BEVERAGE—Jacopo Poli, Miele di Poli NV (Friuli): This honeyed brandy cuts through yet matches the richness of olive oil in the cake. I often dip my cake in a little (like a deconstructed baba), but that's just me!

MAKES 10 TO 12 SERVINGS

2 cups tipo 00 or all-purpose flour

$1/2$ teaspoon baking powder

$1/2$ teaspoon baking soda

Pinch of fine sea salt

3 eggs

$2^{1}/2$ cups granulated sugar

$1^{1}/2$ cups olive oil

$1^{1}/2$ cups whole milk

Grated zest of 3 oranges

Confectioners' sugar for dusting

TOASTED Raisin Biscuit

I have been making this lightly seethed biscuit since I opened Vetri in 1998. Seethed means the batter is gently heated on the stove top but not simmered. I used to cut the biscuit into rectangles, grill them with a little butter, and serve them with our cheese plate. That's still my favorite way to prepare them—even if I'm just having them with an afternoon espresso. Two cool things about the recipe: first, it's all mixed in a saucepan on the stove top instead of a mixer. Second, it's easy to remember: 1 part (6 ounces) each butter, sugar, flour, and eggs to 2 parts (12 ounces) raisins.

MAKES 24 SMALL BISCUITS

3/4 cup (1 1/2 sticks) unsalted butter, softened, plus more for toasting

1 1/2 cups plus 2 tablespoons confectioners' sugar

5 large egg whites

1 1/3 cups plus 2 tablespoons tipo 00 or all-purpose flour

Pinch of fine sea salt

1/2 cup raisins

Preheat the oven to 400°F. Grease a 13 by 9-inch baking pan.

Cream the 3/4 cup butter and the confectioners' sugar in a large saucepan with a wooden spoon. Gently warm the mixture over medium-low heat, stirring in the egg whites, flour, and salt. Do not let the mixture simmer. Remove from the heat and fold in the raisins. Immediately scrape the thick mixture into the prepared pan.

Bake until the top looks dry and the edges are lightly browned, 10 to 15 minutes. Prick the biscuit all over with a fork about halfway through baking to prevent it from bubbling up.

Remove from the oven and let cool completely in the pan on a wire rack. Cut into 1 1/2 by 3-inch rectangles. To serve, melt a little butter in a skillet over medium heat. Add the rectangles and toast until both sides are browned, 1 to 2 minutes, adding butter as needed.

PREP AHEAD

The biscuit can sit in the pan at room temperature, loosely covered, for up to 4 days. Cut into rectangles and toast as needed.

BEVERAGE—Rivetto, Barolo Chinato NV (Piedmont): This is the dessert version of the Piemontese big boy. Rarely produced, it is a blend of almost eighty botanicals mixed with Barolo wine. The result is a full-bodied sweet wine intertwining myriad herb, spice, and dried fruit flavors.

Apple Fritters LOMBARDA STYLE

When fresh, crisp apples come into the market, I love making these fritters. Unlike most fritters, they don't taste like greasy doughnuts with a tiny bit of apple inside. No, these taste more like the whole apple with a light, sweet batter on the outside. If you like cinnamon, sprinkle some in the confectioners' sugar for dusting. The apples are cut into rings, and I like to stack the fried rings on a plate. A slice of raw apple on top and a rosemary sprig garnish makes it look sort of like a whole apple. Honeycrisp and Gala are my favorite apples to use here.

Whisk together the eggs, granulated sugar, milk, the 1/4 cup flour, the baking powder, and salt in a large bowl. Add the apple rings and push them down to soak in the liquid. Put the 1 1/2 cups flour in a shallow bowl.

Add 3 inches of oil to a Dutch oven or deep fryer and heat to 350°F on a deep-fat thermometer.

Working in batches, remove some of the apple rings from the liquid and dredge them in the flour. Drop them into the hot oil and fry until golden brown, 1 to 2 minutes. Adjust the heat as you go to maintain the 350°F oil temperature.

Using a wire skimmer, transfer the apple rings to paper towels to drain and cool until just warm. Dust with confectioners' sugar (mix cinnamon into the confectioners' sugar first if you like).

PREP AHEAD

The apple rings can be cut and soaked in the liquid for up to 1 hour before you fry them.

BEVERAGE—La Spinetta, Moscato d'Asti 2008 "Bricco Quaglia" (Piedmont): Here's a nice, low-alcohol way to end a big meal. Fried sweet desserts need a bit of effervescence, which this naturally sparkling drink has in spades. The apple-pear finish complements the fritters nicely.

MAKES 4 TO 6 SERVINGS

2 eggs

1 tablespoon granulated sugar

1 cup whole milk

1/4 cup tipo 00 or all-purpose flour, plus 1 1/2 cups for dredging

1 teaspoon baking powder

Pinch of fine sea salt

1 pound apples, peeled, cored, and sliced into rings about 1/4 inch thick

Canola oil for deep-frying

Confectioners' sugar for dusting

Ground cinnamon (optional)

Suit the Situation

One of my favorite methods of wine pairing, especially for meals at home, is the situational approach. What is going on around you matters as much as what is on the plate and what is in the glass. Who is coming to dinner? Is this a celebration? What time of year is it? Is the meal black-tie fancy or business casual? These considerations can be as critical as the flavor profile of the meal. Thanksgiving with the family calls for completely different beverages from a company dinner you've chosen to host at your home. Likewise, a quiet evening with your spouse begs for a different drink than the formal sit-down dinner party. I encourage you to adopt this concept for every dish and every meal, but desserts are a particularly good starting point. For instance, we often think of sparkling wine as a celebratory drink at the beginning of a meal, but it works equally well at the end of a casual dinner with something like Apple Fritters Lombarda Style (page 250) or even Mom-Mom's Rice Pudding (page 253). If you have a liquor aficionado at your stylish dinner party and a bottle of top-shelf grappa or another brandy on hand, consider pulling it out for the final course to cut through the richness of something like Olive Oil Cake (page 248). Match the beverage to the situation, and it will blend in seamlessly with the food and the guests to enhance the entire experience.

BUTTERMILK Panna Cotta

Custards top the list of my favorite comfort foods. This one gets a nice sour edge from the buttermilk. I like to serve it with Cherry Jam (page 183) to jazz it up.

Put the cream, buttermilk, and sugar in a small saucepan. Split the vanilla beans lengthwise with a knife and scrape the seeds into the pan. Sprinkle the gelatin over the surface and whisk to disperse it evenly. Put the pot over medium-low heat and gently heat, whisking constantly, until the mixture feels hot to the touch (about 170°F). Do not allow it to simmer.

Set the pan in a bowl of ice water and whisk until the cream is slightly warmer than room temperature, about 90°F. This will take only a few minutes.

Strain the cream and divide it among six 3- to 4-ounce dessert bowls. Cover and refrigerate until set, at least 2 hours. Serve in the bowls.

PREP AHEAD

The panna cotta will keep in the refrigerator, covered in plastic wrap, for up to 2 days.

BEVERAGE—Accornero, Malvasia di Casorzo 2008 "Brigantino" (Piedmont): This off-the-map sweet frizzante red wine lightens the buttermilk richness of the panna cotta. Flavors of candied violets and blackberries make it a fun, lively after-dinner drink.

MAKES 6 SERVINGS

1¼ cups heavy cream

1¾ cups buttermilk

7 tablespoons sugar

2 vanilla beans or 2½ teaspoons vanilla extract

1 tablespoon (1 package) powdered unflavored gelatin

MOM-MOM'S Rice Pudding

Brad Spence brought this recipe to Amis, and it has become a staple. It was his grandmother's recipe, and when she passed away, everyone in the family got a copy of it. She used to make it at Thanksgiving and Christmas, and for all the Spence family gatherings. Mom-Mom was famous for her rice pudding. She liked to put cinnamon and raisins in it, and you can, too, if you like. But I wanted to keep it simple here. For a lighter texture, Brad sometimes folds whipped cream into the pudding just before serving it. He took this rice pudding off the menu at Amis once. Just once. Of course, someone asked for it that very day.

MAKES 8 TO 10 SERVINGS

8 cups whole milk

1 (6-ounce) can sweetened condensed milk

1 cup Arborio rice

4 tablespoons unsalted butter

$1/2$ cup sugar

$1/4$ teaspoon fine sea salt

1 vanilla bean or $1^1/4$ teaspoons vanilla extract

4 eggs, beaten

Combine the milk, sweetened condensed milk, rice, butter, sugar, and salt in a medium saucepan. Split the vanilla bean lengthwise with a knife and scrape the seeds into the pan, stirring until evenly dispersed.

Bring the mixture to a boil over medium-high heat, then reduce the heat to medium-low and simmer until the rice is just tender, about 25 minutes, stirring now and then. Remove the pan from the heat and let cool slightly. Whisk in the beaten eggs. Let cool in the pan and serve.

PREP AHEAD

You can make the rice pudding up to 4 days ahead and refrigerate it in the pan with the lid on. For a lighter texture, fold in about 2 cups whipped cream just before serving.

BEVERAGE—Foss Marai Prosecco di Valdobbiadene "Cartizze" NV (Veneto): While the days of associating Prosecco with an immediate toothache are fading, there are still great examples of these wines with elevated residual sugar, in particular this sparkler from one of the Veneto's only cru vineyard sites.

Blueberry Custard TARTS

These little custards take only a few minutes to assemble, and they really pop with flavor. They're great to keep in the fridge for a few days so you can have a nice-looking dessert ready at a moment's notice. I like blueberries best here, but try whatever other fruits are in season. If you don't have grappa, use another spirit like Cognac or apple brandy. You could even use a liqueur like limoncello, which would add a touch more sweetness.

Preheat the oven to 350°F. Spray six 6-ounce ramekins with cooking spray. Cut a circular piece of parchment to fit the bottom of each ramekin and place inside. Spray the parchment, then put the ramekins on a rimmed baking sheet.

Put the egg yolks, sugar, cornstarch, and grappa in a medium bowl. Split the vanilla bean lengthwise with a knife, scrape the seeds into the bowl, and whisk until the vanilla disperses evenly and the sugar completely dissolves. Add the cream and whisk again.

Pour blueberries into each ramekin to within about ¹/₂ inch of the top. Pour in the custard to barely cover the blueberries.

Put the baking sheet in the oven and pour enough hot water into the pan to come at least ¹/₄ inch up the sides of the ramekins to insulate the custard. Bake until the custard is slightly jiggly in the center and a knife inserted into the center comes out almost clean, 35 to 40 minutes.

Remove from the oven and let cool in the pan for 5 minutes, then remove the ramekins from the water and let cool to room temperature on a wire rack. Cover and refrigerate for at least 1 hour or until cold.

To serve, run a knife around the edge of each custard, shake it loose, and put a plate on top. Invert the plate and ramekin together, then shake the custard from the ramekin as you pull it up and off. Remove the parchment if it sticks to the custard.

PREP AHEAD

The custards will keep in the refrigerator for up to 3 days, but are best within 24 hours.

BEVERAGE—Terre del Granito, Aleatico d'Elba 2006 (Elba): This late-harvest red wine from Southern Italy features notes of chocolate accompanied by dried prune, resulting from a little *appassimento*, a technique of drying the grapes to concentrate their sugars and flavors.

MAKES 6 SERVINGS

8 egg yolks, at room temperature

1 cup sugar

2 tablespoons plus 1 teaspoon cornstarch

2 tablespoons grappa

1 vanilla bean or 1¹/₂ teaspoons vanilla extract

1³/₄ cups heavy cream, at room temperature

2 pints fresh blueberries

Rhubarb STRUDEL

Strudel dough can be a challenge to make, but it's really a fun process. You have to stretch the dough like pizza dough, but so thinly that you can see your hand through it. It's like a test of wills between you and the dough. How far will it stretch without ripping? You have quite a sense of accomplishment when you do it right. Follow the directions here to the letter, and you'll have something truly remarkable to sit down and enjoy.

For the strudel dough: Combine all of the ingredients in the bowl of a stand mixer. Beat on medium speed using a paddle attachment until the dough forms a smooth ball, about 6 minutes. Remove the dough from the bowl, wrap it in plastic, and let it rest in the refrigerator overnight.

For the rhubarb filling: Toss the rhubarb, lemon juice, sugar, and cornstarch in a bowl. Slit the vanilla bean lengthwise with a knife and scrape the seeds into the rhubarb mixture, mixing until incorporated. Let stand for 45 minutes, then strain the mixture through a sieve into a bowl.

To assemble the strudel: Place a cloth (a clean old bedsheet works great) over a large table that you can walk around, like your dining room table, and generously flour the cloth.

Lightly flour a large, separate work surface and roll the dough into a rectangle as large and thin as you can. Carefully transfer the dough to the floured cloth. Remove any jewelry from your hands and wrists, then dip the backs of your hands in flour.

Holding your hands in loose fists with your thumbs tucked underneath, slide your hands under the center of the dough. Gently pull your hands away from each other, stretching the dough between them. Bounce the dough on the backs of your hands to move left or right, so that you can stretch the dough evenly all the way around, like stretching pizza dough. You will need to walk around the table as the dough gets larger. You want to stretch the dough into as thin a sheet as possible. Resist the inevitable desire to pinch the dough in order to thin it—that could cause it to tear. Just keep moving your fists from the center toward the edge, allowing the weight of the dough and the movement of your hands to stretch it thinly. When the dough is so thin that you can see the shadow of your hands through it (or even read a printed sheet of paper through it), trim off the thick edges all around the perimeter with a knife. You should be left with a large rectangle of very thin dough.

MAKES ABOUT 12 SERVINGS

STRUDEL DOUGH

3/4 cup water

3 1/3 cups tipo 00 or all-purpose flour

2 eggs

1 tablespoon grapeseed oil

RHUBARB FILLING

1 1/2 pounds (26 oz) rhubarb, trimmed and cut into 1/4-inch pieces

1/4 cup fresh lemon juice

1 1/2 cups sugar

2/3 cup cornstarch

1 vanilla bean or 1 1/2 teaspoons vanilla extract

1 cup (2 sticks) unsalted butter, clarified (see Prep Ahead, page 257)

PISTACHIO HONEY

3/4 cup honey

1/4 cup chopped pistachios

Preheat the oven to 375°F. Using a pastry brush, splatter the clarified butter evenly over the dough (avoid brushing the dough itself, which could cause it to tear). Arrange the filling in a 4-inch-wide column along one of the short sides of the dough, leaving a 4-inch border all around the column. Starting at the fruited side, use the cloth to fold the 4-inch margin of dough up over the column of filling. Continue picking up the cloth to roll the strudel, jelly-roll style, into a tight roll (avoid touching the dough itself; just pick up the cloth and start rolling).

Put the rolled strudel on a buttered baking sheet and splatter the top with the remaining clarified butter. Bake until brown and crisp, about 35 minutes. Remove from the oven and cool on the pan on a wire rack until just warm, at least 30 minutes.

For the pistachio honey: Heat the honey in a small saucepan over medium heat until warm. Add the chopped pistachios.

Slice the strudel and drizzle with the warm pistachio honey.

PREP AHEAD

The dough needs to rest overnight in the refrigerator, so that gives you a day's jump on things. You can also clarify the butter up to 1 month in advance and refrigerate it in an airtight container. Just warm it up before using it.

To clarify the butter, melt it in a small saucepan over medium heat until it stops bubbling and a white foam forms on the surface. Skim off the white foam and pour the clear golden clarified butter underneath into a small bowl, leaving behind the milky liquid in the bottom of the pan.

BEVERAGE—Canal del Ronco, Picolit 2003 (Friuli): Unlike the majority of the wine selections in this book, Picolit is somewhat scarce, but worth searching for. It's lush with floral aromas and sweet citrus flavors.

Amaretti Semifreddo WITH WARM CHOCOLATE SAUCE

Not everyone has an ice cream machine. Luckily, you don't need one to make creamy frozen desserts at home. Make semifreddo, which means "half-frozen." It's like gelato, but you fold in whipped cream and egg whites into the base before it goes into the freezer so the mixture is light and airy. That way, you don't have to churn it. I like to mix crushed amaretti (Italian almond cookies) right into the semifreddo mixture, like cookies and cream Italian style.

Put the 8 egg yolks and the sugar in a large bowl and whisk until pale and fluffy, 2 to 3 minutes.

Put the egg whites in the bowl of a stand mixer and whisk on medium speed until firm peaks form when the whisk is lifted, 2 to 3 minutes. Pour into the yolk mixture but wait to fold it in.

In the same bowl as the whites were whipped in, whip the cream and amaretti on medium-low speed until the mixture forms soft peaks, about 1 minute. Gently fold the whipped cream and egg white mixtures into the yolk mixture using a rubber spatula. Scrape into quart containers, cover, and freeze until firm, at least 6 hours. To serve, heat the chocolate sauce, stirring often, over very low heat in a small sauce-pan. Spoon 2 or 3 scoops of semifreddo into each dessert bowl, then drizzle with the warm chocolate sauce and sprinkle with the almonds.

MAKES 2 QUARTS; SERVES 6 TO 8

4 eggs, separated

4 egg yolks

$1/2$ cup sugar

2 cups heavy cream

$3/4$ cup crushed amaretti cookies

1 cup Chocolate Sauce (page 276)

$1/4$ cup chopped almonds

VANILLA SEMIFREDDO

Increase the sugar to $3/4$ cup. Omit the amaretti. Split a vanilla bean length-wise with a knife and scrape the seeds into the yolk mixture before proceed-ing with the recipe. Or use $1^1/2$ teaspoons vanilla extract.

PREP AHEAD

You can crush the amaretti cookies in a food processor and store in an airtight container for up to 1 month. Freeze the semifreddo in an airtight container for up to 2 months. Refrigerate the sauce in an airtight container for up to 2 weeks.

BEVERAGE—Librandi, Le Passule 2005 (Calabria): Raisinated Montanico grapes create a light body that is uncommon in sweet wines. Dried fruit with almond and citrus peel aromas blend well with the chocolate and enhance the semifreddo itself.

Waffles WITH NUTELLA AND SEMIFREDDO

My friend Michael Symon came back from a trip to Italy in 2009 raving about some waffles he had in Sicily with gobs and gobs of Nutella on them. So when Michael came to visit, I decided to make him my version of the dish he fell in love with. It has since become my kids' favorite dessert.

MAKES 4 SERVINGS

WAFFLE BATTER

2¹/₂ cups Waffle Starter (page 22)

1 cup milk

1 cup tipo 00 or all-purpose flour

3 eggs

2 tablespoons plus 2 teaspoons sugar

1 teaspoon fine sea salt

1 tablespoon plus 1¹/₄ teaspoons packed fresh cake yeast, or 2 teaspoons instant yeast

1 vanilla bean

1 cup (2 sticks) unsalted butter, melted

TOPPINGS

6 tablespoons Nutella

1¹/₂ cups Vanilla Semifreddo (page 258)

6 tablespoons hazelnuts, toasted, skinned, and chopped (see page 177)

Confectioners' sugar for dusting

For the waffle batter: The day before, combine all of the ingredients in a blender and blend until mixed. You can also blend in a large bowl with an immersion blender. Either way, put the blended mixture into a bowl twice the volume of the batter. Cover and let rise in the refrigerator overnight or for up to 24 hours.

The next day, heat and oil a waffle iron according to the manufacturer's directions and cook the waffles as directed. You can hold the cooked waffles in a 250°F oven for up to 20 minutes to keep them warm.

To serve: Spread 1 tablespoon of Nutella on each warm waffle. Top each with a scoop or two of semifreddo, then sprinkle on 1 tablespoon toasted hazelnuts. Dust with confectioners' sugar.

PREP AHEAD

The waffle batter needs to be made 1 day ahead so it can rise overnight.

BEVERAGE—Ginger Beer Ice Cream Float: This is a kid's dream dessert, so I like to keep that theme going by pairing it with an ice cream float made with ginger beer (Amis serves a homemade version) and some fior di latte gelato. Bring out your inner kid.

Chocolate-Hazelnut TARTUFO

This is a chocolate-lover's dream. It takes a little work but is so satisfying to eat—and to look at! On a round base of rich chocolate cake rests a dome of chocolate and cherry semifreddo studded with candied hazelnuts and enrobed in a firm chocolate shell. It's like a little igloo of chocolate bliss. You'll need some glacé cherries, and six silicone hemisphere molds to form the domes, both of which can be found in specialty culinary shops and online (see Sources, page 279).

For the semifreddo: Put the chocolate in a small metal bowl or the top of a double boiler. Set over gently simmering water and stir until the chocolate melts, 2 to 3 minutes. Keep warm.

Meanwhile, put the egg yolks and sugar in the bowl of a stand mixer and whip on medium-high speed until the mixture runs off the whip attachment in thick ribbons when lifted, 2 to 3 minutes. Scrape the mixture into a large bowl.

In a clean mixer bowl and using the whisk attachment, beat the egg whites on medium-high speed until they form firm peaks when the whisk is lifted, 1 to 2 minutes. Scrape into another bowl and set aside.

Whip the cream in the same mixer bowl on medium speed until it forms soft peaks when the whip is lifted, 1 to 2 minutes. Mix in the cocoa powder on low speed until incorporated.

Scrape the melted chocolate into the yolk mixture and fold until incorporated. Alternately fold in the whipped cream and egg whites with a rubber spatula, folding gently to avoid deflating everything. Fold in the chopped hazelnuts.

Spoon the mixture into six 3- to 4-ounce silicone hemisphere molds until each mold is half full. Freeze until semifirm, at least 10 minutes or up to 30 minutes (put the remaining mixture into the refrigerator to keep it cold). Place 3 cherries on top of each semifirm mixture, then spoon enough of the remaining semifreddo over the top to cover the cherries and fill the mold leveling the tops. Cover and freeze for at least for 30 minutes or up to 1 week. Freeze the remaining semifreddo in an airtight container for up to 4 months. Enjoy at will.

For the chocolate cake: Sift the flour, cocoa powder, and baking powder together into a small bowl. Put the sugar, oil, and eggs in the bowl of a stand mixer and whip until light and lemon-colored, 1 to 2 minutes. Switch to the paddle attachment and add the dry ingredients on low speed in 3 additions, alternately with the cream and milk, mixing well between each addition.

Preheat the oven to 390°F. Coat a 13 by 9-inch baking dish with cooking spray, then line the bottom with parchment paper. Spray the parchment.

MAKES 6 SERVINGS

CHOCOLATE-HAZELNUT SEMIFREDDO

2 ounces bittersweet chocolate, preferably 58 percent cocoa, chopped

6 egg yolks

2/3 cup sugar

3 egg whites

3/4 cup heavy cream

1/4 cup unsweetened cocoa powder

3/4 cup Candied Hazelnuts (page 275), chopped

18 glacé cherries, drained

CHOCOLATE CAKE

1 1/2 cups tipo 00 or all-purpose flour

3/4 cup unsweetened cocoa powder

2 teaspoons baking powder

1 3/4 cups sugar

2/3 cup canola oil

2 eggs

1/2 cup heavy cream

1 cup whole milk

CHOCOLATE SHELL

9 ounces bittersweet chocolate, preferably 58 percent cocoa, chopped

2 tablespoons grapeseed oil

Scrape the batter into the pan and smooth to an even depth of $1/2$ inch. Bake for 10 minutes. Lower the oven temperature to 300°F and bake until a toothpick inserted into the center of the cake comes out clean, 65 to 75 minutes. Remove from the oven and cool in the pan on a wire rack. When cool, run a stiff rubber spatula around the perimeter of the cake and turn out onto the rack to cool completely.

For the chocolate shell: Put the chocolate and oil in small metal bowl or the top of a double boiler. Set over gently simmering water and stir until the chocolate melts, 2 to 3 minutes. Keep warm.

To assemble: Use 2- to 3-inch round cookie cutters (the same diameter as the molds) to punch out 6 circles of the cooled chocolate cake (eat the scraps of the cake or save for another purpose). If necessary, use a serrated knife to trim the rounds and make them sit flat. Just before serving, put the cake rounds on a wire rack set over parchment or waxed paper. Unmold the hemispheres of semifreddo and invert one over each cake to make a dome. Gradually pour the chocolate shell mixture over the top of each dome until completely covered. Let set for 30 seconds, then serve immediately.

PREP AHEAD

Both the semifreddo and the cake can be made ahead, so you can assemble the tartufo just before serving. Freeze the semifreddo in the molds up to 1 week ahead of time and let them soften for a few minutes before assembling. Bake the cake and cut out the cake rounds up to 3 days ahead, keeping the rounds covered in the refrigerator.

BEVERAGE—Santa Sofia, Recioto 2005 (Veneto): Amarone's best-kept secret is the sweet wine that actually preceded it: Recioto. You see, Recioto is the sweeter precursor to drier, more bitter Amarone. With Recioto, you get every flavor in this dessert in liquid form: chocolaty, liqueured fruit notes of cherries in syrup, and dried black mission figs built into a hedonistic, viscous red wine.

Chocolate Zabaione TART

Here is the most elegant dessert in the book. It's a soft and sweet almond tart crust with a dark layer of rich chocolate filling on the bottom and a light layer of creamy zabaione on top. Decorated with a few fresh raspberries, it is simply stunning.

For the dough: Using a mixer, cream the butter and sugar on medium speed until light and fluffy, about 5 minutes. Reduce the mixer speed to low and add the egg, scraping the sides of the bowl with a rubber spatula as needed.

Combine the tipo 00 flour, almond flour, baking powder, and salt in a bowl and stir with a whisk to blend. Add to the mixer bowl and mix on low speed until incorporated. Scrape the dough onto a large piece of plastic wrap, form into a ball, and flatten it slightly. Wrap in the plastic and refrigerate for 1 hour.

Preheat the oven to 350°F. The almond flour gives the dough a very delicate texture. It helps to stick your hands in a bowl of ice for a couple of minutes to get them cold so they don't melt the butter when you handle the dough. With cold hands, roll out the dough on a lightly floured surface to a 12-inch-diameter round. Fold the dough over the rolling pin and transfer it to a 10-inch tart pan with a removable bottom. Unfold the dough and fit it into the pan without stretching the dough. Roll the rolling pin over the top of the pan to trim the excess dough. Line the dough with parchment paper and fill with dried beans or pie weights. Bake for 15 minutes. Remove the beans or weights and parchment and bake until very lightly browned, another 5 minutes. Remove from the oven and let cool on a wire rack.

For the filling: Reduce the oven temperature to 300°F. Bring the cream and milk to a boil in a small saucepan. Remove from the heat and add the chopped chocolate. Let stand for 1 minute, then whisk until melted. Whisk in the egg. Pour the filling into the cooled tart shell and bake for 15 minutes. It will be mostly but not completely set. Remove from the oven and cool completely on a wire rack.

MAKES ABOUT 12 SERVINGS

ALMOND FLOUR TART DOUGH

1/2 cup (1 stick) unsalted butter, softened

1/2 cup plus 2 tablespoons sugar

1 egg

1 1/4 cups tipo 00 or all-purpose flour

3/4 cup almond flour

3/4 teaspoon baking powder

Pinch of fine sea salt

CHOCOLATE FILLING

2/3 cup heavy cream

1/4 cup whole milk

9 ounces bittersweet chocolate, preferably 58 percent cocoa, chopped

1 egg

CHOCOLATE ZABAIONE

3/4 teaspoon powdered plain gelatin

1 1/2 teaspoons cold water

4 egg yolks

1/3 cup sugar

1/4 cup chocolate liqueur, such as Godiva

1/2 cup heavy cream

Fresh raspberries, for garnish

For the zabaione: Sprinkle the gelatin over the water in a small bowl and let stand until softened, 3 to 5 minutes. Whisk together the egg yolks and sugar in a small metal bowl or the top of a double boiler. Set over gently simmering water and whisk in the chocolate liqueur, whisking constantly until the mixture reaches 160°F. Remove from the heat and whisk in the gelatin. Cool the mixture by dipping the bottom of the pan into a bowl of ice water.

Using a mixer or whisk, whip the cream until soft peaks form. Fold the whipped cream into the zabaione mixture with a rubber spatula, then spread over the cooled tart and smooth the top. Refrigerate until set. Garnish the tart with raspberries.

PREP AHEAD

The dough can be made up to 1 day ahead and kept refrigerated in the plastic. You can also bake the crust as directed, let it cool, then keep it at room temperature for 2 to 3 hours before assembling. Or, make the entire tart and store it, covered, for up to 3 days in the refrigerator. Garnish with the berries just before serving.

BEVERAGE—Elio Perrone, Bigaro 2008 (Piedmont): This wine has the best of both worlds: 50 percent Moscato brings pear aromas and syrupy sweetness, and 50 percent Brachetto delivers a slightly acidic fresh berry fruit. As a sparkling dessert wine, it refreshes everything on the plate.

A FEW SUMMERS AGO, I had a corn flan with Corn Crema (page 272) on the menu at Vetri, and one of my cooks had prepared it on a Friday night. During service, someone sent the flan back because he said it didn't taste much like corn. So I tasted the flan and thought, well, he's absolutely right. I asked the cook who made it. "Did you taste the corn?" He replied, "Yes, chef, I did." I asked, "What did it taste like?" He said, "Well, it was yellow and had a light corn flavor." I thought to myself—it tasted yellow? I asked the cook to get some of the raw corn so we could both taste it. I bit into an ear, he bit into an ear, and I asked him what it tasted like. "Not much of anything," he said. "Exactly!" I replied. So I pushed, "Why would you make a corn flan with corn that doesn't taste like much of anything?" He replied, "Well, that's what came in today." So I reminded him of the first rule of cooking: Taste everything you cook with.

SAUCES AND OTHER BASICS

It's always the basics that cooks miss. When new cooks come to train with me, I ask them to make a spaghetti with tomato sauce. Or cook a burger medium-rare. Blanch a carrot. Make a potato puree. Cook dried beans. Or taste this corn and tell me if it is good or bad. I start with the fundamentals. Thankfully, cooks are starting to get reenergized about basic things, like how to butcher animals, bake great bread, pickle vegetables, and make sauces.

These are the skills that I am constantly trying to perfect. The more I cook, the more I realize that a chef should not shy away from mundane things like making a lemon vinaigrette. A chef should take pleasure in them. A chef loves to pick up a ripe piece of fruit and smell it. Whenever I find perfectly ripe peaches, I grab one and let its gentle fuzz caress my nose, then I bite into the fruit until its flesh gives way and its juices dribble down my chin. What you have to realize is that, along with sleep, sex, breathing, and water, food is one of the most elemental requirements of our daily lives. And like those other needs, food should be appreciated, respected, and, above all, enjoyed on a very basic level.

If you like to cook, don't shy away from the basics, like making Garlic Chive Oil (page 269) or Chocolate Sauce (page 276). Embrace them. These fundamentals are the very core of cooking and should capture your imagination for your entire life.

HAND-CRUSHED MARINARA SAUCE

This is the old-, old-, old-school way to make tomato sauce. You want those big hunks of tomatoes in there. And there's no other way to get them than to crush the tomatoes with your hands.

Crush the tomatoes by hand into a bowl, then mix in everything else.

MAKES ABOUT 2 CUPS

1 (16-ounce) can peeled tomatoes, preferably San Marzano

1/4 cup olive oil

1 tablespoon kosher salt

1 teaspoon freshly ground pepper

PIZZA SAUCE

The most important thing about pizza is your ingredients. When you're making something so simple, each ingredient has to be super flavorful. This sauce is just tomatoes, olive oil, and basil. The tomatoes have to be completely delicious. If they're not, the sauce is not going to work. I use La Valle canned San Marzano tomatoes. Avoid brands that say "in the style of San Marzano." That basically means the tomatoes are a fake.

MAKES ABOUT 2 1/2 CUPS

1 (16-ounce) can peeled tomatoes, preferably San Marzano

3/4 cup extra-virgin olive oil

Salt and freshly ground pepper

1/2 bunch fresh basil

Puree everything with an immersion or upright blender. Taste and adjust the seasoning.

PREP AHEAD

You can refrigerate the sauce in an airtight container for up to 4 days.

TOMATO CONSERVA

Try this recipe in late summer when heirloom tomatoes are so plentiful they are falling off the farmers' market stands. Oven-drying them concentrates the flavor and makes them taste even richer.

Preheat the oven to 350°F. Mix the tomatoes, oil, and garlic in a 2- to 3-quart baking dish and season with salt and pepper to taste. Put it in the oven and turn off the heat. Leave the dish in the oven overnight or for at least 8 hours.

PREP AHEAD

You can leave the finished conserva at room temperature for up to 6 hours. Or refrigerate it in an airtight container for up 1 day and return it to room temperature before using.

MAKES ABOUT 2¼ CUPS

3 meaty heirloom tomatoes, cored and coarsely chopped

2 tablespoons extra-virgin olive oil

½ clove garlic, smashed

Salt and freshly ground pepper

PORCINI BÉCHAMEL

I have been messing around with different flavors of béchamels for years. The porcini gives this one a woodsy flavor that I can't get enough of. I use this sauce in all kinds of lasagnas and baked pastas in the fall.

Soak the mushrooms in the hot water in a bowl for 15 minutes.

Melt the butter in a medium saucepan over medium-low heat. Add the onion and cook until soft but not browned, about 4 minutes. Stir in the flour to make a roux and cook for 5 to 6 minutes to cook out the starchy taste, stirring now and then. Gradually whisk in the cold milk. Pluck the mushrooms from the water, squeeze their liquid into the bowl, and set them aside. Pour the soaking water into the roux, leaving any sediment at the bottom of the bowl. Finely chop the mushrooms and stir into the sauce.

Reduce the heat to low and cook until thick enough to coat the back of a spoon, 20 to 30 minutes. Taste the sauce and season with salt and pepper as needed.

PREP AHEAD

Make the béchamel up to 8 hours in advance and reheat it over low heat before using.

MAKES ABOUT 4 CUPS

⅔ cup (1 ounce) dried porcini mushrooms

1⅓ cups hot water

4 tablespoons unsalted butter

⅓ cup finely chopped onion

6½ tablespoons tipo 00 or all-purpose flour

4 cups whole milk

Salt and freshly ground pepper

PISTACHIO PESTO

This isn't your ordinary basil pesto. There's no Parmesan, no garlic, and no herbs. Pistachios are the star. Drizzle it on pizza, pastas, and bread for sandwiches, or use it in Mortadella Tortelli (page 89).

MAKES ABOUT 2¹/₂ CUPS

2 cups shelled pistachio nuts

1 cup extra-virgin olive oil

2 teaspoons aged sherry vinegar

Salt and freshly ground pepper

Put the nuts in a food processor and chop until fine. Add the oil and vinegar and process to a coarse paste. Taste and season with salt and pepper.

PREP AHEAD

Refrigerate the pesto in an airtight container for up to 1 week, or freeze it for up to 2 months.

GARLIC CHIVE OIL

If you don't have garlic chives, use regular chives plus a little minced garlic.

MAKES ABOUT ³/₄ CUP

¹/₄ cup packed fresh garlic chives

¹/₄ cup packed fresh chives

¹/₂ cup extra-virgin olive oil

Buzz the garlic chives, chives, and oil in a small food processor or blender until smooth.

PREP AHEAD

Keep the oil at room temperature for up to 8 hours or refrigerate it for up to 2 days and return it to room temperature before using.

CELERY ROOT PUREE

Here's a little play on potato puree. Celery root lightens the usual mashed potatoes and gives them the savory flavor of celery without the fibrous strings. I like to serve this with Grilled Beef Cheeks (page 206).

Peel and coarsely chop the celery roots and potatoes. Put both in a pot with enough cold water to cover. Cover the pot and bring to a boil over high heat, then reduce the heat to medium-low and simmer until the vegetables are tender, about 20 minutes. Strain out the liquid, then stir the butter into the vegetables. In batches, transfer the celery root and potatoes to a ricer, and push the mixture through. If you don't have a ricer, use a potato masher. Taste and season with salt and pepper.

PREP AHEAD

Make the puree up to 1 day in advance, refrigerate it in an airtight container, and gently warm it over low heat before using.

MAKES ABOUT 3 CUPS

2 small celery roots

2 small russet (Idaho) potatoes

1/2 cup (1 stick) unsalted butter, cut into pieces

Salt and freshly ground pepper

GREMOLATA

You could put this on almost any roasted or grilled meat or fish to add some color and flavor. It's perfect on Grilled Beef Cheeks (page 206).

Mix together the parsley, garlic, and lemon zest on a cutting board and chop until the parsley and garlic are minced and the ingredients are happy together. Put the gremolata in a small container and stir in a small amount of oil to keep the mixture moist. The gremolata should be crumbly, not like a paste.

PREP AHEAD

You can make the gremolata up to 1 day ahead and store it in an airtight container in the refrigerator.

MAKES ABOUT 1/2 CUP

1/2 cup chopped fresh flat-leaf parsley

1 clove garlic, chopped

Grated zest of 1 lemon

Extra-virgin olive oil

SAFFRON PUREE

You can puree almost anything and flavor it however you like. This puree has potatoes at its base, but the spuds are transformed by the rich orange color and haunting aroma of saffron. It looks and tastes good on the plate. Try it with Braised Monkfish (page 209).

MAKES ABOUT 2 CUPS

8 ounces Yukon Gold potatoes, peeled

1 tablespoon saffron threads

1 cup heavy cream, plus more as needed

1/2 cup (1 stick) unsalted butter, cubed

Olive oil as needed (about 3 to 5 tablespoons)

Salt and freshly ground pepper

Preheat the oven to 350°F. Put the potatoes in a large saucepan with enough cold water to cover. Bring to a boil over high heat, then reduce the heat to medium-low and simmer until tender, about 20 minutes. Drain the potatoes and place on a baking sheet. Transfer the sheet to the oven and bake until the potatoes are mostly dried, about 8 minutes.

Meanwhile, put the saffron on a small baking sheet and bake just long enough to dry out the saffron, about 1 minute. Transfer to a spice grinder and buzz into a powder.

Pour the 1 cup cream into a small saucepan and heat over medium heat until steaming. Meanwhile, working in batches, put the dried potatoes and the cubed butter in a ricer and rice them together into a large bowl (you can also put the potatoes and butter in the bowl, then mash with a potato masher). Make a large well in the potatoes and sprinkle 1 tablespoon of the saffron powder into the well. Cover with 3/4 cup of the hot cream and let steep for 2 minutes.

Mix briefly, then use a rubber spatula to push the mixture through a large sieve set over a large bowl. Once all of the mixture has been worked through the sieve, you should have a smooth, bright yellow puree with a nice taste of saffron. Mix in enough olive oil and the remaining 1/4 cup cream to create a silky consistency (keep in mind that the potatoes will stiffen up as they sit). Taste and season with salt and pepper.

PREP AHEAD

You can make the puree up to 1 day in advance and refrigerate it in an airtight container. Gently warm it over low heat before using.

CORN CREMA

Crema is my go-to sauce for spreading on plates, ladling around vegetables or meat, or just licking off the spoon. Try this with everything from cauliflower and celery root to sweet potatoes and zucchini. Use the same method, maybe adding a little milk or cream if you like.

Heat 2 tablespoons of the oil in a large sauté pan over medium heat. Add the corn kernels and onion and cook until soft but not browned, about 5 minutes, stirring occasionally to prevent sticking. Taste and season with salt and pepper. Add the water, cover, and simmer until the onion is very soft and the corn is tender enough to burst easily when you bite into it, about 10 minutes.

Puree everything in a blender until smooth. Stir in the remaining 4 tablespoons oil and the vinegar to taste.

RICH CORN CREMA

Replace the water with milk. Omit the olive oil when pureeing. Just puree the corn and milk and season as directed. It should be thick, like tomato sauce.

SQUASH CREMA

Replace the corn with 1 pound finely chopped zucchini or yellow squash.

PREP AHEAD

Make the crema up to a day in advance and keep it in an airtight container in the refrigerator. Gently warm it over low heat before using.

MAKES ABOUT 3 CUPS

6 tablespoons olive oil

Kernels cut from 5 ears fresh sweet corn (about 3 cups)

1/2 onion, finely chopped

Salt and freshly ground pepper

2 cups water

1/2 to 1 teaspoon sherry vinegar

HORSERADISH CRÈME FRAÎCHE

Along with Pickled Eggs (page 169), this makes Potted Trout Terrine (page 135) a knockout first course for an early-fall meal. Grate the horseradish on a Microplane grater so you get fine shreds instead of big chunks or all juice.

MAKES ABOUT 1 CUP

1 cup crème fraîche

1 to 2 tablespoons finely grated fresh horseradish

Salt and freshly ground pepper

Combine the crème fraîche and horseradish to taste in a bowl. Taste and season with salt and pepper.

PREP AHEAD

Cover and store for up to 1 week in the refrigerator.

LEMON VINAIGRETTE

Add chopped garlic, herbs, a little spice like ground fennel seeds, or whatever you like to flavor this. If you want the vinaigrette to emulsify better, whisk in a speck of prepared mustard.

MAKES 3/4 CUP

Juice of 1 lemon

1/2 cup extra-virgin olive oil

Salt and freshly ground pepper

Put the lemon juice in a bowl. Whisk in the oil in a thin, steady stream until incorporated with the juice. Taste and season with salt and pepper.

LEMON VINAIGRETTE FOR GRILLING

Replace half of the olive oil with grapeseed oil.

PREP AHEAD

The vinaigrette will keep, covered, in the refrigerator for 1 week. Whisk to blend it back together before using.

ROSEMARY-GARLIC BRINE

Here's the basic brine I use for most of my roasted and grilled meats. I change up the herbs and spices to match the meat. This version is especially good for Slow-Roasted Lamb Shoulder (page 190).

Combine the 8 cups hot water, the salt, and sugar in a large saucepan. Bring to a boil over high heat and boil until the salt and sugar dissolve. Remove from the heat and let cool. Chop the garlic and rosemary in a food processor or by hand.

Pour the 8 cups cold water into a small cooler, a tub, a clean heavy-duty trash bag, or another container just big enough to hold whatever it is you are brining. Pour in the cooled sugar/saltwater, the ice, and the chopped garlic and rosemary. The ice will melt as the brine sits. Add the meat and refrigerate or pack with ice in a large cooler for the entire brining time so that the meat stays cold.

PEPPERCORN BRINE

Use 2 cups hot water, 2 cups cold water, 1 cup kosher salt, $^1/_2$ cup sugar, 1 clove garlic, leaves from 1 sprig rosemary, and 4 cups ice. Add 10 black peppercorns along with the garlic and rosemary. Great for Shaved Pork with Summer Fruit (page 195). Makes about 8 cups.

THYME BRINE

Use 2 cups hot water, 2 cups cold water, 1 cup kosher salt, $^1/_2$ cup sugar, 3 cloves garlic, leaves from 2 sprigs rosemary, and 4 cups ice. Add the leaves from 6 sprigs thyme along with the garlic and rosemary. Great for Chicken Halves on the Grill (page 198). Makes about 8 cups.

FENNEL BRINE

This is a large batch intended for Spit-Roasted Suckling Pig (page 192), a whole lamb, or another whole 20-pound animal. Use 1 gallon hot water, 2 gallons cold water, 12 cups (about 6 pounds) kosher salt, 4 cups sugar, 10 cloves garlic, the leaves from 16 sprigs rosemary, and 2 gallons ice. Add 2 teaspoons black peppercorns and 1 tablespoon ground fennel seeds along with the garlic and rosemary. You'll need a 1- or $1^1/_2$-gallon stockpot for dissolving the salt and sugar, and a large cooler for holding the brined meat. Makes about 5 gallons.

PREP AHEAD

You can make the brine up to 1 week ahead of time and keep it covered and cold.

MAKES ABOUT 6 QUARTS

8 cups hot water, plus 8 cups cold water

3 cups kosher salt

1 cup sugar

1 large clove garlic, peeled

Leaves from 6 sprigs rosemary

8 cups ice

CANDIED HAZELNUTS

Use this recipe to candy any nut you like. My kids love to munch on them as a snack. You could also crush them up and mix them into Vanilla Semifreddo (page 258) or Chocolate-Hazelnut Tartufo (page 260).

MAKES ABOUT 3¹/₂ CUPS

3¹/₂ cups (about 1 pound) hazelnuts

1 cup plus 3 tablespoons sugar

2¹/₂ tablespoons water

Nibble a hazelnut to make sure it is fresh and doesn't taste rancid or bitter in the back of your throat. If it does, get new hazelnuts.

Line a rimmed baking sheet with a Silpat or aluminum foil. Stir together the sugar and water in a wide saucepan fitted with a candy thermometer and simmer over medium-high heat until the mixture reaches 240°F, 3 to 4 minutes. Add the nuts, stirring constantly with a wooden spoon. The sugar will crystallize on the nuts. Continue stirring until the sugar melts, glazes the nuts, and turns a light caramel color.

Immediately spread the nuts in a single layer on the prepared pan and let cool completely.

PREP AHEAD

The nuts can be stored in an airtight container at room temperature for up to 1 week.

CHOCOLATE SAUCE

You can't go wrong with chocolate and cream. Sometimes, I add a little shortening or butter to thicken up the sauce. Pour the warm chocolate sauce over gelato or Amaretti Semifreddo (page 258). Or make a chocolate milkshake with it.

Pour the cream into a small saucepan and bring to a boil over medium-high heat. Put the chocolate and butter in a medium bowl and pour on the hot cream. Let sit for 2 minutes, then whisk until the chocolate is melted and the mixture is blended.

In a clean saucepan (I just wash out the small one), combine the corn syrup, sugar, and 4 teaspoons of the water. Set the pan over medium heat until the sugar melts, then whisk it into the chocolate mixture. Whisk until smooth, adding another teaspoonful of water if necessary to thin the sauce.

PREP AHEAD

The chocolate sauce can be refrigerated in an airtight container for up to 1 week before using. Heat it in a metal bowl or the top of a double boiler set over gently simmering water, whisking constantly once it starts to warm up.

MAKES 2 CUPS

$3/4$ cup heavy cream

$7^1/2$ ounces bittersweet chocolate, preferably 58 percent cocoa, chopped

4 tablespoons shortening or unsalted butter, softened

4 teaspoons light corn syrup

$4^1/2$ teaspoons sugar

4 to 5 teaspoons water

CANDIED CITRUS PEEL

I like to candy all kinds of citrus peels, from oranges and grapefruits to lemons, limes, and citron. If you like bitter tastes, include a little of the white pith under the zest, the colored part of the rind. Otherwise, peel carefully to avoid it.

Put the citrus peels in a saucepan with cold water to cover and bring to a boil over high heat. As soon as the water boils, drain the peels and cover again with cold water. Repeat the process to blanch the peels 3 times.

Drain and pat the blanched peels dry. Combine the sugar and water in a small nonreactive saucepan and add the peels. Cook over low heat until the peels look translucent, about 30 minutes.

Remove the candied peels from the syrup using a slotted spoon and spread on waxed paper to cool. Save the citrus-scented syrup for another use. Roll the cooled peels in superfine sugar.

PREP AHEAD

Make the peels up to 1 month ahead and keep in an airtight container at room temperature. The citrus syrup you end up with will keep in an airtight container in the refrigerator for weeks. Use it for drizzling over Apple Fritters (page 250), Olive Oil Cake (page 248), or Baked Peaches with Almond Frangipane (page 247). By the way, if you can't find superfine sugar, make your own by grinding granulated sugar in a clean coffee grinder or blender until very fine.

MAKES ABOUT 1 CUP

1 cup 1/4-inch strips citrus peels

1/2 cup sugar

1/4 cup water

Superfine sugar for dusting

SOURCES

MOST OF THE EQUIPMENT AND INGREDIENTS called for in this book are widely available. Here are some of the purveyors I use or recommend. You can also find similar products at markets near you.

BREADS AND PIZZAS

ALLEN CREEK FARM

P.O. Box 841
Ridgefield, WA 98642
Phone/Fax: 360-887-3669
www.chestnutsonline.com
Chestnut flour.

DI BRUNO BROTHERS

930 South Ninth Street
Philadelphia, PA 19147
Phone: 215-922-2876
888-322-4337
www.dibrunobrothers.com
Parmigiano-Reggiano, Gorgonzola dolce, mozzarella di bufala, fresh ricotta, mortadella, prosciutto, pancetta, and other Italian foods.

FORNO BRAVO

The Monterey Peninsula
744 Neeson Road
Marina, CA 93933
Phone: 800-407-5119
Fax: 707-515-7396
www.fornobravo.com
Tipo 00 flour, pizza stones, and pizza-making supplies.

IL MERCATO ITALIANO

P.O. Box 9751
Green Bay, WI 54308
Phone: 877-202-8881
Fax: 206-339-2598
www.ilmercatoitaliano.net
Bottarga, salted anchovies, La Valle San Marzano tomatoes, amaretti cookies.

KING ARTHUR FLOUR

135 U.S. Route 5 South
Norwich, VT 05055
Phone: 802-649-3361
800-827-6836
Fax: 802-649-3365
www.kingarthurflour.com
Sir Galahad flour, King Arthur all-purpose flour, durum flour, semolina, almond flour, glacé cherries, SAF instant yeast, gram scales, and baking supplies.

PREVIN

2044 Rittenhouse Square
Philadelphia, PA 19103
Phone: 215-985-1996
888-285-9547
Fax: 215-985-0323
www.previninc.com
Ring molds, terrine molds, and other baking supplies.

WEBSTAURANT STORE

Phone: 717-392-7472
www.webstaurantstore.com
Vollrath stand mixers, baking stones, baking sheets, baking molds, pizza dough dockers, and other kitchen equipment.

PASTAS

BUON ITALIA

75 Ninth Avenue
New York, NY 10011
Phone: 212-633-9090
Fax: 212-633-9717
www.buonitalia.com
Tipo 00 flour, semolina, and other dry goods.

EURO GOURMET

10312 Southard Drive
Beltsville, MD 20705
Phone: 301-937-2888
800-799-EURO
Fax: 301-937-8214
www.eurogourmet.biz
Fresh sheep's milk ricotta, burrata, buffalo mozzarella, and other cheeses.

FANTES

1006 South Ninth Street
Philadelphia, PA 19147
Phone: 215-922-5557
800-443-2683
Fax: 215-922-5723
www.fantes.com
Garganelli combs and boards, chitarras, pasta machines, and other pasta-making supplies.

KITCHENAID

Customer Satisfaction Center
P.O. Box 218
St. Joseph, MI 49085
Phone: 800-541-6390
www.kitchenaid.com
Stand mixers, extruded-pasta presses, pasta rollers, pasta cutters, meat grinders, sausage stuffers, and other attachments.

LA TIENDA

3601 La Grange Parkway
Toano, VA 23168
Phone: 800-710-4304
888-331-4362
www.tienda.com
Baccalà (salt cod).

SALUMI

BUTCHER & PACKER

P.O. Box 07468
Detroit, MI 48207
Phone: 313-567-1250
800-521-3188
Fax: 313-567-8938
www.butcher-packer.com
Sausage-making supplies.

THE GROW ROOM

8 Bridge Street
Nyack, NY 10960
Phone: 845-348-8811
800-449-9630
www.greenair.com
In-line hydrostats and thermostats.

THE SAUSAGE MAKER, INC.

1500 Clinton Street, Building 123
Buffalo, NY 14206
Phone: 888-490-8525
716-824-5814
Fax: 716-824-6465
www.sausagemaker.com
Sausage-making supplies.

PICKLES AND PRESERVES

INDIAN BLEND

Phone: 888-753-4299
www.indianblend.com
Pure mustard oil.

MEATS AND FISH

BARBECUE WOOD

P.O. Box 8163
Yakima, WA 98908
Phone: 509-965-0123
800-379-9663
Fax: 509-965-3553
www.barbecuewood.com
Oak, hickory, and other woods for grilling, roasting, and smoking.

COUNTRY TIME FARM

3017 Mountain Road
Hamburg, PA 19526
Phone: 610-562-2090
www.countrytimefarm.com
Pork.

D'ARTAGNAN

280 Wilson Avenue
Newark, NJ 07105
Phone: 973-344-0565
800-327-8246
www.dartagnan.com
Duck, rabbit, lamb, suckling pig, and other meats.

JAMISON FARM

171 Jamison Lane
Latrobe, PA 15650
Phone: 800-237-5262
Fax: 724-837-2287
www.jamisonfarm.com
Lamb.

SAMUELS & SON SEAFOOD COMPANY

3407 South Lawrence Street
Philadelphia, PA 19148
Phone: 800-580-5810
Fax: 215-336-0251
www.samuelsandsonseafood.com
Halibut, tuna, monkfish, swordfish, squid, and other seafood.

SPITJACK

268 Boston Turnpike
Shrewsbury, MA 01545
Phone: 800-755-5509
508-425-3261
Fax: 508-755-8818
www.spitjack.com
Spit-roasters and grilling supplies.

WELLS MEATS

982 North Delaware Avenue
Philadelphia, PA 19123
Phone: 215-627-3903
800-523-1730
Fax: 215-922-7648
www.wellsmeats.com
Duck, rabbit, oxtails, lamb, suckling pig, and other meats.

VEGETABLES AND FRUITS

BLUE MOON ACRES

P.O. Box 201
Buckingham, PA 18912
Phone: 215-794-3093
Fax: 215-794-2406
www.bluemoonacres.net
Lettuces, microgreens, and herbs.

CAYUGA PURE ORGANICS

18 Banks Road
Brooktendale, NY 14817
Phone: 607-793-0085
www.cporganics.com
Freshly milled organic polenta, buckwheat flour and other flours and grains like farro.

GEORGE RICHTER FARM

4512 70th Avenue East
Fife, WA 98424
Phone: 253-922-5649
Fax: 253-926-0621
Fresh berries.

GREEN MEADOW FARM

130 South Mount Vernon Road
Gap, PA 17527
Phone: 717-442-5222
Fax: 717-442-5065
www.glennbrendle.com
Vegetables and fruits.

LINVILLA ORCHARDS

137 West Knowlton Road
Media, PA 19063
Phone: 610-876-7116
www.linvilla.com
Apples, pumpkins, and vegetables.

MAXIMUS INTERNATIONAL FOODS

15 Bicknell Road
Weymouth, MA 02191
Phone: 617-331-7959
Fax: 781-335-5416
Wild and cultivated mushrooms.

POTIRONNE

120 Thornwood Road
Georgetown, TX 78628
Phone: 512-635-3742
Fax: 303-681-0221
www.potironne.com
Canned snails.

DESSERTS

AMAZON

Phone: 866-216-1072
www.amazon.com
Forno Bonomi ladyfingers, hemisphere silicone molds.

ACKNOWLEDGMENTS

My FATHER TOLD ME a long time ago that if the whole world goes right, I'll go left. He was absolutely right! That's why compiling a list of people to "acknowledge" for helping to write this book makes me want to run the other way. It just seems silly to me. It's not enough to write someone's name down, thank them, and then move on to the next person. It's meaningless. No one would expect that from me, and quite frankly, I don't want to disappoint! The fact is, there are hundreds of people to thank for my entire being leading up to this point in my life, including this book. I'll do my best to set the record straight.

My mother and father are two of the greatest people on the planet. From reading me Leo Buscaglia books to encouraging me to never give up—all of my dedication, work ethic, perseverance, attitude, strength, and will are a direct result of how they raised me. They taught me invaluable lessons and always had my back. I only hope to instill in my children the compassion, drive, understanding, and passion for life that they taught me and still teach me every day.

If I could add one more recipe to the book, it would be the recipe for a happy life. When you're young and looking for someone to spend the rest of your life with, choose a person who surpasses you in every way imaginable. Choose someone who makes you work harder because she or he is so good. Choose someone who makes you strive to be a better human being. I was lucky enough to be given that opportunity and to make that choice. Megan, I love you more than life itself. You are my everything!

> The hardest battle you're ever going to have to fight
> is the battle to be just you.
> —LEO BUSCAGLIA

First, make yourself a reputation for being a creative genius.

Second, surround yourself with partners who are better than you are.

Third, leave them to go get on with it.

—DAVID OGILVY

I'll admit I am creative. But a genius? I'm not so sure. I am also a very hands-on person, so I'm still working on the third part of this quote. But I'll tell you this, when it comes to restaurant partners, mine are second to none!

As a chef, I look for inspiration. I often find it in Italy, but I also find it on trips to eat at my colleagues' restaurants in the States. I can't tell you how many times I've gone to Chicago or Boston, New York or Los Angeles, New Orleans or Colorado, eaten at a friend's restaurant, and then felt like I wasn't worthy to be washing their dishes. My colleagues, chefs and restaurant owners from around the country, are the people who inspire me the most every day. They cheer me up when I need cheering; they rejuvenate me when I'm in a rut; they inspire me when I need inspiring; and they are the first ones to help out others in a time of need. It is an industry of the most generous, chivalrous, noble, self-effacing, tireless workaholics on the planet. And I couldn't be prouder to be a member!

Outside the restaurant world, three people have had more of an impact on my life in recent years than anyone else. They are Alex, Liz, and Jay Scott. They taught me that one person can truly make a difference in this world. Thanks to them, I see things more clearly, I feel things more vibrantly, I involve myself more passionately, and I understand the real meaning of the saying, "When life gives you lemons, make lemonade!"

Finally, David Joachim, you're just da bomb. 'Nuff said!

Countless other people helped me write this book. You all know who you are. You all know I appreciate you more than words can say. And when I see you again, I'll give you a big hug.

Voglio bene a tutti voi!

—Marc

INDEX

Copyright © 2011 by Marc Vetri
Photographs copyright © 2011 by Kelly Campbell

Library of Congress Cataloging-in-Publication Data
Vetri, Marc.
    Rustic Italian food / Marc Vetri with David Joachim ; beverage notes by
Jeff Benjamin ; photography by Kelly Campbell ; foreword by Mario Batali.
        p. cm.
Summary: "The second cookbook from acclaimed Philadelphia chef Marc Vetri,
featuring recipes for staples of the hand-crafted Italian Kitchen like bread, pasta,
pizza, and salumi"— Provided by publisher.
    1. Cooking, Italian. 2. Cookbooks. I. Joachim, David. II. Title.
    TX723.V484 2011
    641.5945—dc23

                            2011015301

ISBN 978-1-58008-589-2
Printed in China
Cover and text design by Nancy Austin
Prop styling by Sarah Cave and Theo Vamvounakis

10 9 8 7 6 5 4 3 2 1
First Edition